BUILDING BRAND AUTHENTICITY

BUILDING BRAND AUTHENTICITY

7 Habits of Iconic Brands

Michael Beverland

Professor of Marketing, RMIT University

First published 2009 by
PALGRAVE MACMILLAN

Palgrave Macmillan in the UK is an imprint of Macmillan Publishers Limited, registered in England, company number 785998, of Houndmills, Basingstoke, Hampshire RG21 6XS.

Palgrave Macmillan in the US is a division of St Martin's Press LLC, 175 Fifth Avenue, New York, NY 10010.

Palgrave Macmillan is the global academic imprint of the above companies and has companies and representatives throughout the world.

Palgrave® and Macmillan® are registered trademarks in the United States, the United Kingdom, Europe and other countries

ISBN-13: 978-0-230-58031-2

This book is printed on paper suitable for recycling and made from fully managed and sustained forest sources. Logging, pulping and manufacturing processes are expected to conform to the environmental regulations of the country of origin.

A catalogue record for this book is available from the British Library.

A catalog record for this book is available from the Library of Congress.

10 9 8 7 6 5 4 3 2 1
18 17 16 15 14 13 12 11 10 09

Printed and bound in Great Britain by
CPI Antony Rowe, Chippenham and Eastbourne

To Emma

CONTENTS

List of Figures and Tables   xi
Acknowledgements   xiii

Chapter 1   The New Brand Reality   **1**
    Introduction   1
    What is Wrong with Brands Today?   4
    Book Structure   6
    Conclusion   10
        Side Bar: *Zippo* – Still the Best Lighter Money Can Buy   10
        Side Bar: Data and All That   11

Chapter 2   Why Authenticity?   **13**
    A Tale of Two Brands   13
    What is Authenticity?   15
    Who Determines Brand Authenticity?   17
    Why Do Consumers Look for Authenticity in Brands?   21
    How Do Marketers Build/Destroy Authenticity?   25
    Conclusion   27

Chapter 3   The Authenticity of Stories
    Weapons of Mass Destruction and Wooden Chassis   29
    Why Do Brand Stories Create Authenticity?   33
    The Ten Stories Behind Authentic Brands   37
        Founding   37
        Side Bar: Burt and His Bees   40
        Family   42
        Conflict and struggle   44
        Triumph and tragedy   46
        Creation   48
        History   51
        Side Bar: Life during Wartime   52
        Community   54
        Place   56
        Consumers   58
        Product/service   59
    Conclusion   60

Chapter 4   Appearing as Artisanal Amateurs   **63**

Altoids and the P&G Effect   63

    Side Bar: Less is more – returning *Cracker Barrel* to its roots   65

'Amateurs', 'Artisans', and 'Appearances'   66

What Makes a Brand Appear Artisanal and Amateurish?   68

    One: Emphasizing craft traditions   68

    Two: I wasn't formally trained   70

    Three: We don't do marketing   72

    Four: I love what I do!   73

    Five: Luck played a big role   74

    Six: Admit failure   76

    Seven: We just want to have fun!   77

    Eight: Not bad for no budget   80

The Other Half of the Story   81

Conclusion   82

Chapter 5   Sticking to Your Roots   **85**

Taking Photos at Melbourne Airport   85

What Sticking to Your Roots Doesn't Mean   87

How to Stick to Your Roots?   88

    Side Bar: The other *Dr Pepper*   89

    One: Stylistic consistency   90

    Side Bar: *Tiger Balm*   91

    Two: Retaining tradition   93

    Three: The founding spirit   95

    Four: Telling moralistic tales   96

    Five: Returning to or continuing roots in periods of transition   98

    Six: Retaining community traditions   99

    Seven: Engaging in focal activities   101

Conclusion   101

Chapter 6   Love the Doing   **103**

Ayn Rand and James Dyson   103

Why Do We Love The 'Lovers of Doing'?   105

How to Demonstrate a Love of Doing   106

    One: Product/production orientation   107

    Two: Experiencing production   109

    Three: Leaders involved in production   111

    Four: Espoused love of craft   113

    Five: The quest for excellence   115

    Six: Being design-led   118

Conclusion   120

Chapter 7   Market Immersion   **121**

Right Wing Customers   121

    Side Bar: *Tata Motors*   123

How to be Immersed in Your Market 124
 One: Employ your customers 124
 Two: Live in the market 128
 Side Bar: Hans Beck and *Playmobil* 130
 Three: Trust your gut 131
 Side Bar: *Alessi* 135
 Four: Allow employees to dabble 135
 Five: Seed the fan base 138
Conclusion 139

Chapter 8 Be at One with the Community 141
Chateau Margaux's Cows 141
Authenticity is Local (Even when the Brand is Global) 142
How to be at One with Community 145
 One: Nation 145
 Two: Region 147
 Three: Industry 149
 Four: Culture 152
 Five: Subculture 154
Conclusion 157

Chapter 9 Indoctrinate Staff into the Brand Cult 159
Gordon Ramsay 159
How to Indoctrinate Your Staff into the Brand Cult 160
 One: Select carefully 160
 Two: Look after their welfare 162
 Three: Tell their stories 164
 Four: Manage non-performance early 165
 Five: Encourage creativity 167
 Six: Immerse staff in the brand's culture 169
 Seven: Lead by example 171
Conclusion 173

Chapter 10 What Can You Do? 175
Faking it is Hard 175
Don't Just Say it, Show it! 177
Embrace the Tension at the Heart of Authentic Brands 179
Product, Product, Product (or Service, Service, Service – or Both) 180
Be Part of the Consumers' World 181
Avoid the Temptation to Exploit Your Brand for
Commercial Gain 183
Employ a Brand Historian 184
Don't be Afraid of Letting Consumers in 185
Be Open and Honest 187
 Side Bar: What about B2B? 189
Conclusion 190

CONTENTS

Bibliography   191

Author Index   203

Brand Index   207

Subject Index   215

LIST OF FIGURES AND TABLES

Figures

1.1 Building brand authenticity 6
1.2 *Zippo* has long been a US soldier's most desired possession – a relationship honoured in this design 11
2.1 Authoring brand meaning 18
2.2 Authenticating brands 24
3.1 *Bruichladdich*'s Weapons of Mass Destruction (WMD II) 30
3.2 Stories are at the heart of whisky producer *Bruichladdich* 31
4.1 *Altoids* packaging appears old world and amateurish when compared to the brand's plastic, manufactured competitors – that's part of *Altoids'* charm 64
4.2 *Altoids* advertisements are as collectible as their tins. The ads reinforce the brands playful, irresistible, deviant nature 64
4.3 The instantly recognizable face of *Dilmah Teas* – Merrill J. Fernando 75
4.4 The sign says it all – *Virgin* gyms encapsulate Richard Branson's laid-back fun image (unlike all those other corporate gyms) 79
6.1 Eagerly awaited by collectors, *W. Britain*'s return to the Delhi Durbar range kicks off with this lovingly crafted, and carefully researched, Jaipur elephant 114
7.1 *Phil and Ted*'s Inline Buggy – a product improved through direct feedback from staff-as-parents 125
7.2 Hans Beck's *Playmobil* figures were developed after observing how children draw faces and figures 131
7.3 Dyson married cutting edge technology and design with tradition in the firm's new take on the washing machine – the *Contrarotator* 133
7.4 Now a staple of kitchens and airports, the Dyson Airblade is another example of how the firm constantly challenges traditional thinking in designs 134
10.1 Thousands visit the *Zippo Visitors Centre* every year 186

Table

3.1 Ten stories behind authentic brands 38

ACKNOWLEDGEMENTS

No book about being true to oneself can fail to acknowledge the many people that have helped me along the way. First and foremost, I'd like to thank my co-authors who have played a critical role in honing some of the ideas covered here. A big thank you to my main partner in crime, Francis Farrelly (Monash University), as well as Sonia Dickinson-Delaporte and Julie Napoli (Curtin University), Mike Ewing (Monash University), Adam Lindgreen (Hull University Business School), Pascale Quester (University of Adelaide), and Michiel Vink for their respective contributions to various articles on authenticity. Second, a big thanks to Emily Chung and Kay Laochumnanvanit for helping with consumer data collection. Third, a big thanks to all the supportive editors of various journals that have nursed my (often rough) ideas through the review process. Thanks to John Deighton and Eric Arnould (*Journal of Consumer Research*), Candace Jones, N. Anand, and Josè Luis Alvarez (*Journal of Management Studies*), Barry Babin (*Journal of Business Research*), Russell Laczniak, Tom Duncan, Don Schultz, Charles Patti, and Marla Royne (*Journal of Advertising*), Catherine Dalton (*Business Horizons*), Nick Lee (*European Journal of Marketing*), Matt Coney (*Idealog*), Abbie Griffin (*Journal of Product Innovation Management*), and Thomas Walton (*Design Management Review*) for their patience, support, and insights (and acceptance). Fourth, thanks also to all the anonymous reviewers that provided constructive insights on each of my papers. Throughout the development of my ideas, a number of people have provided encouragement and critical insights that have proved very useful. These include Linda Price (University of Arizona), Tandy Chalmers (Queen's University), Mark Ritson (Melbourne Business School), Richard Elliot (University of Bath), Kelly Tian (University of New Mexico), Steven Kates (Simon Fraser University), Mark Uncles (University of New South Wales), Carla Taines (University of Melbourne), Peter Danaher (Melbourne

Business School), Tim Fry and Mike Reid (RMIT University), and Steve Charters (Reims Management School).

This book would not have been possible without generous funding. In many cases grant bodies were asked to provide funds for what seemed, on the face of it, rather questionable projects – such as conducting research on luxury wineries in France. Without the support of various reviewers and chairpersons, the research necessary to bring these ideas to life would have been impossible. Thanks therefore to the Faculty of Business and Economics Research Committee at Monash University, the Faculty of Economics and Commerce Research Committee at University of Melbourne, the School of Economics, Finance and Marketing Research Committee at RMIT University, the Australian Research Council (DP0985178 & DP0664943), and Phil Bretherton who as Head of School at Unitec, Auckland signed off on many research requests that ultimately generated case data for this book.

Although funds were critical, this book would never have appeared were it not for the informants. There are too many to thank, and many more gatekeepers and connectors whose names I've forgotten who helped secure me interviews with busy people (especially in France). However, I'd like to thank the following people for providing me with approval to use the photographs in the book: Anton Brown (*Virgin Active* Australia), Matthew Parkin (*Morgan Motor Co*), Mark Reynier (*Bruichladdich*), Richard Walker (*W. Britain*), Jamie Dickinson (*Playmobil*), Jeni Golomb (*Altoids* on behalf of *Wm. Wrigley Jr. Company*), Pat Grandy (*Zippo*), Dilhan C. Fernando (*Dilmah*), and Richard Shirtcliffe (*Phil & Teds*).

Thanks must also go to the publications team at Palgrave Macmillan including Eleanor Davey-Corrigan, Stephen Rutt and Imran Shahnawaz (any errors that remain are mine). Thanks also to my doctoral student Jo En Yap for editing and developing the index, my colleagues at RMIT for putting up with a less than attentive discipline leader during the writing phase of this book, the guys at *Switchboard* Café in the Manchester Unity building (where much of this book was planned out and edited) for great coffee (and remembering I have two Long Macciato's every morning), my good friends Anish, Elison, Julie, and Liliana (keep it real pink shirts) for keeping me grounded, and my loving partner, Emma, for her understanding and support.

Here's the book, hope you like it.

CHAPTER 1

THE NEW BRAND REALITY

Authenticity is the benchmark against which all brands are now judged.

John Grant, *The New Marketing Manifesto*

INTRODUCTION

Would anyone care if your brand disappeared? As I write this, the *Morgan Motor Company* (a small UK-based car manufacturer) is about to celebrate its centenary. Morganeers around the world (from as far away as New Zealand) are shipping their 'Mogs' to the village of Malvern Link to take part in this once in a lifetime celebration of a brand many business consultants predicted wouldn't see out the end of the twentieth century. At the same time, the 'Big Three' (*Chrysler, Ford,* and *General Motors*) are receiving financial aid (much to the consternation of the American taxpayer) from the US government. *Chrysler* has filed for bankruptcy protection (with *General Motors* likely to follow) as part of a merger deal with *Fiat*. The contrast in fortunes between the two sets of companies is as obvious as the contrast between their respective resource bases, including budgets for marketing and research and development.

In its 100-year history, *Morgan* has released seven different models of car (and you can still buy cars that were effectively designed in the 1950s), whereas barely a year goes by without a new model from the US automakers. Over the last 100 years *Morgan* has done little in the way of marketing and only recently (2005–6) started formalizing their brand position with the strap line 'Driven at Heart'. In contrast, the US automakers have invested enormous sums into marketing

1

and design. While *Ford*, *Chrysler*, and *General Motors* were regularly exemplified in MBA classes, business books, and the *Harvard Business Review*, *Morgan* gained little attention from those seeking to identify best practice. In fact, at one time *Morgan* was pilloried as an example of 'all that is wrong with British industry' (Laban 2000). What is going on here?

Not everyone was oblivious to the enduring nature of the *Morgan* brand. Prior to his death Soichiro Honda predicted the car industry would eventually consist of just six manufacturers. He then paused and said 'oh, and Morgan' (Laban 2000, p. 59). Similar examples abound across the globe – remember Michael Dell's comment about closing *Apple* and returning the money to long aggrieved stockholders? Which stock would you rather own now? Why do consumers pay exorbitant sums for collectable *Altoids* tins, proudly display their *Dyson* vacuum cleaners as taste markers, get tattooed with *Apple* or *Harley Davidson* logos, trek to the ends of the earth to pay homage to their favourite brands of beer, whisky, and/or wine, and so on? What is it about these brands that make them so attractive to large numbers of consumers while more conspicuous brands (such as *Microsoft*, *Ford*, and *Pepsi*) struggle? How is it that brands which profess to 'hate marketing', 'do no market research', or 'make nothing for the customer' endure, while those that prostrate themselves before customers struggle (or are at best regarded as functional necessities)? This book proposes consumers love these brands because they are authentic.

Wait a minute. Isn't the notion of 'authentic brands' contradictory? Doesn't the very act of branding render a person or object inauthentic? How can one have authenticity when one is tainted by crass commercial motives? This book identifies how a large number of brands manage to simultaneously achieve market success while denying any interest in marketing, branding, or commercial motivations. The people running these brands paint themselves as perpetual underdogs, fighting against the blandness produced by modern marketers and the standardization of modern life. Rather than investing heavily in marketing, these brands focus on getting on with the job of making great products, seeking perfection, solving difficult problems, or offering great service. In doing so, this book offers an alternative to standard branding advice. I urge marketers to stop revelling in their expertise, stop playing safe, and reject consistency of message. Instead, marketers need to imbue their brands with a warts and all humanity and use the tools at their disposal to tell, and help others tell, stories. As Global Managing Director for *Jack Daniel's*, Gus Griffin states:

> Brands can have multiple storytellers. In our advertising, the brand is the storyteller, however, the most powerful storyteller over the history of the brand has been pop culture. The stories told by pop culture have very effectively communicated the independence and masculinity values of the brand, while much of our advertising has communicated the values of authenticity and integrity. (Drummond, 2008, pp. 20–1)

Just as *Jack Daniel's* has gained iconic status by becoming part of popular culture, so too other brands have prospered from allowing consumers and society to become co-authors in their meaning. *Adidas*'s rebirth in the 1980s provides a compelling example. Largely viewed as a soccer (football to non-Americans) brand, the adoption of the three stripes by hip hop act Run DMC breathed new life into the ailing icon. Touring North America, the band noticed that many of their fans were wearing *Adidas* gear to their concerts. The band invited some *Adidas* marketing executives to their Madison Square Garden concert and during the performance of their song 'My Adidas' (which is not actually a homage to the brand but an attempt to counter the view at the time that street culture was synonymous with gang violence) they encouraged fans to wave their *Adidas* shoes in the air. The marketing team was smart enough to realize what was happening and promptly signed a sponsorship deal with the band (before they had their first breakthrough worldwide-smash with 'Walk this way'). The brand was reborn – from preppy lifestyle brand in the 1970s to edgy street wear in the 1980s and beyond. By allowing the brand's story to be shaped by a hip hop group, their fans, and the street subculture, *Adidas*'s ailing fortunes were reversed, at relatively little cost (Courtney 2008).

Still not convinced? If examples don't suffice hopefully consumer research will. A recent study conducted by my colleagues identified that brand authenticity is a better predictor of purchase intentions than brand love, trust, and credibility (Napoli et al. forthcoming). Therefore, more authentic brands have higher levels of equity in their category than other comparable brands. Other research supports these findings, with a brand authenticity index identifying that authentic brands are more likely to attract a higher share of big spending consumers and gain word-of-mouth support (Principals-Synovate 2008). That is, authentic brands gain higher margins at lower promotional cost (it is not unusual for many of the brands covered here to do little or no advertising).

WHAT IS WRONG WITH BRANDS TODAY?

Why are marketers now talking about authenticity and 'authentic brand strategies'? After all brands used to be highly respected institutions – the darlings of the share market, talented employees, business schools, and customers. Consumers trusted brands (particularly big brands) because they consistently delivered superior benefits over time. Although brands were obviously commercial objects, they operated above politics and personal prejudice (after all brands that discriminate on racial or other grounds give away potential profits), and were seen as benevolent actors in the community because they provided employment with above-market conditions. Globally, brands remained above the fray – the Communist Bloc may have expressed a desire to destroy the capitalist West, but their people desired western brands. Brands such as *Coca Cola* were seen as iconic representations of freedom among oppressed peoples around the world (Pendergast 2000). Western brands were embraced in new developing nations because they provided people with a conspicuous sign of success. We even began to identify the global brand as the ideal business model (Levitt 1983).

Currently, large brands are not thought of so positively. Large brands such as *Starbucks*, *McDonald's*, and *Wal-Mart* face a community-led backlash under the banner of 'not in my neighbourhood' (Holt 2002; Thompson et al. 2006). While in the past the arrival of such brands was often seen as a vote of confidence in the community, many large brands are now viewed in parasitical terms – big brands exploit community members, shut down local businesses, offer poor paying jobs, and when times get tough, pull out with no regard for the wider social impact of their decisions. The very disinterest in local affairs and political issues exhibited by brands in the past is now viewed as a fault rather than a virtue. No longer can brands appear to be above the fray, or separate from issues of national politics. For example, while *Coca Cola* was once a symbol of freedom around the world, in some Middle Eastern countries it is now seen as a symbol of oppression, with the locally produced *Mecca Cola* representing (in the eyes of the brand's founders) 'a little gesture against US imperialism and foreign policy' (Henley and Vasagar 2003).

No longer garnering the respect they once did, brands are blamed for a range of societal ills including environmental degradation, poverty, war, visual pollution, and overconsumption. Naomi Klein's *No Logo* (2000) began a whole new genre in anti-brand discourse. Klein compared the espoused statements of large global brands with their actions, and found them wanting. *Nike* for example, failed to honour its stress on personal excellence and achievement when it used Asian contractors that engaged in exploitative work practices. *Starbucks'* emphasis on creating an authentic communal coffee house was contrasted with the perceived decline in local coffee houses resulting from the brand's dominance. The rebranding of *British Petroleum* (BP) to 'Beyond Petroleum' was seen as a cynical exercise in greenwashing given how little the company invested or made from sustainable energy sources. In short, brands were inauthentic – their aspirational claims were little more than cynical impression management.

I argue that the traditional branding model is partly to blame. The traditional 'mind-share' branding model with its focus on individual rational consumers fails to account for the sociocultural context within which consumers draw their identity (a point illustrated in Chapter 2 with the opening two examples) (Holt 2004). As a result, too much market research focuses on understanding whether consumers are aware of brands, or understand the marketer-driven meaning of the brand. However, research reveals that consumers imbue brands with their own meaning, which may be the opposite of what marketers intended. Such meanings are usually reflective of consumers' identity goals, which themselves reflect wider sociocultural myths (Beverland and Farrelly, forthcoming; Thompson 1997). There is little point in telling consumers that 'brand meaning resides in the mind of the consumer' when marketers pay so little regard to the role such brands play in the consumer's life world. Brand authenticity is actually derived from an ongoing interaction between the firm, its stakeholders, and society, as identified in Figure 1.1. Authenticity is not just another brand attribute to be explicitly used by marketers to differentiate their offer from others. This book offers an alternative approach to branding that will hopefully return brands (and branding) to a more illustrious status.

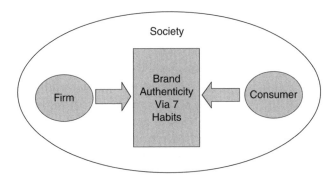

FIGURE 1.1 **Building brand authenticity**

BOOK STRUCTURE

This book consists of three parts. The first part (Chapter 2) grounds the rest of the book by examining the changing nature of authenticity, why and how consumers attribute authenticity to brands, and why marketers should care about building authenticity. The second part (Chapters 3–9) details the seven habits that increase a brand's authenticity. The final part (Chapter 10) provides a guide to action for brand managers, identifying eight of practices needed for enhancing a brand's authenticity. Examples from a wide range of brands and nations will be used throughout.

Chapter 2 discusses the nature of authenticity. Debates have raged for centuries over the nature and meaning of authenticity, and where authenticity can be found. Historically authenticity was seen as something objective. That is, objects, people, places etc. either were authentic or not. Under this view, authenticity was typically something universal and dictated to people by experts, laws, or institutions. However, research reveals that people find authenticity in a range of things including mass-produced items, everyday objects, reproductions, contrived or staged events, and even the obviously fake. As a result, in the postmodern era, what is authentic is highly subjective. For marketers, understanding how and why consumers attribute authenticity to some objects and not others is of paramount importance. Chapter 2 focuses on an emerging body of research examining consumer attributions of authenticity, marketer attempts to produce authenticity, and the benefits of building brand authenticity.

Part II is primarily based upon the author's decade-long research project examining the nature of enduring brands (see 'Data and All That'). Using primary and secondary research data, I identify seven 'habits' of authentic brands. The term 'habit' is used because it focuses on actions that are second nature to the people behind the brands covered in the book. The story of *Zippo Lighters* provides an early *entrée* into these habits (see *Zippo* – Still the Best Lighter Money can Buy). Marketers are good at espousing values yet often fail to live up to them, resulting in negative consumer experiences and increased cynicism towards marketer claims. The seven habits are:

1. Story telling
2. Appearing as artisanal amateurs
3. Sticking to your roots
4. Loving the doing
5. Market immersion
6. Being at one with community
7. Indoctrinating staff into the brand cult

Chapter 3 focuses on the role of stories in branding. Typically, marketers tell extremely simple stories that focus on functional, emotional, or experiential benefits. In contrast to the great stories of humanity, brand stories are usually devoid of conflict, flaws, and intrigue. And, all-knowing marketers solely author them. In contrast, authenticity is built through rich, multilayered stories featuring brand heroes that struggle, stumble, fail, and triumph against impossible odds. These stories are replete with rich characters, hilarious incidences, tragedy, stupidity, and passion. At their core, authentic brand stories feature conflict. Finally, authentic brand stories have several authors – marketers, consumers, and society (see Figure 1.1).

Chapter 4 examines the founders and people behind the brands. Rather than revelling in their professionalism – their marketing expertise, quality investments, strategic documents, and other standard business practices – these people play up their amateurish qualities (lack of commercial motivation, lack of training, and lack of planning). Such images lend the brand a sense of authenticity because they downplay the very real commercial practices and motivations in favour of more personal, human qualities. Paradoxically, these brands gain the outcomes of professionalism, including high brand awareness, loyalty, and equity. These brands are seen as standard setters in their field and regularly innovative while appearing to be stuck in the past or benefactors of lucky breaks. I go behind the scenes of these brands to understand how one can appear the amateur while remaining the consummate professional.

Chapter 5 identifies how authentic brands remain committed to their roots. With research identifying brands losing equity when they stray from their roots – whether it is core values, founding activities, or subculture, I identify how authentic brands remain relevant while reaffirming traditions. Authentic brands reinterpret their roots for the times, adding new stories and layers of richness to their histories. When such brands fail, returning to the brand's roots becomes crucial. When combined with the material in Chapters 6 and 7, I identify how brands build authenticity through balancing tradition and innovation.

Chapter 6 examines how brands build authenticity by expressing a love of doing – that passion for craft and product/service. The people in charge of and behind authentic brands love their work. They are skilled craftspeople that revel in perfecting their skills and products/ services. Others are enthusiasts for their product or focal activity. Therefore, the brand gains authenticity because employees have direct experience with the customer's world. Consumers find this enthusiasm infectious because it reflects their own level of passion for the brand and such love lies in direct contrast to the disinterest they see in employees of other brands. Brand authenticity is therefore reinforced through stories and messages that communicate involvement in, and love of, production.

Chapter 7 examines a further paradox surrounding authentic brands – how do their people produce things consumers love while rejecting any role for customer influence in innovation. I identify how customer-driven innovations have seen authentic brands stumble, while new releases seemingly derived from creative intuition score success. I identify this as a process of market immersion. Market immersion involves actively living in the life-world of the consumer – one effectively absorbs ideas rather than asks consumers directly for new insights (that often they can't give). As a result, new products and services released by authentic brands result from being in the market, rather than being of the market. When combined with Chapters 5 and 6 market immersion results in a stream of seemingly timeless innovations that enable the brand to espouse distance from the market, creative genius, love of tradition and craft, and relevance.

Authentic brands are part of the cultural landscape – whether at the national, regional, industry, or subcultural level. Chapter 8 identifies how brands gain authenticity by contributing to (as opposed to exploiting) their relevant communities. By becoming one with the community, brands build sincerity and communal bonds, which provide critical points of difference against larger, more moneyed rivals. In contrast to other brands that try to exploit communities when they are cool, authentic brands play a core role in founding subcultures and have often been a genuine partner with community members' struggle for legitimacy. Rather than engage in overt commercial activities such as sponsorship, authentic brands develop sincere ways to 'give back' to the community supporting them.

The final chapter of Part II focuses on the cult-like nature of leadership behind authentic brands. Outsiders often wonder why staff put up with overbearing, demanding, and seemingly ungrateful leaders. Behind the scenes however, leaders of authentic brands create an environment in which talent can flourish. Critical to this creative environment is the early management of poor performance. Such an environment reinforces the other six habits and creates an image of passionate people working hard to achieve the impossible. Staff passion for the brand is nurtured in other ways including careful selection, looking after their welfare, telling their stories in brand communications, encouraging creativity and risk taking, induction programmes, and through leading by example.

Part III identifies practical implications arising from the seven habits. To build brand authenticity eight practical strategies or mindsets are required. First, marketers should focus on being authentic through their actions rather than stated values. Second, managers need to embrace the tension at the heart of authentic brands by learning to manage paradox and conflict. Third, managers should stress innovation and commitment to timeless elegance in product design or service standards. Fourth, brand managers, founders, and staff should immerse themselves in the consumers' world. Fifth, managers should be wary of short-term fashions or gimmicks. Sixth, firms should retain all their brand archives and employ brand historians for branding purposes. Seventh, brand managers should allow consumers to see the inner workings of the firm and to take ownership of brand stories. Finally, brand managers need to remain open and scrupulously honest in their actions, including dealing with failures and moral lapses, as well as giving credit were it is due.

CONCLUSION

Building brand authenticity is essential to increasing brand value. However, doing so requires a different approach to brand building – in fact one has to try to build brand value while appearing not to be commercially motivated and preferably not use words like 'brand'. Building authenticity requires adopting seven habits and eight strategies. Although these will be explored in detail in Chapters 3–9, the next chapter will examine authenticity in more detail. Just what do I mean by authenticity? How do consumers attribute authenticity to brands? And, what cues help and hinder this process? Finally, assuming brand managers care about authenticity, what can they do about it?

Side Bar:
ZIPPO – STILL THE BEST LIGHTER MONEY CAN BUY

Zippo lighters have all the hallmarks of authenticity (over 400 million have been made). George Blaisdell founded the firm in the 1930s after he saw a local businessman using an awkward looking Austrian-designed lighter. Asked why he chose that lighter, the businessman replied, 'because it works' (Meabon 2003, p. 11). This reply struck George as imminently sensible and he founded *Zippo* with the aim of producing a one-handed lighter than was reliable and windproof. Released in 1933, the first lighter reflected George's motto that has made the company famous, 'Build your product with integrity, stand behind it 100 percent, and success will follow' (Meabon 2003, p. 7). These values formed the basis of the brand's famous guarantee – 'it works, or we fix it for free' – a practice *Zippo* continues to this day. The *Zippo* guarantee has one other advantage. When consumers return lighters for repair, this information can be used in new product innovations and improvements (which is why George spent more time in the repair workshop than any other part of the business).

Like other authentic brands, *Zippo* lighters have played their part in US history, being used (and prized) by US troops in World War II, Korea, Vietnam, and both Gulf Wars (Figure 1.2). Special edition lighters have been developed, drawing on the designs of troops who engraved their lighters. Consistent with other authentic brands, *Zippo* always looked after its employees, viewing them as the firm's biggest asset. In 1946 when a serious problem with lighter flints was discovered,

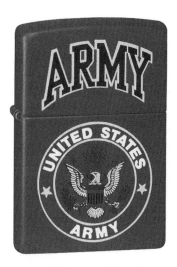

FIGURE 1.2   *Zippo* has long been a US soldier's most desired possession – a
relationship honoured in this design

George ceased production and shipping immediately in order to fix
the problem. During this time he continued to pay his employees
even though no revenue was coming in. The factory remains located
in Bradford, Pennsylvania (handprints of Blaisdell family members
are set in concrete at the firm's main office to remind visitors that the
family still stands behind the brand), where the brand plays a major
role in community life. Fans (who may be members of the *Zippo Click
Club*) pay homage to their beloved lighters every year when they visit
the Zippo Visitors Center in thousands.

Side Bar:
DATA AND ALL THAT

Like many ideas, and some of the brands covered herein, I came upon
the notion of authentic brands by accident. In 2002 I undertook a
series of case studies on iconic French wineries in Bordeaux, Burgundy,
and Champagne. Initially I was interested in understanding luxury
brands. However, what struck me at each of these wineries was how
sincere and passionate the people I was interviewing were. However,
sincerity and passion didn't quite capture what I was seeing in my data.
A year later I noticed a call for papers on authenticity in the *Journal
of Management Studies*. Immediately I knew that I'd found the term

I was looking for. Since that time, I have conducted numerous studies on the consumption and production of authenticity (several of these are listed in the Bibliography), supervised several research theses on the topic, interviewed over 100 consumers, conducted ethnographic research with food, wine, motoring and toy consumers, visited factories, been an audience member in multiple sales presentations, and interviewed over 100 experts, designers, owners, and staff. As well, my research for my doctorate (conducted throughout 1997–2000) was also reviewed as it was judged relevant to my emerging thesis on authenticity.

So how did I judge a brand authentic? Initially it was firm employees who stated the importance of authenticity to their brand's identity. I then identified a number of attributes of brand authenticity (early versions of those covered in Chapters 3–9) that I then explored further through reading published histories on each brand, and reviewing advertising and marketing materials. I would then triangulate these insights with consumers, experts, and further data (such as ethnographic research, personal experience, fan sites, or club magazines). As my initial ideas started to unfold, I became more specific in my research, picking out brands and consumption contexts that I reasonably thought would be judged authentic (or selecting those which I thought wouldn't be). Throughout this process, I read streams of research on authenticity, presented my ideas to academics and practitioners through informal discussions and formal presentations at conferences and submitted papers for review to leading international journals (which often forced me to rethink my initial views). Finally, along with colleagues, I developed a scale to measure a brand's authenticity to help validate the theory developed in this book.

CHAPTER 2

WHY AUTHENTICITY?

Where there's so much crap customers are craving authenticity.

(Hall 2004, p. 42)

People who are dedicated to wearing chucks never call them sneakers; chucks have always been a step apart from common or generic athletic shoes.

(Peterson 2007, p. 2)

A TALE OF TWO BRANDS

Under the stewardship of *Quaker Oats*, *Snapple* shouldn't have failed – not if you believe in branding and marketing. *Quaker's* strategy was simple – take a brand that had been built by amateurs to the next level through the application of marketing's famous four P's (price, product, promotion, and placement). The *Quaker* team did a superb job of developing market-driven innovations, accessing mass retailers, and investing in mainstream advertising. How could it be that four years after buying *Snapple* for US$1.7 billion, *Quaker* was forced to sell it for the markdown price of US$300 million (and some thought this too much)? Simple, the *Quaker* team forgot that consumers drank *Snapple* because of its quirks – consumption of this drink was a reaction to impersonal mass production and mass marketing. Drinking *Snapple* was a powerful cultural display in an age of conformity and artificiality (Deighton 2003). The very marketing amateurism evident in the pre-*Quaker* days gave the brand authenticity – the central driver of its equity.

Contrast *Quaker's* approach with Australian-based *Pacific Brands'* revival of the iconic *Dunlop Volley* shoe. After starving the brand of marketing investment (in innovation, channel support, and advertising) for years, *Pacific Brands* decided to reposition the shoe as an entry-level quality brand that people were not ashamed to own. These seemingly modest expectations belied the extent of the challenge facing *Pacific Brands.* Although the shoe had once been the only choice for Australian consumers and sportspeople, *Nike* and other global competitors had outflanked *Dunlop* by focusing on quality and fashion, dramatically shifting consumer expectations of athletic footwear. From number one seller in the early 1970s, by the 1990s the *Volley* was viewed internally as a commodity, by low-priced retailers as a loss leader, by specialist sports retailers as an anachronism, and by consumers as something the 'old man wore when mowing the lawns'. In short, the brand was a cash cow fast turning into a dog. *The Pacific Brands* team aimed to turn this around; although never in their wildest dreams could they have planned for what happened next.

During the late 1990s, Australian teens 'borrowed' their fathers' worn out *Volleys* from the garden shed and proudly began to wear them. Innovative teens were wearing this shoe as a semi-political statement – a rejection of *Nike's* and *Adidas'* big budgets, high prices, and large sponsorship deals. *Pacific Brands* started to receive requests from editors of street managzines run by innovative teens, for advertising and free shoes. Suddenly the *Volley* was the hottest item on the street and in dance clubs. *Dunlop* could have exploited the shoe's sudden cool with a retro-inspired mass-marketing campaign. Such a campaign would have had short-term benefits – the shoe would become the latest fad – with no lasting impact on the brand's image.

Pacific Brands decided not to exploit the *Volley's* adoption by teens. Instead they provided free shoes to street artists for sculptures, giveaways at raves, and unique shoes designed by up-and-coming teen designers. Eventually the in-crowd moved on. But the effect was obvious – the brand was seen as a reborn local icon – an authentic object reflective of the Australian way of doing better with less. The authentic response of the *Pacific Brands* team to teens resulted in increased brand equity at low cost (Beverland and Ewing 2005).

The contrast between these two brands sets the scene for this chapter. First, these examples raise questions about the nature and authorship of authenticity. Second, they suggest that a brand's authenticity is important to consumers, and therefore brand equity. Third, the examples suggest that brands are more than just a bundle of functional benefits; rather they are important to consumers' identities. Finally, the different outcomes experienced by the two brands suggest marketers can build or destroy authenticity. These four issues form the basis of this chapter.

WHAT IS AUTHENTICITY?

The term 'authentic' is derived from the Latin *Authenticus* and Greek *Authentikos* and means 'worthy of acceptance, authoritative, trustworthy, not imaginary, false or imitation, conforming to an original' (Cappannelli & Cappannelli 2004). Under this traditional view, authenticity was determined by authorities or experts (in the case of artworks) and was often an objective part of the object. As well, authentic objects were rare and carried special status. As a result, what was authentic was often contrasted with mass produced objects or everyday objects precisely because these items were common.

This view has been called 'the objective ideal of authenticity' (Postrel 2003). Such a view is non-personal and holds that what is authentic cannot involve alterations, dilution, and staging. That is, authenticity requires conforming to original principles, traditions, function, and nature. In this view, commercial objects struggle for authenticity unless they are exact replicas of historic designs (such as licensed copies of an *Eames* chair), continue established traditions (such as traditional brewing methods for beer), or adhere to 'form follows function' (where the look of an object is solely determined by its purpose – resulting in simple designs). Finally, any hint of staging – usually seen in terms of self-interest or role playing (such as that employed by *Disney* service staff) is inauthentic.

This historic view has a number of limitations. First, underpinning so-called claims of objectivity are subjective judgements, self-interest, and institutional influence. Related to this is the fact that traditions are often invented to reinforce existing power structures. For example, the famous 1855 Bordeaux wine classification that established quality tiers (with resulting status and price premiums) was initiated to protect the pricing differentials of existing wineries rather than being reflective of intrinsic differences in estate quality (Markham 1998). Second, the objective view of authenticity ignores the role played by people (consumers, critics, marketers, cultural authorities, and trendsetters) in conferring authenticity to an object. For example, small firms play up claims of authenticity to position their brands against larger rivals. Research also reveals consumers find authenticity in a range of objects, including those they know to be fake, mass-market items, and obviously staged events such as reality television (Rose and Wood 2005). In fact, consumers are very active in constructing impressions of authenticity that conform with preconceived views of 'how things ought to be'. In doing so, they often attribute more authenticity to obviously fictional objects than genuine ones (Grayson and Martinec 2004).

These findings suggest authenticity is subjective, socially constructed, and given to an object by consumers, marketers, and others. Subjective forms of authenticity include formal harmony, balance and delight, connection to time and place, and self-expression. Authenticity as formal harmony, balance and delight results from objects that seem to 'work' or give pleasure (Postrel 2003). Thus nostalgic updates of old brands such as the *Mini*, *VW Beetle*, or *Fiat 500* are judged authentic because they look good and bring joy (even though they are only tenuously related to the original design). Authenticity as connection to time and place is important because it reaffirms tradition. Many Australian consumers view *Vegemite* spread in this way – consuming it reaffirms family traditions and marks one out as a 'true Australian' (Beverland and Farrelly forthcoming). Finally, authenticity as self-expression involves consumers' desired self-identity. In this view, objects that express an inner personal truth are authentic, or 'I like this because I'm like that' (Postrel 2003). For example, some consumers may view *Apple* products as authentic because they reflect a sense of creativity and design-led innovation that reaffirms their desired identity (i.e., 'I want to be creative so *Apple* is for me').

Another dominant theme in discussions of authenticity involves sincerity and genuineness of intent. For example, research reveals service staff are viewed as authentic if they demonstrate a genuine interest in individual consumer problems (Arnould and Price 1993; Grandey et al. 2005). Likewise, artists are viewed as authentic to the extent that they ignore commercial considerations (Fine 2004). Sincerity is also important to the authenticity of brands. For example, fine wine consumers judge products seemingly untainted by commercial concerns as more authentic than mass-market products. Lack of commercial interest may be demonstrated by overt statements of disinterest in marketing, commitments to place, organic production techniques, continuing craft traditions, and the passion of winemakers for their products (Beverland 2006). Other consumers may attribute more authenticity to craft products, particularly if they reflect cultural (usually non-Western) traditions because this reflects less materialistic motivations (MacCannell 1976). Research also suggests sincerity can be projected onto commercial objects by consumers seeking to achieve important identity goals (Beverland and Farrelly forthcoming; Rose and Wood 2005).

In this book, authenticity refers to the manifestation of the search for what is real (Berger 1973). This definition accepts that authenticity is subjective, socially constructed, dynamic, and possibly created, imagined, and invented. In seeking to solve problems or construct an identity, consumers gravitate to certain brands and in doing so confer authenticity on them. However, since notions of authenticity are socially constructed, consumer-expressions of authenticity often reflect wider social norms (Beverland and Farrelly forthcoming). Therefore, despite the subjective nature of authenticity, it is possible to identify consistent themes or expressions of authenticity across cultures and subcultures. This leads us to examine the role played by different people and groups in creating brand authenticity.

WHO DETERMINES BRAND AUTHENTICITY?

Traditional brand models emphasize that brand meaning resides in the mind of the consumer. The dominant branding approach is the Customer-Based Brand Equity model (Keller 2003) or 'mind-share' model (Holt 2005). Under this model, the consumer determines brand equity or brand value, although paradoxically, consumers are given little role in constructing brand meaning. This role is left to marketers whose job it is to build positive brand associations with consumers through one-way, top–down communication strategies (Holt 2004). Brand marketers' main job is to measure the gap between how consumers *should* view the brand (brand identity) and how they currently see it (brand image). Strategies with names like 'reinforce-ment', and 'repositioning' are then used to close this gap (Keller 1999). As part of this approach, brands must 'stay on message' by repeating their core message – change, ambiguity, or inconsistency should be avoided (Holt 2004). However, this so-called best practice has rarely been subject to empirical validation (Holt 2005), contradicts the approach adopted by high-profile iconic brands (including *Nike*, *Harley Davidson*, *Mountain Dew*, and *Corona* – see Holt 2004), and ignores sociocultural influences on brand equity and meaning. After all, the *Quaker Oats* team followed this advice when repositioning *Snapple*, and look what happened.

When we actually look at how consumers interact with brands we find that for some brands (like those in this book), meaning is derived from three sources – consumers, marketers, and social forces (see Figure 2.1). Harley Davidson provides a classic example. Clearly marketers play a role in feeding the myth of Harley Davidson through their advertising, brand events, and sponsorship. However, the brand would not enjoy its iconic status without its fan base. Consumers, for example, give the brand significant meaning. For example, middle and upper class consumers (called 'rich urban bikers') adopt the brand because they want to experience the freedom often denied to them in their day-to-day jobs. Lesbian bikers (who identify with the name 'dykes on bikes') adopt the bike because they are co-opting the ultimate symbol of male chauvinism. Working-class bikers adopt the brand as a means of expressing their love of America, and in particular their support for American manufacturing (Schouten and McAlexander 1995).

The wider subculture also feeds the myths surrounding the brand. First, freedom is an enduring theme in American discourse and the outlaw bikie experiencing freedom on the road is simply an updated version of the cowboy riding off into the sunset. Second, the brand (after a management buyout in 1981) survived the onslaught of Japanese imports (largely due to a return to historical quality levels; Scott 2003) and thus represents the triumph of the American spirit. Third, the brand gains significant and positive associations through

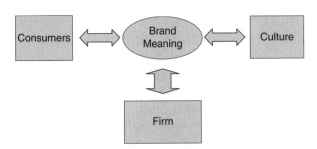

FIGURE 2.1 **Authoring brand meaning**

18

being used in movies such as *Easy Rider* that sympathetically portray bikers as the last representative of free spirits in corporate, middle class America. Much of the advertising supporting the brand, including its core position (freedom) is derived from consumers and the wider socio-culture surrounding the brand. Can we imagine the brand without its association with bikie gangs, rituals such as bikers taking pleasure in destroying Japanese bikes, and iconic images such as Peter Fonda and Dennis Hopper riding on their *Harley's* in search of the real America? The brand meaning of *Harley Davidson* is embedded in a variety of subcultures, without which it would be little more than an overpriced and underperforming motorcycle brand.

Other brands derive significant meaning from subcultures. *Absolut*, *Levi's*, and *Coors'* status within the North American gay community reflects the extent to which these brands are seen as legitimate partners in the struggle for gay rights (Kates 2004). *Absolut* and *Levi's* advertised to the gay community, supporting community events and publications long before this subculture became a legitimate segment to target. *Levi's* extended medical and other benefits to same-sex partners, and discontinued relationships with organizations that discriminated against homosexuals (such as the *Boy Scout* movement). In contrast, *Coors'* attempt at targeting the gay market has failed. The *Coors* family's donations to anti-gay organizations ensure the brand is banned from many bars in gay areas. *Coors* is viewed as lacking legitimacy because it seeks to profit from a community while donating to causes that seek to deny human and legal rights to community members.

The cases of *Dunlop Volley* and *Snapple* provide two further examples. Snapple lost brand equity because the marketing team at *Quaker Oats* failed to understand that consumers embraced the brand because of its countercultural status. The brand had originally been built with the support of rebels such as Rush Limbaugh and Howard Stern. As part of the strategy to reposition the brand to the mainstream, such luminaries were deemed too controversial. With Stern referring to Snapple as 'Crapple' on air, the brand's core consumer base deserted it in favour of niche offerings, leaving the brand little of the cultural capital needed to appeal to more adventurous mainstream consumers (Deighton 2003). As such, the brand had little by way of differentiation against other fruit juices. In contrast, *Pacific Brands* sought to understand the place of the *Volley* in the teenage rave subculture, resulting in a more sensitive marketing approach and eventually elevating the shoe beyond its functional position to one of a local, edgy icon (Beverland and Ewing 2005).

Today, consumers have even greater impact on brand meaning since they are highly connected through technology such as 3G mobile phones, blogs, and websites such as *Twitter, Facebook, YouTube,* and *Myspace.* These platforms allow consumers to access large amounts of information regarding brands (not all of which is favourable). Consumers also engage in culture jamming whereby they ironically poke fun at brands or co-opt the original brand message for the opposite effect than that intended. For example, to make a point about body image and racial bias, consumers have posed and changed the *Barbie* doll to present her as a teenage single mom, sorority slut, and drug addict (see www.hecklers.com). *Starbucks'* logo has been subject to multiple parodies by *Adbusters* including surrounding the mermaid with the words 'Consumer Whore'. *Absolut* has suffered similar parodies of their campaigns with activists linking the brand with death, obesity, alcoholism, and impotence. Such actions eventually find their way into popular culture and mainstream discourse with increasing frequency (especially in today's highly connected age), impacting on how consumers view the brand (Thompson et al. 2006).

Academic research examining brand authenticity identifies how consumers actively create personal brand meaning. Rather than being passive receivers of marketing information, consumers actively construct brand meaning and brand authenticity in order to achieve desired identity goals (Beverland and Farrelly, forthcoming). Such activities may involve acts of imagination, suspension of disbelief, projection, selective information processing, and negotiation of paradox. Figure 2.1 demonstrates how consumers attribute authenticity to a brand. When seeking to build their identity, consumers look for authentic brand partners – that is, brands that reflect inner personal truths (Postrel 2003). For example, many *Apple* fans choose the brand because they want to reflect a desired identity – that they are creative, anti-establishment, liberal individuals (Belk and Tumbat 2005). Such a desire leads some fans to tattoo the *Apple* logo onto their skin, sticker their cars and offices with the brand mark, and even add an *Apple* sticker to non-*Apple* products in order to enhance its perceived performance (Kahney 2004a). Conferring authenticity to a brand involves an act of transformation involving the active use of particular cues (such as taglines or symbols), the use of strategies (such as imagination or selective processing), and the application of subcultural standards (e.g., does this brand support anti-gay causes?).

When consumers want to identify with a particular community they often seek out brands that will mark them out to other members. In doing so they confer authenticity to certain brands, while rejecting others. Let's say a consumer wants to be identified as a 'hard-core' skateboarder. Many brands are targeted at this activity, but not all are viewed as authentic brands by skaters. The wrong brand may have the opposite effect – it may mark you out as an inauthentic member of the community, thus hindering your ability to join and engage with others. The first thing the aspiring skater may do is engage in strategies such as placement (being near other skaters), mimicking (examining what others wear), and projecting the information gained from encounters with skaters onto brands. The aspiring skater may conclude that skateboarders desire freedom from the rules and formality of mainstream sports, and also enjoy breaking the rules by skating where it suits them and engaging in difficult feats with little care for themselves.

This information may be projected onto brand cues. Thus edgy imagery such as graffiti-styled text, and symbols such as death's heads, skull and crossbones and devils are selectively processed as being representative of an authentic skate brand. Into this mix, subcultural standards are applied. First, the aspiring skater may learn that certain brands are 'not hard-core' and that their imagery is used to appeal to fashion-conscious consumers who do not skate. Second, she may learn about the superior performance of certain brands such as shoes. Since performance is critical in this community, these cues become essential to judgements of authenticity. Finally, she may learn that true skaters care little for what others wear (except for those brands that are definitely out) and that she should seek out her own style (Beverland, Farrelly and Quester forthcoming). These standards are used to filter marketing messages and along with strategies of projection and imagination help transform certain brands into authentic partners that help her achieve her desired identity goal (an authentic skater).

Since consumers actively create brand authenticity, it is worth considering why they do so.

WHY DO CONSUMERS LOOK FOR AUTHENTICITY IN BRANDS?

Brands are ubiquitous. As such, they are one of the most dominant institutions in consumer society. Why does this matter? Well, most other institutions that used to shape our identity are in decline. For example, notions of class, family, race, nationality, and place are undermined by macroeconomic, social, and demographic changes (Arnould and Price 2000). Most people will have worked for more than one employer over the course of their work life. Social institutions where people used to gather (church, school meetings, local sporting events, and pubs) are also in decline in many nations (Boyle 2003; Firat and Dholokia 1998). Those institutions that remain more often than not divide people. In contrast, brands reign supreme (Brown 2003; McCracken 2005). They welcome all comers. After all it is branded spaces that have been identified as the 'third place' of postmodern life (the place we frequent after work and home) (Oldenburg 1989). And, they bring people together who may otherwise disagree on a range of different issues. As one young fan of *Chuck Taylor* shoes stated, '[chucks] are the great unifier' (Peterson 2007, p. 5). Rock stars, college students, athletes, and anyone who loves the brand wears the shoes (in fact estimates suggest at least 60 per cent of Americans have owned a pair of chucks in their lifetime; Peterson (2007)). *Tupperware* is also universally loved. Why?

> Tupperware design is emancipated design, it is intercultural and universal – but the most important thing is: it can inspire people with enthusiasm, trigger emotions, find passionate devotees – right across all strata of the population, age groups and on every continent. Tupperware design is truly democratic design. (Tupperware 2005, p. 39)

Furthermore, research reveals that consumers can imbue everyday mass-produced objects with rich personal meaning. One study revealed that up to 85 per cent of the objects consumers considered 'sacred' (and therefore irreplaceable) were mass-market items (Grayson and Schulman 2000). These common items were deemed sacred because consumers had transformed them into authentic objects. In a more recent ethnographic investigation of a London neighbourhood, the objects people surrounded themselves with at home often reflected deep personal meanings including memories of loved ones, joy and loss, life-changing events, and major coming-of-age rituals (Miller 2008). Objects, not all of them mass-produced, have also taken on iconic status in many societies (Sudjic 2008). A pair of *Converse White High Top* (Taylor's personal favourites) *Chuck Taylor* shoes is housed in the *Smithsonian* (Peterson 2007), while a *Dyson Dual Cyclone* vacuum takes pride of place in the *Victoria and Albert Museum* in London. It is not uncommon for consumers to protest against the loss of loved items (the author is currently a member of several 'bring back' groups on *Facebook*), wear T-shirts featuring advertisements for local iconic products, buy histories of famous commercial objects and brands, attend brand museums, take factory tours, or attend exhibits of famous brands such as *Armani, Bugatti, Chanel, Manolo Blahnik, Tupperware,* or *Vivienne Westwood* in art galleries.

Arnould and Price (2000) contend that three characteristics of postmodern societies have reshaped how and where we find identity and authenticity.

1. *Globalization*: With an increase in cross-border trade and migration, and the increasing exposure of local economies to global forces, individuals may struggle to understand their place in the wider global order since faraway forces can change personal circumstances with little notice. The current financial crisis provides an example with many people struggling to understand how their lives can be so affected by decisions made by stockbrokers and banks halfway across the globe.
2. *Deterritorialization*: As people move from one nation to the next (through tourism or migration), and are exposed to different cultural experiences such as art, entertainment, and food, they lose connections to place and associated rituals that helped form their identity. For example, Japanese American children are often surprised to find that their beloved sushi is available in Japan when they visit.
3. *Hyperreality*: The increased stylization of everyday life results in increasing difficulties in telling real from fake, especially given increases in advertorial, viral, and guerrilla marketing campaigns (that beautiful person sidling up to you at a bar could very well be a brand ambassador looking to encourage you to try their new product).

The loss of traditional sources of identity and the increased dominance of image in everyday life gives rise to rituals that affirm an individual's authentic self and their desired collective identity. Increasingly these rituals involve brands, branded spaces, or activities involving brand identity markers (such as skateboarding). For example, consumers may seek out regional or niche brands, or engage in communal activities that feature brands in order to reconnect to a sense of place or community. For example, Jewish bikies formed a *Harley Davidson* club called Star of Davidson to encourage social interaction (Scott 2003). Finally, consumers may use branded images and stories to create a sense of authenticity outside oneself. Figure 2.2 identifies how consumers engage in creative acts to generate new 'truths' when conferring authenticity to brands. Thus, as members of brand communities or even society in general, the ability to share in ritualistic discussions of television shows, viral advertisements, *YouTube* videos, and stories surrounding brands provides a sense of reality outside oneself.

Brands are particularly important in allowing people to reconnect to a sense of time, place/space, and shared culture. First, communities of like-minded individuals have often formed around brands. These 'brand communities' bring together a range of diverse individuals, all of whom shared a love of *Apple, Harley Davidson, Star Trek, VW Beetle, MG, Morgan,* comics, films and television shows, musicians, and so on. Brands such as *Starbucks* and *Borders* attempt to create social spaces where people can congregate and meet one another. Second, many communities were founded by brands, or gained legitimacy following brand support. This is particularly the case with extreme sports such as *Burton* and snowboarding, *Quiksilver* and surfing, *Schwinn* and cycling, and *Vans* and skateboarding. Third, few public spaces are free of brands. In some countries it is not uncommon for brand advertising to feature at school, while institutions such as universities, churches and museums have engaged in branding to bolster flagging finances (Twitchell 2004).

Finally, brands may also help consumers achieve important identity goals (e.g., an older consumer may wear a pair of *chucks* 'to feel young again'; Peterson 2007, p. 22). Recent research suggests diverse expressions of authenticity can only be understood in light of consumer identity goals. Many societies insist that individuals achieve practical

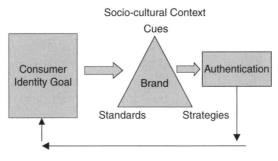

FIGURE 2.2 **Authenticating brands**

outcomes in their everyday life, participate in communal events, and obey a few universal moral laws. Brands, or our rejection of them, allow us to manage these multiple and often conflicting identities. As Star of Davidson spokesman Ray Eichler stated:

> The appearance of the riders mimics the outlaw look – a mean look, but really for our riders it's just one way to express themselves. If you are a doctor, then on the weekend you can become a different person. That's what makes it so romantic. You can get on the bike and be somebody else. (Scott, 2003, p. 118)

Consumers may select product leader brands to help them achieve practical goals, use mass-market items to allow them connect to others or achieve communal identities, and select or reject brands that conform or breach societal codes of morality (Beverland and Farrelly forthcoming). Given that brands are used by consumers to achieve authenticity, how do marketers enhance or diminish the authenticity of their brands? The next section examines the emerging stream of academic work on this issue.

HOW DO MARKETERS BUILD/DESTROY AUTHENTICITY?

Although marketing *per se* does not diminish a brand's authenticity, how one markets products and services is critical. Overall, research suggests consumers confer authenticity to a brand through selective and creative use of marketing cues and other brand-relevant information (Beverland and Farrelly forthcoming). Consumers may use a building block approach where they look for specific cues that indicate authenticity, or they may search for evidence that suggests a lack of authenticity (Beverland et al. 2008; Chalmers and Price 2009). In both cases, consumers have a mental picture of what authenticity means in a given context; all that differs is whether a brand has to reach a certain minimum threshold to be considered authentic, or whether the mere existence of one offending cue is enough to damn the brand as inauthentic (Beverland et al. 2008; Chalmers 2007). What is clear is that overt claims of authenticity render a brand suspect immediately. For example, when Belgian Trappist Monasteries used the slogan 'Authentic Trappist Product' to identify their products, consumers reacted negatively, immediately considering the products suspect (even though they genuinely desired a real Trappist beer) (Beverland et al. 2008). Similarly, *Starbucks'* overt claims of being an authentic coffee house have backfired (Thompson et al. 2006).

So what cues should marketers use when seeking to build brand authenticity? I have defined (Beverland 2005a, p. 1008) brand authenticity as:

> A story that balances industrial (production, distribution and marketing) and rhetorical attributes to project sincerity through the avowal of commitments to tradition (including production methods, product styling, firm values, and/or location), passion for craft and production excellence, *and* the public disavowal of the role of modern industrial attributes and commercial motivations.

In telling such a story, brand owners develop sincerity by connecting their brand to a sense of place, using traditional production techniques, stylistic consistency, drawing on history and culture, and appearing above commercial considerations (Beverland 2005a; 2006). Gilmore and Pine (2007) suggest authenticity can be built by referring to nature, originality, uniqueness, significant others, and achievement. Brand managers should seek to fit their brands or product categories to the relevant cues. Therefore, brands such as *REI (Recreational Equipment Inc.)* should reference nature because they sell outdoor sporting equipment whereas luxury fashion brands should draw on cues that signal uniqueness, originality, and adoption by significant others.

A recent quantitative study has identified three core attributes of a brand critical to consumer judgements of authenticity (Napoli et al. forthcoming). These are:

1. *Quality Leadership*: Quality leadership is the belief that behind the brand are passionate artisans using the finest quality materials and meeting exacting standards to continually push the barriers of product excellence. Examples include *Apple, Chanel, Dyson*, and New Zealand's *Weta Works* (producer of *Lord of the Rings, Chronicles of Narnia*, and *King Kong*).
2. *Heritage*: Heritage is the belief that the brand is connected to time, place, and culture. The brand exudes commitments to traditions, reminds consumers of a golden age, and is based on timeless designs. Examples include the *Morgan Motor Company, Chateau Margaux, Louis Vuitton*, and *In-N-Out Burger*.

3. *Sincerity*: Sincerity is the belief that the brand lives up to its espoused values and commitments. Examples include *The Body Shop, Lonely Planet, Zippo, Untouched World,* and *Champagne Bollinger*.

The specific mix of cues chosen are driven by consumer-goals. Advertising research identifies three forms of authenticity – pure or literal, approximate, and moral. Literal authenticity is important when consumers desire the genuine article and need to make an on-the-spot decision about a brand's authenticity. In these situations, consumers are more likely to look for cues signalling inauthenticity, as well as cues providing a clear link between the brand name and its focal activity. When using approximate authenticity, consumers were seeking to reconnect to an idealized image of time and place. Thus more stylized cues reflecting general notions of a particular period or place were sought. Finally, when seeking moral authenticity consumers desire brands that reflect their personal beliefs. In these cases, cues that signalled sincerity, and the lack of cues signalling commercial motivations are critical (Beverland et al. 2008).

So far, academic research has focused on the cues that suggest or diminish authenticity in an advertisement or brand. However, building an authentic brand requires more than just manipulating the right cues. As my definition above suggests, marketers must craft a rich story that balances competing perspectives and pressures on the business. Also, consumers authenticate brands that deliver the high performance standards associated with modern industrial production and marketing practices, even though overt promotion of these strategies diminishes authenticity (Beverland 2006; Beverland et al. 2008; Beverland and Luxton 2005). This requires marketers to engage in a delicate balancing act involving behind the scenes investments in quality, 'right type of marketing', and the promotion of a rich story that downplays these very investments – all the while maintaining impressions of sincerity. Part II identifies how marketers achieve this balancing act to achieve lasting brand authenticity.

CONCLUSION

Authenticity involves the manifestation of the search for what is real. One critical manifestation of consumers' search for authenticity is brands. Consumers are extremely creative in authenticating brands, often drawing on their imagination, collective myths and stories, and personal predilections to when judging brand-related cues and information. Although the authenticity of a brand is highly subjective, research identifies a number of consistent themes or characteristics of brand authenticity. The main three characteristics of consumer-based brand authenticity are quality commitments, heritage, and sincerity. Failing to understand this can result in rapid declines in brand equity (as was experienced by *Snapple*), while brand managers that understand the sociocultural role of a brand can enhance their status and equity (as was the case with the *Dunlop Volley*). Since brand authenticity involves creating a rich story, we now examine the nature of such stories in Chapter 3.

CHAPTER 3
THE AUTHENTICITY OF STORIES

For the consumer, Champagne's mystique is in stories.

(Fabrice Rosset, CEO *Champagne Deutz*, quoted in Farmer 2005/2006, p. 36)

Every entrepreneur is a great *storyteller*. It is storytelling that defines your differences.

(Anita Roddick 2005, p. 41)

WEAPONS OF MASS DESTRUCTION AND WOODEN CHASSIS

For the past 90 minutes Lynne McEwan held the Melbourne-based audience in the palm of her hand as she regaled us with stories of *Bruichladdich* (pronounced 'Brooke Laddie') – the Islay distillery resurrected by her father and legendary whisky maker, Jim. This was no corporate-sponsored, power point-based whisky tasting; rather this was akin to listening to a saga of old, where the audience added their own stories about the brand (many had been to the distillery) to Lynne's narrative. Being a marketing researcher, one story in particular appealed to me. Such is the love that customers have of *Bruichladdich* single malts that webcams are placed in the distillery so fans can monitor the progress of each batch (it really is a thrill a minute). Lynne recalled the day the sales staff received an email inquiry from the US wondering when a faulty camera would be repaired. Staff replied that the camera would be running soon and asked, 'Are you a single malt fan?' The reply was unexpected – 'no we are not single malt fans, we are the Defense Threat Reduction Agency (DTRA) and believe you are making weapons of mass destruction!' The agency had been training their staff on the production of biological and chemical weapons using the webcams.

The story met with mass laughter from the audience, coming as it did after the ill-fated search for 'weapons of mass destruction' in Iraq. Such a story confirmed the generally held belief by many Australians of the incompetence of government intelligence services, and a common disdain for bureaucrats. There was a purpose to this story however – it provided the background to *Bruichladdich*'s 2003 bottling of their 1984 single malt entitled 'WMD 1 – the Weapons Inspectors'. Lynne left it up to audience to decide whether WMD stood for weapons of mass destruction, or whisky of mass distinction (as used on the bottle's label). The original release now sells for UK£350 per bottle (it was around £50 on release). The WMD story doesn't stop there however. In 2005 a fishing vessel hauled up a British Navy yellow mini-submarine seven miles away from *Bruichladdich*. Following a much-publicized spat between the fisherman and the British Navy (that denied losing the submarine), the submarine was returned to the government. *Bruichladdich* used this story – not only were the Americans spying on sleepy old Islay, now the Brits were at it too. The resulting whisky, WMD II (Figure 3.1), was released with a picture of the unfortunate yellow submarine on the front.

Bruichladdich are master storytellers, using the unique events and circumstances at hand to craft an authenticity that others find difficult to replicate. In fact, while competitors release standard line-ups of

FIGURE 3.1   *Bruichladdich's* Weapons of Mass Destruction (WMD II)

10-, 20-, 30- and even 40-year single malts, *Bruichladdich* release an ever-expanding range of products, each with a unique story (Figure 3.2). The *PC* releases celebrate the efforts of individual staff members at the distillery, the *Celtic Nations* range celebrates the Celtic diaspora by bottling whiskies from around the world, the *Links* range celebrates the world's famous golf courses, the *Rocks*, *Waves*, and *Peat* range make a virtue out of Islay's unique environment (that contributes to the flavour of the whisky), while the *Sixteen's* range makes a virtue out of being stored in discarded wine barrels supplied by the world's great wine estates. Masters distiller Jim McEwan is an innovator in new whisky styles, particularly the use of wine (instead of bourbon or sherry casks) barrels for storage and importantly for flavour. Recalling an early experiment with wine casks, Lynne noted how one batch of whisky was turned pink because it was left too long in a wine cask. Rather than dump the product, it was relabelled *Flirtation* and local newspapers ran headlines stating 'Bruichladdich makes whiskey for women and gays'.

Stories also form the backbone of the *Morgan* brand. Although, as CEO Charles Morgan stated, not all authentic stories are developed by the marketing team:

Rather than a brand I think it's more an attempt to interest the cult and keep the cult going. We like providing stories that people can tell in the pub and feel that that makes them part of the family. And

FIGURE 3.2 **Stories are at the heart of whisky producer *Bruichladdich***

so our brand is made up around a series of myths, some of which are true, *some of which are owned*. The one about the wooden chassis in France, we have tried and tried to get rid of that, but it still persists. And I think eventually we're going to have to say ok yeah yeah yeah it's true.

Charles' quote identifies the subjective nature of brand authenticity. *Morgan* builds traditional English sports cars. Part of the body is made of wood, although the chassis certainly is not. Despite this, French fans of the brand continue to believe the chassis is made of wood, a point *Morgan* no longer sees any reason in denying. As Charles notes, central to *Morgan's* brand stories are myths – some that are true, and others that are created and owned by consumers. The French consumers' view is an example of a story that is not true, but provides an element of mystique that is alluring. Critically, *Morgan* has given up trying to tell these consumers what is authentic; rather they are happy to allow consumers to create stories that work for them precisely because they help the brand.

Authentic brands are simply collections of stories – as Charles Morgan and Jim and Lynne McEwan are so clearly aware. Although marketers regularly tell stories, often these are simple ('*Ajax* drives away germs'), or extremely sanitized versions of events that provide no emotional connection with consumers. Marketers and public relations staff are encouraged to smooth out the rough edges of corporate histories (such as the whitewashing by many German firms of their use of slave labour between 1933–45), diminishing a brand's human-like quality. Also, marketers are taught to remain in control of their brand's story, even though today's Internet connected age makes such attempts futile. As such, marketers worry if consumers and the public reinvent the brand's image in a way they do not intend (Thompson et al. 2006). Instead, the marketers behind authentic brands allow and even encourage consumers to tell their own stories about the brand. As Charles Morgan noted, such stories may not be true, but they do hold meaning for the consumers involved (and thus for them are truthful).

All the brands covered in this book use storytelling in a number of ways. First, they create stories from their surrounds and circumstances. Second, they take advantage of lucky events (*Bruichladdich* and Weapons of Mass Destruction). Third, they allow others to tell stories for them. This can include consumers, publics, or even artists (such as *Harley Davidson* and *Easy Rider*). Fourth, they draw on the stories of their respective subcultures. Fifth, they provide their brand attributes to consumers so that they can create their own stories. Why do such actions create authenticity? Brand stories provide a context that most of us can share. As a result, storytelling has become the 'new black' in branding circles (Mathews and Wacker 2008; Sisodia, Wolfe, and Sheth 2007). We explore this issue in more detail next, before turning to the nature of authentic brand stories.

WHY DO BRAND STORIES CREATE AUTHENTICITY?

A person's identity is not to be found in behavior, nor – important though this is – in the reactions of others, but in the capacity to keep a particular narrative going. (Giddens 1991, p. 54)

Every culture has stories. In fact stories are some of our oldest documents, whether they be paintings on rocks by cavemen, ancient sagas (such as Homer's *Iliad*), oral histories, myths, or religious texts. Such stories form part of our collective identity and are canonized because they are seen as essential to global, national, and/or regional identity. The structure of stories (plot, theme, and setting) often cross national, racial, and religious boundaries (Booker 2004) providing the basis for a shared context and therefore mutual understanding. Stories are powerful simply because they bring people together – they provide a shared context that allows us to connect, not only to each other, but also across time and place. However, changes rendered by globalization, deterritorialization, and hyperreality have undermined our shared context (some refer to the current world as 'context-less'; Arnould and Price 2000), reducing the identifying and unifying power of traditional canons.

Yet our need for identity and connection remains, and this is where brands come in – they allow us to keep personally relevant identity narratives alive (which as Giddens' quote above states, is essential to self-authentication). The very ubiquity of brands is what makes them important unifying institutions. Love or hate a particular brand, such attitudes increasingly reflect inner personal truths (Postrel 2003) and allow us to connect with like-minded others. *Apple* consumers often describe themselves as 'Apple people' in contrast to 'PC people' (in contrast, some of my tech-savvy students view *Apple* as dumbed-down computers) and see themselves as more creative, free thinking, and independent (even though these descriptors are attributes generated by the brand's marketing team) (Belk and Gumbat 2005). The *Apple* brand unites these diverse people, while the stories surrounding the brand provide the basis for further sharing and connecting.

Stories are viewed as more authentic than other forms of information because they mirror how we (and others) communicate things about ourselves, others, places, events, cultures, and experiences. Often we use stories when communicating with loved ones, close friends, family members, or trusted colleagues. When we tell stories, we often move 'off script' revealing personal secrets, fears, desires, or histories (or, we let our guard down). In contrast, much of our public life (particularly at work) involves staying 'on script', remaining wary of others views, sensitivities, impressions, and judgements (Goffman 1959). Societal norms also shape how we act in public. For example, societies have different 'rules' on what is on and off-limits, how much emotion can be displayed, how one should act in certain situations, and so on. For many of us restrictions imposed by roles, firms, culture, and society limit our authentic expression. In contrast stories allow us to reveal our true self (they are also useful for inducting new members into cultures and subcultures).

Brands also reflect this tension between off-script and on-script behaviour. As former *Coca-Cola* CEO Sergio Zyman states:

> Leaving things up to the consumers' imagination is something you *never* want to do. Customers are dangerous, and if you let them decide how they want to be satisfied, you're going to have a terrible time living up to their dreams. It's better if you can control both the promise and the delivery. (quoted in Wipperfürth 2005, p. 8)

Zyman's view is consistent with much traditional brand advice, but is simply not practical in a postmodern environment when consumers do decide how your brand should satisfy them. Many brands stick strictly to a script, often defining how employees should dress, look, behave, and respond emotionally. Such behaviour often undermines the credibility of claims regarding customer sensitivity, customer orientation, particularly when things go wrong. Worse still is when firms attempt to limit consumers' abilities to tell their own stories about the brand they love (for fear of losing control they don't actually have). *Facebook* provides a recent example. Following user pressure to back down over the social network site's decision to claim ownership over user content, founder Mark Zuckenberg remained on marketing script when he noted that users' concerns would be addressed in a revised version of *Facebook*'s terms and conditions. Failing to understand how people bonded with the site, Zuckenberg chastised users for believing they should simultaneously share personal information with friends (personal sites are in fact closed to those friends people invite on) on the site and continue to demand control and ownership over this content (Stafford 2009).

Compare this approach to Peter Jackson, director of the *Lord of the Rings* trilogy and founder of *Wingnut Film Studios* in New Zealand. When fans (called *Ringers*) of the trilogy raised concerns about a virtually unknown director being responsible for translating Tolkien's books on screen, Jackson (an unabashed Tolkien fan) set up a website that addressed these concerns. As the films started to develop, Jackson let fans in on his decisions to include or exclude scenes (from the books), adapt material, and flesh out characters. Turning long novels into films necessitates cuts to the original material, while a visual medium also requires shifting material around to ensure on-screen continuity. By making himself available, listening to fan concerns and criticisms, and explaining his decisions, Jackson effectively went off-script, enhancing the authenticity of the final films in the eyes of fans (Sibley 2006).

Jackson's approach is reflective of how brands, or in his case, people and artworks, gain an aura of authenticity. Recent books on using stories or authenticity as a branding tool simply represent a different form of staying on script marketing. These approaches may help with brand positioning and provide a form of differentiation, but they are unlikely to generate lasting authenticity particularly since the authors advocate inventing stories (even if they have no shred of truth), staying on message in the face of contradictory evidence or ignoring or 'correcting' consumer stories like that created by French *Morgan* owners about the wooden chassis (Mathews and Wacker 2008). Rather than picking on a few well-constructed, consistent stories to form part of a brand script, the brands covered in this book take a different approach. Essentially, they use a broad range of stories to add ever-deepening layers to the brand's richness. The result is a strong aura or impression of authenticity, rather than a series of well-defined brand associations (that constantly require renewal). This aura reinforces consumers' 'gut feeling' about the object, which is the essence of a great brand (Neumeier 2003).

Authentic brands collect stories the way a hurricane draws energy as it moves over water. Just as the force and size of a hurricane differs according to climate and topography, so too authentic brands draw on their surroundings to create a powerful aura. Authentic brands draw energy from the three authors of meaning covered in Figure 2.1. Authentic brands are essentially made up of stories created by the firm, told by others, borrowed from elsewhere, and co-created by the firm, society, and/or consumers. For example, the *Bruichladdich* brand consists of stories created by the marketing team – such as stories about the role of Islay's unique natural features (water, peat, and rocks) in the production of their whiskys, or the celebration of distillery staff in their *PC* series. Stories are also told by others including consumers and critics – a classic example being the *Flirtation* line which was christened as a whisky for women and gays by the press – a story that has since become part of the brand's folklore. Other stories are borrowed, such as those behind the *Celtic Nations* range, which locate the brand in a global diaspora of Celtic peoples who have taken the knowledge of whisky production from Scotland and Ireland to North America, Australia, and New Zealand. Finally, the WMD range is an example of co-creation – crafting a unique story out of serendipitous events that reflects consumers' biases regarding government competence. Which story is the most important? Who can say – or rather, different consumers connect to the brand in different ways, including creating their own story (my own relates to Lynne jokingly (I think) threatening to 'do in' some rowdy customers at a 2008 Melbourne tasting).

Although the hurricane metaphor does not capture the lasting power of authentic brands (thankfully hurricanes dissipate), it does capture the force-of-nature like presence these brands have among their devoted consumers. These brands are powerful transmitters of authenticity, constructed naturally, and a constant presence on the wider landscape – just as hurricanes are seasonal, we anticipate and prepare for releases from *Apple*, the fine wine estates, whisky houses, fashion houses, movie directors, car manufacturers, and the other brands covered here, which are often major news events in their right. The metaphor is also useful in another way – a hurricane's power or size is the product of all the energy it consumes. Authentic brands are similar – they are a product of all the stories they create, receive, or co-create over time. Authentic brands in this sense are the sum of their parts, although they cannot be encapsulated in a single tagline, or distilled into a small number of attributes.

In contrast to mainstream brands that have a forever-set-in-stone position and meaning, the owners of authentic brands often struggle to define their brand's position, falling back on a series of stories that help communicate some of the brand's mystique. In my research with fine winemakers and their marketers in France I soon discovered how difficult it was for these informants to answer the question 'how would you define your brand?' Since many of the informants had some knowledge of formal brand models, they realized what I was after and often rejected the notion that they had brands at all. Like Charles Morgan in the opening quotation of the chapter, these winemakers and marketers often started telling stories – stories of place, people, time, culture, failures, struggles, luck, triumphs, passion, and so on. Further historical research on these estates revealed that many of these brands had histories stretching back 200 years or more (in one case over 600 years) (Beverland 2005a). As a result, these brands, as with all authentic brands, represent collections of idiosyncratic stories that collectively produce a powerful mystique or aura over time.

THE TEN STORIES BEHIND AUTHENTIC BRANDS

Debates rage on the number of different stories brand managers can tell. Some favour seven key plots that characterize all human stories (Booker 2004), while others suggest 20 and even 36 different storylines (see Mathews and Wacker 2008 for review). Recent examinations of brand-based stories suggest five key stories (Mathews and Wacker 2008), five genres of authenticity (Gilmore and Pine 2007), or four key elements of storytelling (Fog, Budtz, and Yakaboylu 2005). Although the hurricane metaphor suggests authentic brands are indiscriminate collections of stories, there are ten consistent themes that emerged from my research. These are summarized in Table 3.1, and discussed in order below.

Founding

The founding story of *Sony* is well known – Akio Morita and Masaru Ibuka struggling to make ends meet in their radio repair shop in a bombed out building in postwar Japan (Nathan 2001). We may struggle to identify with the global behemoth that *Sony* has become, but we can easily identify with the struggles, and critically, the humanity, of Akio and Masura. All brands have foundation myths that include stories of start-up challenges, the role and motivation of key personnel

TABLE 3.1 Ten stories behind authentic brands

Story	Forms	Brand benefit	Consumer benefit
Founding	1. Start-up and early challenges. 2. Founding 'myths'. 3. Motivation for founding.	1. Roots brand to time, place, human experience, and values.	1. Provides connection to the past. 2. Provides basis for storytelling.
Family	1. Family members and dynasties. 2. Generational changes. 3. Stewardship.	1. Roots brand to continued traditions and values. 2. Provides brand with stories of renewal.	1. Provides connection to people behind brand name.
Conflict and struggle	1. Conflict with others, self, authorities, competitors, forces of history, and nature.	1. Heightens emotional interest in brand resulting in stronger bonds to brand. 2. Enhances brand differentiation. 3. Increases loyalty in times of difficulty.	1. Consumers identify brand with their cause or values. 2. Provides central rallying point.
Triumph and tragedy	1. Successes as well as their failures. 2. Personal and national triumphs and tragedies. The struggle for acceptance. 3. Seeing off competitors, the break-up of key teams in the firm, disasters, struggles with launching new products or services, and community struggles for recognition.	1. Humanizes the brand. 2. Creates brand myths.	1. Connects brand to reality of consumers' own experiences. 2. Connects brand to community struggles.
Creation	1. Link people behind products and service and brand. 2. Problem solving and innovation. 3. Challenging conventions and solving paradoxes. 4. Love of production and craft.	1. Enhances perceptions of quality leadership, heritage, and sincerity. 2. Differentiates brand from larger 'faceless' corporations.	1. Self-authentication: helps build identity of creative, rule-breaking consumer.

History	1. The role of the brand and people behind it in historical events. 2. Use of brand by major historical figures. 3. Role of history in shaping brand (and vice versa). 4. Brand history. 5. Evolution of product/service and processes. 6. History of supportive communities.	1. Enhances heritage. 2. Ensures iconic or institutional status for brand. 3. Brand seen as part of the social landscape and cultural identity.	1. Connects the brand and its consumers to time, place, and culture.
Community	1. The role of the brand in community-founding myths. 2. Mutual relationship between brand and community or nation.	1. Enhances perceptions of heritage and sincerity. 2. Enhances legitimacy and status.	1. Connects to time, place, and culture. 2. Identity creation.
Place	1. Role of place in shaping product. 2. Link to nature. 3. Substantive link to somewhere. 4. Link to birthplace. 5. Context of performance.	1. Enhances brand's heritage. 2. Gives brand physicality. 3. Enhances brand's uniqueness.	1. Builds connections to place. 2. Provides background for performances and experiences.
Consumers	1. Personalized versions of other stories. 2. Self-authentication. 3. Fantasy. 4. Innovation.	1. Enhances authenticity through sincerity and providing non-firm voice to brand story. 2. Lowers cost.	1. Personalizes and strengthens brand connection. 2. Self-authentication. 3. Allows for connection. 4. Social identity.
Product/service	1. Performance. 2. Creation. 3. Failures. 4. Love for product/service.	1. Builds perceptions of quality commitments.	1. Goal achievement. 2. Creativity. 3. Mastery. 4. Identity.

in the brand's early days, and key events that shaped the brand (see the Sidebar on Burt's Bees). These myths are critical for authenticity because they connect the brand with time and place, and also everyday human desires and emotions. Founding stories demonstrate that great companies were once struggling start-ups, suggesting that such greatness may be possible to each of us. Finally, stories of founding enhance the aura of authenticity surrounding the brand by adding to the brand's mystique (especially when histories eventually become contested, as they usually do with the passage of time).

For example, *Apple*'s foundation myth concerns the relationship between Steve Jobs and Steve Wozniak, the choice of logo, founding the company in Jobs' bedroom (and later his garage), and the early decisions to emphasize aesthetics as well as performance. According to legend, *Apple* was funded by the US$1300 gained from the sale of Wozniak's scientific calculator and Jobs' *Volkswagen* van. *Apple* (the name was taken from the Beatles record label whom Jobs admired) was founded in 1976 with the release of the *Apple 1*. Jobs credits key aspects of *Apple*'s design to luck – although he dropped out of college he continued to drop in on classes, one of which was calligraphy. As Jobs' states, 'If I had never dropped in on that single course in college, the Mac would have never had multiple typefaces or proportionally spaced fonts' (14 June 2005).

Side Bar:
BURT AND HIS BEES

The *Burt's Bees* brand was built on stories – stories of the founder, the bees, place and nature, and a rags-to-riches tale that saw a cottage industry grow into a major brand. The story started when struggling part-time waitress Roxanne Quimby met unassuming beekeeper Burt Shavitz in Garland, Maine in 1984 at a flea market. Quimby had a store at the flea market to try and earn extra money while Burt had a stall selling honey. Since Burt stockpiled his beeswax, Quimby suggested he turn it into candles. One thing led to another, and soon the pair was producing lip balm, creams and the brand was born (allowing Burt to buy a prized classic motorbike). Although Roxanne originally positioned the brand around quality, she quickly realized that it was storytelling that would differentiate her product. In particular, Burt's stories were what consumers loved. Describing him as a 'sage' Roxanne quickly got Burt to meet consumers, retail buyers, and talk about his products (and even sign T-shirts for fans) (Rosica 2007, pp. 15–16).

Burt even featured in the firm's packaging, although it is the bees that rightly take pride of place in the firm's logo. How many other personal care companies are able to do the same thing?

Stories around the brand began immediately with Wozniak's decision to price the *Apple 1* at US$666.66, controversially corresponding to the number of the beast in the Bible – Wozniak chose this number because he liked repeating digits and the price was $US500 plus 33 per cent mark up (Wozniak and Smith 2006). Jobs' roguish reputation is also a key part of *Apple*'s folklore – particularly the story regarding how Jobs' cheated Wozniak out of his US$2200 share of some initial work for *Atari* (Jobs told Wozniak that the total paid by *Atari* was US$600 – the pair had agreed to a 50:50 split) (Young and Simon 2005). These are just a handful of the thousands of stories concerning the founding of this iconic brand (and just as many have probably faded with time). What do these founding days say about the brand? First, they connect the brand to two individuals, both of whom were passionate about computers. Second, they connect the brand to the early days of Silicon Valley and the development of the personal computer. Third, they provide early evidence of the values that would later shape *Apple* – artistic values, entrepreneurial spirit, roguish charm, Jobs' involvement in all aspects of the firm, the love of design, and the desire to shake up the system. Together these foundation stories tie the brand to the history and development of the industry, thereby connecting it to time and place. As well, these stories connect the brand with real people – people who embody human imperfections (passion, desire, hard work, audacity, dishonesty). Such stories enhance the heritage aspects of the industry, and allow consumers to connect to time, place, and the spirit of adventure that characterized the early days of the industry.

All brands have founding myths, but authentic brands choose to tell and retell these myths. The older the brand, the more the founding myths gain potency and change with losses in records, people, deliberate forgetting (such as *Jack Daniel's* claim they have no memory of where their famous *Old Number 7* label came from; Krass 2004), and deliberate embellishment (such as the centrality of Jobs' to the original success of *Apple*). Some brands' foundation myths are literally lost to history such as the early days of iconic French winery *Chateau Margaux*. Although the brand is around 600 years old, the vineyard was planted well before that, with some tracing the lineage to Roman times (Faith 1988). Such foundation myths also change with each retelling, much like a game of Chinese whispers – often generating their own literature and fierce debates between opposing camps in the brand community, all of which enhances the bond between consumer and brand, and the brand's mystique.

Family

Many old brands are named after their founding family, or founded and maintained by families. Examples include *L.L. Bean, Gucci, Honda, Chateau Margaux, Krug, Morgan, In-N-Out Burger, Ferrari, W. Britains, Bruichladdich*, and *Prada* (among many others). Stories regarding family involve the role of family members in the business, the contribution of each family member to the success or decline of the brand, inter-generational change, family tragedies and triumphs, and notions of continued stewardship. Brands often lose something special when the last surviving family member leaves the firm – a moment that often evokes press comment.

Stories of family are often used during times of renewal. In particular, the continued stewardship of the brand under family members provides comfort to long-time fans that important traditions will continue even when change is necessary. Because family members often grow up around fans, and are inducted into the business at an early age, they intuitively know why customers bond with the brand. For example, when Leon Gorman (grandson of L. L. Bean) took over the running of the Maine based outdoor sportswear retailer, he understood that commitment to service, customers, product quality, and product endorsements by staff who used the products in the same outdoor pursuits as their consumers, were critical to the brand's heritage and strategy of renewal. Instead of radical repositioning towards fashion or modernization, Leon recommitted to these values that had declined in L. L.'s dying days. The product range was slashed, service standards, warehousing, and logistics were improved, and Leon and his staff increased their involvement in outdoor activities. Leon also returned to L. L.'s quirky style of product endorsement in their catalogue, continuing the personal touch that had made the company famous. Although the family is no longer involved in the day-to-day management of the firm, Leon's actions left the brand's authenticity and equity stronger than ever (Gorman 2006).

Solutions to family tension or conflict are often viewed as a critical phase in the brand's evolution. Such a story sits at the heart of the renewal of one of Australia's oldest wineries, *Yalumba*. Although the winery was one of the first in Australia, and was a major player in the domestic market in the late 1960s and early 1970s, by the 1980s the brand was viewed as an outdated, fading star due to lack of investment, lack of strategic focus, family quarrels, and the emergence of exciting new producers. One of the major problems facing the brand concerned the fragmentation of share ownership that had occurred over the years as the family grew and shares were inherited and owned by large numbers of people, many of whom had little interest in the business. Few of these shareholders had the ability to recapitalize the business, but all wanted a say in how it was run. To break this paralysis, fifth generation CEO Robert Hill Smith took a controlling interest in the company and changed the family ownership structure as part of a larger strategy of renewal. Today, Smith's decision is seen as crucial to the survival and prosperity of this famed winery.

Family stories are critical to the authenticity of the *Morgan* car brand. Often the firm's history is told in terms of cycles that relate to each generation. The first period involved founder HFS Morgan who developed the original 3-wheeler car and the first version of the still-in-production 4/4 (later changed to +4). The second period involved HFS' son Peter who saw the company through the difficult post-war period by increasing export markets with a modernized version of the +4, the iconic +8, and the poorly received +4+. The third and current stage involves HFS' grandson Charles who has lifted quality standards and contributed his own two models – the *Aero* and *Aeromax* (and currently experimental electric *LIFEcar*), as well as further evolving the +4 and morphing the +8 into the *Roadster*. All three founders were avid car enthusiasts and race drivers. Charles has continued the tradition of innovation began by HFS as well as ensuring his own cars and leadership contribute to the ongoing legacy of the brand. (The next generation is already being immersed in the business – Charles commissioned a special *Morgan* car shaped bed in 2006 for his young son).

What do these stories tell us? Stories of family enhance the heritage of the brand and emphasize the brand's evolving tradition of stewardship under the watchful gaze of family members all too aware of the obligation they have to past, present, and future generations. For consumers, the ability to meet family members, either founders, or descendants of founders provide a real connection between the brand

and the people behind it. South Australia's *Cooper's Brewery* (founded in 1862) emphasizes this link in its advertising messages that stress, 'you can still meet a Cooper' – in contrast to the major corporate breweries such as *Fosters*. Finally, consumers often tell stories of meeting family members, and affectionately refer to them on a first-name basis. For example, toy soldier collector William McDade noted it was 'an indescribable thrill' to meet *W. Britains'* (one of the largest manufacturer of collectible toy solders) third generation toy maker Dennis Britain ('described by William as '[a] wonderful gentleman') at the company's centenary dinner in 1993 – William noted he became Dennis' 'pen pal' after this event (up until Dennis' death in 1996) (McDade 2009, p. 27). Such stories have an impact on others because they reinforce our own passion for the brand.

Conflict and struggle

The most effective stories involve conflict – whether with nature (*Moby Dick* or *The Perfect Storm*), other people or beings (*The Fountainhead* or *Alien*), or self (*Lord of the Rings, A Perfect Mind*). Put simply, no conflict makes for boring stories:

> Imagine Jaws without a hungry white shark, Superman without kryptonite, or the tale of Red Riding Hood without a ferocious wolf: the teenagers would have had a great summer at the beach, Superman would not have a worry in the world, and Little Red Riding Hood would visit her grandmother and then go home. Boring and predictable springs to mind! Movie director Nils Malmros once said, 'Paradise on a Sunday afternoon. ... Sounds great, but it sure is boring on film.' In other words, too much harmony and not enough conflict makes for a story that is about as exciting as watching paint dry. (Fog, Budtz, and Yakaboylu 2005, pp. 32–3)

The right amount of conflict is critical in the context of branding. Functional brands have too little conflict at the heart of their story – while fighting germs may be an important benefit for *Ajax*, it hardly engenders intense emotion among consumers. Too much, and the brand is an advocate, such as *People for the Ethical Treatment for Animals* (PETA) that ends up preaching to the converted and alienating the rest of us.

Richard Branson often uses a David and Goliath story when entering a new category. The message is simple – offering better service for less won't be easy when we're up against large, entrenched, protected, and arrogant competitors, but if we all pull together we'll win. Branson's recent (February–March 2009) entry into the Australian fitness market is one example. Asked whether it was a good time to start a business (due to the 2008–9 financial crisis) Branson reaffirmed his David role, identifying that the need for flexible, quality, low-cost fitness centres was even more important. Continuing, Branson expressed outrage at how anti-customer entrenched players were, with their lock-in contracts, their insistence on a personal interview before allowing customers to exit, and so on.

Once, again, Branson was reprising his role as friend of the consumer (one billboard for the brand stated 'More Richard than Gym'), fighting for their interests and freedoms. As a second billboard noted, 'That's right, you and us, we're going to be good together. We're going to treat you well, never take you for granted, and always support you; whatever your health goals. This isn't a gym membership – it's a healthy relationship. We're in it together.' Such a motivation drove *The Body Shop* founder Anita Roddick (2008, p. 37) too:

> In the cosmetics industry at that time [1976] you had no choice of sizes, so you were browbeaten into buying what you didn't really need. It seemed ridiculous to me that you could go into a sweet shop and ask for an once of jelly babies, but if you wanted a body lotion you had to buy a much larger amount.

Likewise, James Dyson recounts how company after company turned down his *Dual Cyclone* vacuum cleaner, so he 'bet the house' and started his own firm. James Dyson was angered by the fact that the basic technology behind vacuum cleaners had not changed since the first vacuum was invented. Modern vacuum cleaners therefore continued to lose suction after a few uses, resulting in poor cleaning perform-ance. Like Branson and Roddick, what angered Dyson more was the consumer was being exploited by large lazy corporations who (instead of investing in innovation) focused on superficial style changes and marketing campaigns. So successful has he been that a new generation of consumers no longer uses the word 'Hoover' to refer to vacuum cleaners (Dyson 2002).

Central to the authenticity of the *Lord of the Rings* franchise is Peter Jackson's struggles to remain true to Tolkien's vision and produce three films rather than try to condense the story into one because studios believed moviegoers desired instant gratification. Jackson struggled for years to gain financial backing for the venture, produce the films in his native New Zealand, and retain artistic control. Further struggles ensued when filming started including the difficulties involved in creating a new world, bringing certain characters and creatures to life, remaining on schedule and budget, and dealing with fans and even actors who were dissatisfied with some of Jackson's editorial choices. The very public struggles, conflicts, and ultimate triumph enhanced the authenticity of Jackson's vision and resulted in *Wetaworks* and *Wingnut Films* gaining a stream of commissions.

Conflict and struggle are part of life. Too often marketers downplay, remove, or avoid conflict in their brand's story out of concern that such struggles will present the brand as less-than-perfect. In doing so however, they strip the brand of interest, humanity, and authenticity. Since we as consumers are not perfect, how can we relate to brands that pretend to be (and all too often are not)? In contrast, authentic brands surround themselves with stories ridden with conflict. This conflict heightens interest in, builds passion towards, and strengthens the emotional bond the consumer forms with the brand. Since brand managers acknowledge the legitimacy of conflict, they are also more open to multiple views, and more skilled in managing tensions between stakeholders. This all adds to the brand's authenticity. As a result, consumers are often devoted to these brands and rally around it in times of trouble (examples include *Apple* fans in the 1990's, *Star Trek* fans, and those of other cancelled series such as *Farscape* and *Firefly* (see fan DVD *Done the Impossible: The Fans' Tale of Firefly & Serenity* [2006]), and *Harley Davidson* when the brand was facing bankruptcy).

Triumph and tragedy

Stories of triumphs and tragedies take many forms including the struggle for acceptance, seeing off competitors, making disastrous mistakes, straying from one's values, product successes and failures, failed new businesses, personal/consumer/staff successes and failures, and community struggles. Although stories regarding triumphing against the odds are central to the legends surrounding authentic brands, these brands do not ignore their failures. In fact, failures are often used to reinforce the legend and/or provide a moral warning to employees and potential new owners. As such, these stories, and those involving triumphs form part of the brand's legend, often reinforce perceptions of quality commitments and more importantly, sincerity. Such an approach stands in stark contrast to the practices of other brands whose public relations departments attempt to spin every failure into a success, or sweep them under the carpet.

For example, *Quaker Oats'* treatment of *Snapple*, and the brand's subsequent increase in equity when its new owners returned the brand to its roots serves as a powerful example to be wary of tampering with a brand's authenticity (Deighton 2003). Richard Branson also uses his many failures in a positive way – to reinforce *Virgin's* image of always trying to shake things up to benefit customers (Branson 2005). Likewise, *Apple's* many failures throughout the 1990s often provided the technical basis for successful innovations such as the *iMac* (Levy 2000). *Krispy Kreme's* decision to tamper with the ingredients of its famous doughnut due to cost considerations is used to reinforce the importance of commitments to producing the best possible quality product (Kazanjian and Joyner 2004). Similarly, *Morgan's* failed +4+ in the 1960s was a reminder against tampering with both the iconic design and production of the open-top, hand-crafted, wooden framed car in order to follow other manufacturers' forays into closed top, fibreglass sports cars (Laban 2000). Dyson' failure with its *Contrarotator* washing machine reminds employees to ensure new innovations have easy-to-experience benefits (Carruthers 2007).

Although not ignoring failures and tragedies are unique to authentic brands, brands that constantly stumble and fail rarely last long. Most attractive to consumers is the consistent triumphs of these brands. Many of these brands and their founders attract a large number of detractors, so success is seen as a vindication of their vision and their audacity, reminding consumers that better things are possible. *Dyson's* market share triumph over the very firms who rejected his iconic *Dual Cyclone* vacuum design is central to his brand's story. James Dyson's success also came at a time when concerns were being raised that Britain no longer made things; rather the country focused on superficial services such as finance and marketing (Dyson 2002). His success in creating value through substantive investments in research and development reminded Britons of their glorious manufacturing-based past, and inspired a whole generation to consider a career in design and manufacturing (Carruthers 2007).

The story that best epitomizes the role of triumph and tragedy in building brand authenticity is the history of *Chanel*. Coco Chanel overcame prejudice against her background as well as many personal tragedies to completely reshape notions of women's fashion by the end of World War I. She pioneered the practice of designers extending their name into accessories with the development of the world's most iconic perfume *Chanel No. 5*. Shunned by society following her affair with a German officer during World War II, Chanel was written off as irrelevant following a self-imposed exile from designing. Following savage reviews of her 1954 relaunch, Chanel returned to her status as pre-eminent designer by immersing herself in her work and craft. Despite her death, Chanel, and the brand named after her retain their aura of authenticity and mystique to this day (Charles-Roux 1995).

Triumph and tragedies add authenticity in several ways. First, triumphs inspire us to strive to achieve our goals and fight for our values and beliefs. In concrete form, they demonstrate to us that we too can follow our passion regardless of the many barriers against us. As such, triumphs are essential for self-authentication. Second, by associating with triumphant brands we create an identity based on success. Third, because of the nature of a brand's many triumphs, we forgive the failures, and often recast these in terms of moral lessons or learning experiences. Fourth, the triumphs motivate us to fight for the brand in times of trouble. Fifth, triumphs often involve issues of acceptance for ostracized communities (such as gays or in the case of *Burton*, snowboarders). Tragedies also enhance authenticity by humanizing the brand and the seemingly infallible creators behind it. As well, they serve an important moral lesson in cases where they involve brand's straying from their core values.

Creation

Behind every authentic brand is a creative genius (or geniuses), whether it is James Dyson, Steve Jobs, Steve Wozniak and Jonathan Ive, John Galliano, Marc Jacobs, Peter Jackson, Muccia Prada, Coco Chanel, and so on. These geniuses regularly solve problems that mere mortals cannot, and they usually do so in innovative ways. Authenticity has long been linked to the intuition, vision, or passion of creative people (Beverland 2005a). Creative people (such as designers) also see their authentic self in terms of perfecting their vision, working on meaningful projects, creating breakthrough products, and challenging conventions (Beverland 2005b). Stories of creation are a prominent feature of all authentic brands. After all, brands that lack creativity are usually me-too or follower brands that although functional and cheap, fail to inspire us. Stories of creation typically involve problem solving and innovation, challenging conventions and solving paradoxes that confound larger, more moneyed rivals, expressions of love of craft and the passion of people behind the products and services at the heart of the brand.

Stories of creation help form a connection between the brand and an identifiable person. The wine industry provides a great example. It is not uncommon for large conglomerate wineries to downplay the role of individual winemakers in the production of their brands, instead emphasizing the corporate brand, or the company team as whole (Beverland 2002). This strategy limits the influence of any one winemaker over the firm, which is often critical for organizations seeking to make consistent, standardized products year-on-year. As a result sales and marketing staff run public tastings. In contrast, their founders or winemakers often promote the brands of small wineries. Here, tickets to public events often sell out quickly because fans of particular labels want to be close to their heroes – wine marketers don't have the same allure (much to the disgust of the many I have met over the years). Similar experiences occur in other industries – witness the sell out presentations by Gordon Ramsay, *BMW* designer Chris Bangle, *elBulli* chef Ferran Adrià, and *Apple*'s Steve Jobs at *MacWorld*.

Stories around creation and creativity also involve accounts of difficult feats. Such stories often identify how creative people overcame problems that had confounded others. In particular, they often recount how leaders and their teams challenged conventions and in doing so, reshaped the market. Thus, *BMW*'s designer Chris Bangle refuses to accept that one should give up the brand's driving experience when developing a hybrid or non-petrol powered car. Since hybrid or electric engines are quiet, the standard industry view is that the traditional driving experience will have to change – with predictable howls of protest from motoring traditionalists (such as *Top Gear* presenter Jeremy Clarkson). In contrast, *BMW* is working with different fuel technologies and engines that will provide the thrill and sound *BMW* is known for while also lessening the impact on the environment. Through their *LIFEcar, Morgan* are doing the same – challenging conventional views of the company as traditional old world carmaker by leading the world in new fuel cell technology (and turning their traditions – the use of wood and aluminium – into strengths by emphasizing their lightness and renewable nature). *Virgin* takes a similar approach to conventions in the service industry.

Stories of creation also include a focus on the craft of production and the genius of the designer or design team behind the brand. Because these designers downplay rational production methods and the voice of the customer in innovation, their creations marvel us even more because they are perceived as being derived from intuition and the deep insight of a master craftsperson (Beverland 2005a, 2005b). Some, such as James Dyson and Muccia Prada, go as far to state that marketing is what holds back true innovations. For example, pre-eminent Australian designer Collette Dinnigan was lambasted when she began to 'play it safe' with her clothes collections because she was worried about losing loyal customers. Critics at the time questioned whether her status as an international fashion designer was deserved (Beverland 2005b). In contrast, stories celebrating creation often focus on the natural love and passion designers, craftspeople, and others behind the brand have for their work.

How do stories of creation enhance a brand's authenticity? First, such stories reinforce perceptions of quality commitments. Consumers view quality commitments in many ways, but one important aspect relates to the belief that behind the brand is someone dedicated to 'pushing the envelope' (in effect they have 'the right stuff') and constantly improving products they love. For example, many sportspeople gravitate to brands that are run by people engaged in the sport. Surfers for example, may select the *Quiksilver* brand because of their continued investments in surfboard and wetsuit technology (Beverland, Farrelly and Quester, forthcoming). Cyclists may select the *Campagnolo* brand for the same reason (Beverland and Farrelly, forthcoming). Since surfers and cyclists run these brands, the designers are motivated to provide products that reflect the desires for excellence or performance of consumers.

Second, these stories reinforce perceptions of heritage. Heritage in this case concerns an established track record of innovations that changed the world (or life world of the consumer). A strong track effectively means the brand has 'paid its dues' – a feeling critical to judgements of authenticity (Beverland 2005; Caves 2000). Examples include *Apple* with the *Apple 1*, *Macintosh*, *iMac*, the mouse, *iPod*, *iPhone* and so on. In services, *Virgin* has established a track record of creating successful businesses against the odds by defying convention. Third, these stories reinforce notions of sincerity because the people behind the brand are viewed as lovers of their craft and are therefore motivated by the pursuit of perfection rather than money. Finally, since the people behind these brands defy convention to see their creations realized, they speak to the desire in many people to do the same – to transcend the boundaries of their daily roles and follow their dreams. As such, the purchase of authentic brands allows people to achieve self-authentication because it reflects deep inner truths (Postrel 2003).

History

The company started in 1785 and used to tailor to the military, dressing the likes of Wellington and Lord Nelson – handmade catalogues used to be rowed out to boats for captains to peruse. (James Whislaw, Gieves & Hawkes No. 1 Savile Row, quoted in Dent 2003, p. 58)

The brand image of *Sony*, *VW* and *Vespa* are inevitably tied to images of the post-war reconstruction of Japan, Germany, and Italy (respectively). The great wines of Bordeaux were regularly purchased by historical figures such as Thomas Jefferson, while the Tsars of Russia and European royalty consumed vast amounts of champagne. *Chanel* changed women's fashion and as such changed how women behaved in public. *Virgin* made its mark by releasing the Sex Pistols' *Never Mind the Bollocks* album at the height of the punk movement. Both *Apple* and *Morgan* are intertwined with the early days of the computing and motoring industries. *Coke* followed *GI*'s into Europe during World War II and has been celebrated as an image of freedom ever since. *Hermès* named their famous Kelly bag after actress Grace Kelly. *Gucci* continues to promulgate the myth that they were saddle makers to the Medici (Forden 2001). *Louis Vuitton* retains the historic estate of the brand's namesake to communicate to new staff members and consultants the rich heritage of the brand that is at stake. *Quiksilver* and *Vans* also draw their authenticity from the founding days of the surf and skateboard communities, while *Absolut* supported the gay community's fight for equal rights.

These are just a few of the historic stories that enhance the authenticity of brands. The Sidebar entitled 'Life during wartime' identifies some more. Since it is often difficult to tell real from fake, brands with strong historical associations allow consumers to reconnect to notions of time, place, and culture. Thus consumers of traditional Trappist beers will go to extreme lengths to verify the authenticity of each product. This is particularly the case given that many large breweries have entered the traditional beer market with religious looking beers (called 'Abbey Beers') that attempt to mimic the religious affiliations of Trappist beers (often they are named after fake abbeys, abbeys that have long since been destroyed, or abbeys that no longer produce beer or house a community of monks) (Beverland, Lindgreen and Vink 2008). Authentic brands collect historic associations in the same way that a hurricane gathers strength over water. As such, they enhance perceptions of heritage.

Side Bar:
LIFE DURING WARTIME

Authentic brands are part of history, including war (*Zippo* lighters are still among soldiers' most prized possessions, while *Leica* cameras used by the Luftwaffe are among the most prized by 'Leicaweenies'; Lane 2007). Stories of wartime are often particularly powerful, especially in the victorious nations because the brand is seen as patriotic. *Hershey*, *Coke*, and *Cadbury* have a history of providing troops with confectionary during major conflicts. Troops carrying these products often gave these away to children in liberated countries, thus providing the basis for international expansion, and importantly, building the association between freedom and the brand (an association *Coke* still has to this day).

Other brands also played their part in wartime struggles, including *Dunhill* (who received orders from relatives on behalf of their sons fighting abroad), *Harley Davidson*, *Schwinn* who made radar equipment, *Morgan* and *Rolls Royce* who converted their factories to assist with weapons production. Stories abound of French winemakers hiding wines from looting Nazis, as well as joining the ranks of the resistance. *Hermès* staff also often 'lost' orders from high-ranking Nazi officials. Reflecting the stoicism and dedication of Londoners during the Blitz,

Alfred Dunhill set up shop immediately after an air raid that destroyed his store. An image provided in Nick Foulkes' (2005) historical account of the brand identifies Alfred sitting on at a burnt desk in front of a ironic (given that the shop was completely destroyed) handwritten sign ('Dunhill's Enquiries Within') serving soliders on leave who desired a pipe for the front line.

Historic stories take many forms. Some brands refer to historic periods for their identity. Ralph Lauren, for example, seeks to bring the style of upper class 1920s East Coast North America (as described so lavishly in F. Scott Fitzgerald's novel *The Great Gatsby*) to a modern audience. He did so at a time when American fashion was influenced by the 1960s hippy movement. Lauren desired to bring quality and style back to men's fashion. To this day his collections and flagship stores reflect this historical era. This also explains his decision not to exploit the sudden cool status of his clothes among rappers and teens. As Lauren notes, he provides 'style not fashion' (Gross 2003), thus reinforcing his image as a carrier of history. *Burberry* makes a similar virtue out of history with the continued production of its iconic trench coat – a product that traces its lineage back to the trenches of World War I.

Many of the famous events of the twentieth century (and those of the twenty-first) have been photographed with one camera – *Leica* (the M3 was named 'top gadget of all time' by *Stuff Magazine*; Lane 2007). A *Leica* was the tool of choice for many of the twentieth century's most famous photographers including Aleksandr Rodchenko, Andre Kertesz, Cartier-Bresson, and Robert Capa. As Lane (2007, p. 165) stated:

> Even if you don't follow photography, your mind's eye will be full of Leica photographs. The famous head shot of Che Guevara, repro-duced on millions of rebellious T-shirts and student walls: that was taken on a Leica with a portrait lens – a short telephoto of 90 mm – by Alberto Diaz Gutierrez, better known as Korda, in 1960. How about the pearl-grey smile-cum-kiss reflected in the wing mirror of a car, taken by Elliot Erwitt in 1955? Leica again, as is the even more cele-brated smooch caught in Times Square on V-J Day, 1945 – a sailor craned over a nurse, bending her backward, her hand raised against his chest in polite half-protestation. The man behind the camera was Alfred Eisenstaedt, of Life Magazine.

Notions of history are critical to judgements of authenticity (Beverland 2005a). Consumers respond to the use of historic stories – especially those that feature them and the struggles of their community – because they root the brand to time and place. More importantly, by being part of history, the brand gains associations (positive and negative) from the people that adopt it, the uses to which it was put, and so on. Even negative associations give the brand a certain notoriety, which often enhances its aura. For example, no one minds that racist skinheads as well as anti-racist gay and left wing protesters (nor for that matter rich yuppies in the 1980s) adopted the working class boot *Dr Martins* as part of their uniform. The fact that various social movements have continually adopted such a humble item adds to the brand's colour, aura, and status, and suggests it has become part of the shared historic landscape. As a result, the brand becomes part of the culture or subculture.

Community

In Australia, when someone tells a white lie (or tall story), people call it a 'furphy.' Where did this word come from? Would you believe that it is the name of a brand of water tank? *J. Furphy & Sons* was started by John Furphy in 1873 and became famous for its water cart. These carts were used in Australian army camps during World War I and this is where the legend started – Australian troopers would gossip around the water carts, and the drivers of these carts became carriers of rumour from one camp to another. The brand then featured in the 1915 Gallipoli campaign (often described as a founding event in Australian history) with journalists referring to rumours of spies as 'Furphy's Gazette', and the brand was immortalized in various poems written by returned servicemen (Barnes 1998). Lamborghini reversed this situation when they named one of their cars the 'Countach', which in Lombard (where the firm is based) dialect means 'something sublime and unusual'.

When snowboarding started, many ski runs banned snowboarders. Burton, a brand now synonymous with the sport, sponsored events and pushed for official recognition of snowboarding at the Olympics. Subsequent efforts by ski manufacturers to enter the snowboard market have met with resistance from consumers because of the bitterness still felt towards them for trying to stamp out snowboarding. *Dunlop*

Volley sponsored grass roots sports ignored by the major brands and has played a part in reversing the decline in participation in communal sports events (Beverland and Ewing 2005). Notions of community are often central to discussions of authenticity. Concerns that community spirit is being lost, or communal bonds are being lost (resulting in greater fragmentation and loneliness) are tied up in debates about the loss of authenticity in the postmodern world (Irwin, C. 2005; Putnam 2001).

Although the market is often blamed for the loss of authenticity, consumers often form communities around brands. Brands such as *Harley Davidson, Morgan, Apple, Burton, Quiksilver, Schwinn, BMW,* and so on all have extensive fan communities that bring together diverse groups of people to celebrate the one thing they share – love of a brand. *Morgan* owners often comment that the most unexpected pleasure gained from their car is that they are suddenly part of a community of people they would not normally have met (Beverland 2009). Communal activities including drive tours, racing events, challenges, and celebrations of the brand itself are regularly reported in *Morgan* publications (started by the fan clubs), online communities, and local club gazettes. Such is the importance of community to the brand that Charles Morgan sponsored an *Aero 8 Club* when the new model car was released. Communal activities, members' exploits, historic changes, infighting, and successes feature in many stories surrounding authentic brands.

Pokémon is an example of a brand that is synonymous with a fan community. Essential to success in America was the development of a complex trading card game. Fans collect these cards but it is the trading aspect that is so critical to sustaining interest in the brand. Through clever licensing the brand was effectively driven by its increasing numbers of extensions, often themselves developed by collectors. At one point 50,000 children took part in a brand related communal event that focused on education, trading, and game playing. Unofficial websites started up and provided a communal space for fans to discuss cards, characters, and conduct trades (Fournier 2001). Although criticized for fuelling materialism and taking time away from education, the attractiveness of *Pokémon* lies in its communal aspects – the brand provides the basis for young kids to share, trade, learn, and bond. As a result, the brand has avoided the fate of other fashionable phenomena and continues to increase in sales and fuel demand for videogame consoles and television series.

Why do brands tell stories, and allow stories to be told, of community? First, these brands draw strength from these communities. Second, communities *per se* are attractive to non-members seeking to connect with others. Thus brand communities attract new consumers and fans to the brand (thus helping it renew and survive). Third, since communities celebrate the brand, stories of community are authentic expressions of consumers' love for the object (as opposed to paid sponsorship). Fourth, just as authentic brands become part of history, they naturally become part of the communal landscape. Consuming such brands often marks one out as a genuine community member. Therefore, eating *Vegemite* makes one a true Australian, just as support for *Absolut* and *Levi's* are essential identity markers for North American gays. Finally, many brands, such as *Dunlop* and Trappist beer brands such as *Chimay* and *La Trappe* play a major role in supporting social activities and therefore improving the lives of community members. This all adds to perceptions of sincerity, while sustained associations with particular communities reinforce notions of heritage (Dickinson, Beverland and Lindgreen forthcoming).

Place

> What are you most likely to remember – some ludicrous advertising claim that you know to be a lie or the fact that the cream you are buying comes from nuts gathered by a women's cooperative in Africa? (Roddick 2005, p. 82)

Bordeaux, Champagne, Tennessee, Scotland, Marlborough, Southern California, Detroit, Malvern, Miramar, Silicon Valley, Cognac, Tuscany, Maine: these places, and many others, are all synonymous with certain brands or product classes. Seemingly old-fashioned *In-N-Out Burger* reflects their Southern California roots in their products, diners, service, and family values. Weary of expanding too far beyond this geographical place for fear of losing their connection to place, the brand is content to remain relatively small in the fast food industry. And, why not! *In-N-Out* charges some of the lowest prices, pays the highest wages, records the highest profits, and does not suffer from the level of staff turnover that characterizes the sector in the US (Moon 2003). In an age of globalization and cyberspace, real connections to place are critical sources of authenticity and brand equity.

Authentic brands retain links to geographic place. While stories of community involve locating the brand within a wider socio-culture, stories of place celebrate particular physical areas. Not surprisingly, stories of place are central in cases where local characteristics give rise to unique product aspects. At *Chateau Margaux*, the vineyard is the star; so focused on ensuring the wines are an expression of place that the estate has its own herd of cattle to produce local manure for the vineyard (Faith 1988). More extreme are the vineyards of Burgundy who label their wines after places – seen as unintelligible by many, the diversity of places is central to the enduring fascination (and high prices) of these wines with collectors and consumers (Beverland 2006). Stories of place are also central to other food and beverage brands including Scotch Whiskey, Tennessee Bourbon, European cheese (and other products), and Artisanal waters such as New Zealand's *Antipodes*.

However, place is also central to non-food and beverage brands. Fashion brands in particular tell stories of place. Iceland brand *66 Degrees North*, New Zealand's *Icebreaker*, and Australia's *Hard Yakka* draw connections between the rugged country from which they were spawned and product qualities such as performance, warmth, durability, and style. Surf brands such as *Quiksilver* continue to reference their place of founding as well as other physical places where surfing occurs. Given the tendency of surfers and other sportspeople to embellish tales regarding their own performance in extreme conditions (terrain, beaches, temperature), it is perhaps natural that such stories form part of the enduring legends of these brands (Jarrat 2006). Since the peak experience desired by these sportspeople must occur in a particular place, referencing place in brand-related stories reminds users that these products were forged in the very place where performances occur (Beverland, Farrelly and Quester forthcoming).

Even hi-tech brands such as *Apple*, and car brands such as *Ferrari*, *Mercedes*, and *BMW* tell stories of place in their histories, identifying with the spirit of time and place (*Apple* and Silicon Valley; Hertzfeld 2005) and/or physical attributes and design characteristics (car brands) (Butterfield 2005; Kiley 2004; Williams 2001). Place also adds to the mystique of the brand. *Jack Daniel's* is still distilled in Lynchburg Tennessee, which paradoxically is a legal dry area – no alcohol can be consumed in the home of the brand (Krass 2004). This seeming quirk adds to the legend of brand, as do images of countryside in the rural South, the original estate and the notion that Mr. Jack still keeps an eye over things (even though he died long ago). Sri Lanka's *Dilmah Tea* provides another story of place – the desire on the behalf of the founder to capture the uniqueness of place in a cup of tea rather than allow these characteristics to be diluted away in a commodity tea blend.

Why do stories of place resonate so strongly? Place reinforces notions of heritage, quality, and sincerity, and is usually seen as central to claims of authenticity, even when there remain only tenuous links between a particular place and the brand (Beverland 2006). Identifying with real physical places also provides a means to connect to the 'real' in an age when globalization has undermined place-based notions of identity. In the context of food and beverages and even some textiles such as wool, stories of place enhance the uniqueness of the product. Place is so powerful that many consumers undertake pilgrimages to famous regions in order to enhance their own experience of the brand. For example, tens of thousands of fans visit tiny Dublin, Texas to see the world's oldest *Dr Pepper* bottling plant, *Dublin Dr Pepper*.

Consumers

Consumers tell their own stories regarding authentic brands and have their stories told (not stolen) by brand owners. Consumer stories take many forms including personal versions of the other stories identified in this chapter and in Chapters 4–9, and stories of personal achievement, love, anger, surprise, and fantasy. Such stories are part of the process of self-authentication and identity formation, and allow consumers to find authenticity in an age characterized by globalization, deterritorialization, and hyperreality. While all authentic brands allow consumers to create their own stories, some go as far to include them as part of their canon, even using them to inform innovations. The earlier example involving the resurgence of *Dunlop Volley* demonstrates the power of consumer stories in enhancing brand authenticity and equity.

Although authentic brands often have their own websites, unofficial fan websites also proliferate. These sites celebrate the brand, trade in rumour and gossip, and provide a running commentary on the current status of the brand. Such sites even spring up around seemingly old-fashioned brands such as *Morgan*. So powerful are some of these communities that they even have the ability to shape products including later versions of the *Harry Potter* series (Brown, 2007), revised versions of *Star Wars*, *VW Beetle* (Brown, Kozinets and Sherry 2003), and the

Lord of the Rings (Jones and Smith 2005). Web-based communities have also breathed new life into cancelled entertainment franchises such as *Farscape*, *Firefly*, and *Star Trek*. These stories are themselves often celebrated in fan-developed documentaries. Once again, the hurricane like nature of authentic brands gathers strength from these stories.

Most brands pay homage to their fans in a variety of ways, often citing consumer support and thanking particular consumers for ongoing loyalty. Some go so far as to provide the context for consumers to enact their own stories or fantasies. For example, US-based *Sci-Fi Channel* provides background footage of their award winning *Battlestar Galactica* series to fans so they can create their own movies. These movies are then uploaded onto the *Sci-Fi Channel* website for other fans to vote and comment on. Such stories keep interest in the franchise alive during the off-season. Such fan actions represent what Arnould and Price (2000) call an authoritative performance whereby consumers engage in public displays or brand rituals as part of a search for authenticity and identity.

Consumer stories are also used by brand managers to enhance perceptions of authenticity and to communicate to others (often new staff) the responsibility they have towards ensuring the brand performs. Legends abound about *Manchester United* fans being willing to swap their wives for tickets to critical league games. Such stories become part of the urban legend surrounding the brand. Consumer stories are essential to authenticity in many ways. First, consumers use these brands to express their identity and therefore stories are often public displays of their affection and commitment. Second, consumers consider they have some claim over the brands they love, and thus expect to have their views heard by brand managers. Third, such stories are critical to brand communities and connecting with like-minded others (in many cases they represent important rituals and even currency in communities). Fourth, acknowledging the role of fans in the brand story recognizes the reciprocal relationship between the firm and consumer in the brand's success.

Product/service

The final set of stories involves the real stars of the show – the products and services that form the basis of every great brand (Fournier 1998). Marketers often forget that consumers bond with products and services and not brands *per se*. It is only through eating a freshly made *Krispy*

Kreme doughnut that we experienced the promise of the brand. Many of the stories above celebrate the creative act behind great products, love of craft, product history, performance, and use. Appliance manufacturer *Fisher and Paykel* channels James Dyson when they stress the importance of design innovation over marketing. Central to the firm's success are iconic products such as the groundbreaking *Dish Drawer* dish washing machine. In fact, so many stories have developed concerning this innovation that even company employees have difficulty in telling fact from fiction.

Authentic brands also collect stories of products and services, with some such as *BMW*, *Dublin Dr Pepper*, *Zippo*, *Vespa*, and *Mercedes* going so far as to include these in their brand museums. Winemakers, consumers, and critics will wax lyrical about great vintages, while fans of toy soldiers will also discuss various collections, pieces, and the merits of matt versus gloss paint. Ugly ducking examples also find their fans – such as communities surrounding the *Apple Newton* (Muñiz and Schau 2005) or the historical revisionism of the Morgan +4+ (now a true collectible given that only 24 were ever built). In services, stories of amazing encounters form part of the brand legend, particular around iconic retailers such as *Shanghai Tang*, *Nordstrom*, *Neiman Marcus*, and *Fortnum and Mason*, the great hotels of the world, or *Virgin Atlantic*.

Stories of products are also reflected in the role collectors' play in the overall brand story. Authentic brands usually have secondary markets where collectors trade rare items. These include everything from *Leica* cameras, *Schwinn* cruiser bicycles, *W. Britains* toy soldiers (and those of other traditional makers), *Zippo* lighters, fine wines, and whiskies, right down to limited edition tins of *Altoids* mints, old *Crayola* crayons, *Hermès* scarves, as well as other brand related memorabilia. Collectors keep the brand visible and alive, and pass on brand rituals and brand love to new generations and new fans. With quality commitments being so central to a brand's authenticity, it is not surprising that stories celebrating individual product lines, great service encounters, and individual service personnel form around brands that make substantive investments in innovation.

CONCLUSION

None of the ten stories behind authentic brands is more important than the other. Each story adds another layer of richness to the brand's meaning. Some of these stories are told in formal marketing communications and therefore represent the official history of the firm. More often than not, these official histories are revised to take account of the stories generated by consumers and society about the brand. Over time, the brand gains a certain mystique or aura of authenticity because of this blend of voices and stories. As the brand grows older and more powerful, new stories are told, while old ones decline or are challenged by brand historians and other 'authorities'. This process of storytelling differs fundamentally from traditional models of brands management because it represents an open, pluralistic, emergent process as opposed to the rigidly planned and managed process of most brand strategies. This point, and the ten stories above are reflected in the other six habits covered in Chapters 4–9.

CHAPTER 4

APPEARING AS ARTISANAL AMATEURS

The maturation process is quite a complex process, there are something like 500 flavour components. Surely if you start with a few good whiskies and take a little of each you're bound to get a good result? You can mix six classics from different Scottish regions and the result can be truly awful. It's like an artist painting a picture: you first paint the canvas with grain whisky, then you add the colours with the malt whiskies.

(Gordon Bell, Master Blender, *Johnny Walker*, April 4–5 2009)

ALTOIDS AND THE P&G EFFECT

Altoids mints are a great example of an authentic brand. Introduced in the nineteenth century as a remedy for indigestion (largely due to the poor state of British food), *Altoids* (the 'curiously strong mint' (Figure 4.1)) achieved cult status through their old-fashioned tins (introduced in the 1920s), quirky promotion, weird flavours, and high-quality paper wrapping (Morris 2004). In fact, *Altoids* advertising and collectible tins are highly sought after by collectors on *ebay* (Figure 4.2). In a remarkable article, Claudia Kotchka (VP of Design, *Proctor and Gamble*) identified why *Proctor and Gamble* (*P&G*) couldn't produce brands with the authenticity of *Altoids*. Recalling *Snapple*, Kotchka (2006) noted how *Altoids* brand authenticity would be destroyed by the '*P&G* effect'. First to go would be the *Altoids* tin. Tin is more expensive than plastic, is heavier (thereby increasing shipping costs), is old fashioned, and the unique moulded design is difficult and expensive to change in response to changing trends. Second to go would be the high-quality paper inside the tin that protects the

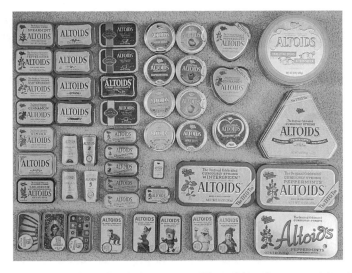

FIGURE 4.1 *Altoids* packaging appears old world and amateurish when compared to the brand's plastic, manufactured competitors – that's part of *Altoids'* charm. http://commons.wikimedia.org/wiki/File:Altoidstins1b.jpg

FIGURE 4.2 *Altoids* advertisements are as collectible as their tins. The ads reinforce the brands playful, irresistible, deviant nature

This Altoids Ad is owned by Wrigley and is used with permission

mints from being damaged when the tin is shaken. Again, too many parts, too much expense, and paper would be unnecessary in a newly designed plastic container.

Third to go would be the wacky flavours – after all no market test would highlight mass interest in liquorice mints, ginger mints, and cinnamon mints. Fourth to go would be the strength of the mints themselves as this puts many people off. Finally, the shape and size of the mints would be standardized with new production processes because focus groups disliked their rough seeming hand-cut shape. Kotchka concluded that the result of this attempt to 'smooth out the edges' of *Altoids* would be to destroy the product's value in the eyes of its customers. Much like *Quaker Oats* and *Snapple*, P&G would have turned an authentic brand into a me-too one.

Why has a brand that changed little over the last century been so successful in a highly cluttered category? Why would *P&G's* hypothetical attempts to professionalize the brand backfire? One habit of authentic brands is their seeming amateurism when compared with other 'mainstream' players. For example, while *Microsoft* talks up the skills of their programmers (including that of Bill Gates), Steve Jobs reminds people that he can't write code (Levy 2000). *Ralph Lauren* and *Manolo Blahnik* regularly note that they received no formal training in fashion and shoemaking respectively (Gross 2003; McDowell 2000). Similarly while mainstream brands celebrate their marketing prowess, authentic brands such as *Burt's Bees, Columbia Sportswear,* and *The Art of Shaving* are happy to be referred to as 'accidental brands' (Vinjamuri 2008). The sidebar on *Cracker Barrel* provides an example of how this can be done. While mainstream brands talk of efficiency and quality production, authentic brands often revel in craft traditions, presenting themselves as passionate artisans deeply committed to their subject matter. As such, appearing as artisan amateurs is a central habit of authentic brands.

Side Bar:
LESS IS MORE – RETURNING *CRACKER BARREL* TO ITS ROOTS

Cracker Barrel products have long been a staple in American homes. The brand, which traces its roots back to 1969 recently desired to recapture its authenticity through careful package redesign. Concerned that the packaging was plain and middle of road (not to mention inconsistent), the brand team sought to remake the entire line by going back to the future. In seeking to capture the brand's authenticity, the design team practiced restraint. Chief creative Paul Brourman (Ebenkamp 2008, p. 13) stated:

You can say "I'm authentic," but to actually live it you've got to do the homework of understanding the era. We read a lot of books and studied packaging from earlier times [to better understand] the sensibilities. We did a lot of deep study on texture and colors. ... We enjoyed the fact that the intent was to have it feel more minimalistic.

Rather than seek to throw all the marketing bells and whistles at the brand's redesign, leaving things out became the order of the day. Rejecting the glossy colours used on the old packaging, new packaging uses matt colours and simple typography to reflect a classic American heritage. The results? An estimated 25 per cent increase in sales.

'AMATEURS', 'ARTISANS', AND 'APPEARANCES'

The central defining characteristics of amateurs are they are unpaid and not formally trained. The word is derived from French and roughly translates to 'lover of' (Wikipedia 2008). Rather than doing something because they are paid to, amateurs engage in activities because of their personal passion. For example, members of the open-source movement (behind *Linux*) contribute time and intellectual property for free because of their love for the activity, the belief that the Internet should be open (as opposed to owned by corporations), and because they are part of a group of like-minded people who contribute to a community. Amateurs often generate innovations (like *Linux*) that are better than their rivals and often do so on much smaller budgets. This lack of resources and training often results in new approaches to old problems. Amateurism also has a downside however – performances may be subpar. This is where artisans come in.

Historically the term 'artisan' was given to skilled craftspeople. In the Middle Ages, artisans could earn higher wages than unskilled labourers because of their ability to produce unique high-quality objects. Today, the term artisan refers to unique goods produced by hand. Typically these goods are produced in small batches, in contrast to mass-produced mainstream brands. While mass-produced goods are standardized, artisans are believed to impart individual qualities to each product or batch because these outputs are subject to the differences that come with handcrafted production. Since artisans dominated manufacturing and services prior to the industrial revolution, references to this term conjures up images of simpler and more authentic times (Sennett 2008). As *Hermès'* Christian Blanckaert (Hume 2004, p. 39) states, 'We want to be the last artisans; our strategy is to be the last of the Mohicans'.

Authentic brands therefore combine the passion of the amateur with the skill of the artisan. This approach is consistent with what Stebbins (2007) calls 'serious leisure.' The term 'serious' evokes the commitment to excellence and passion of the artisan and the sincerity, earnestness, and importance given to the activity by the amateur. Such an approach differentiates the people behind authentic brands from hobbyists or volunteers, or pleasure seekers, who are seen as less committed to and involved in a pursuit over the long term. Serious leisure expresses the individual's authentic self and results in deep self-fulfilment. Such an approach characterizes the actions of many founders of authentic brands including Steve Jobs, HFS, Peter and Charles Morgan, Manolo Blahnik, Peter Jackson, L. L. Bean, J. Peterman, Paul Pontallier (*Chateau Margaux*), and is also embodied by their staff.

Finally, why do I use the term 'appearance' in this chapter's title? Authenticity involves the deliberate downplaying of behind-the-scenes activities that are critical for the brand's performance, but may run counter to claims of handcrafted, small batch production, and accidental branding (Beverland 2005a). High-profile Australian winemaker Charles Melton put me on to this approach when he discussed the importance of people believing he was 'still the guy mucking about on the tractor in the vineyard' – an image and story that was central to the initial success of the brand. Charlie noted that although business growth meant he rarely had time to spend in the vineyard (although he is still chief winemaker), it remained critical for people to *believe* that he was still getting his hands dirty by being involved in day-to-day production (Beverland 2002). At a time when many in the Australian wine industry were writing off amateurish operations like Melton's because of their lack of market orientation and high production focus, Melton was enhancing the authenticity of his brand. Currently, the scientific-marketing driven Australian industry is suffering declines in margins, sales, and general interest – in contrast, critics, consumers, and retail buyers were demanding more of the Melton approach (Ritson 2007).

WHAT MAKES A BRAND APPEAR ARTISANAL AND AMATEURISH?

In analysing the marketing communications, stories, and histories of various brands, eight sub-themes emerged that reinforce perceptions of artisanal amateurism. These themes involve messages, stories, statements or myths that emphasize craft traditions, lack of training, downplaying business expertise, passion, luck and accidents, love of failures, fun, and great results on low budgets. Together these eight themes generate perceptions of authenticity because they provide a direct comparison to more professional, staged, marketing-driven brands (which increases perceptions of sincerity), enhance claims of quality, and also relate the brand back to perceptions of a golden age (reinforcing perceptions of heritage).

One: Emphasizing craft traditions

The facility itself was old so Billie turned its age into another marketing attribute. What had previously been only an incidental post script on advertising – 'founded in 1891' – was now shouted across every billboard, magazine or newspaper ad as 'the oldest Dr Pepper bottling plant in the world. ... Billie could not expect a return on his investment if he upgraded equipment ... so he boasted of his antique bottling equipment, making it a point of honor that bottling was still done the same way and in the same location where it had been since the plant was founded. He was fond of saying that the old machines were held together with gum and baling wire, a line he meant to be quoted. (*Dublin Dr Pepper* and advertising, taken from Wright 2006, p. 129)

Why do people now write in *Moleskine* notebooks in an age of PDAs (this book was conceived in several of them)? Why have mechanical Swiss watches become such a must have item? In the 1970's the Swiss watch industry virtually disappeared due to the emergence of cheap, high-quality Japanese produced battery-powered quartz watches. Yet today, it is mechanical watches that are in high demand, along with other seemingly archaic products of the past such as fountain pens, leather bound notebooks, and record players. Why? As McSpeddin (2005, p. 71) explains:

> Part of the explanation lies in what we might call the contradictory current of progress: just as the car made the horse a luxury, as did the biro the fountain pen, so too has the cheap and ubiquitous quartz watch transformed the status of its mechanical predecessor.

The desire for authenticity has always been a reaction to 'progress' (Campbell 2005). Niche producers have long emphasized craft traditions, including hand-made products and batch production, to differentiate themselves from larger, mass-producers (Beverland 2005a). Legendary car producer *Lamborghini* continues to make cars largely by hand – in fact *Ford* produces more cars in a single eight-hour shift than *Lamborghini* will in a year (Eisenstein 2002). *Hermès* workers use tools not dissimilar to those used by founder Thierry Hermès in the nineteenth century (Hume 2004). Consumers also respond positively to such claims, emphasizing notions of hand-made, traditional production methods and craft when making assessments of authenticity (Beverland 2006; Beverland et al. 2008). Likewise, commitments to craft traditions and the involvement of identifiable individuals in production are critical to assessments of quality commitments and sincerity – both critical to consumer assessments of brand authenticity (Napoli et al. forthcoming). Finally, authenticity has been previously defined as involving a deliberate emphasis on craft traditions while simultaneously downplaying scientific and industrial production methods (Beverland 2005a).

When we conjure up images of the great wine estates of the world, immediately we think of timeless tradition – an image repeated in the movie *Mondo Vino*. Tours of great Champagne houses such *Krug*, *Bollinger*, *Louis Roederer*, and *Pol Roger* emphasizes hand production, intuition, and tradition. One enduring image is that of skilled artisans hand-turning (riddling) champagne bottles during their years of maturation. As the publicity brochure of *Champagne Krug* states:

> Due to their unusual shape, the [brand name] Champagne bottles are positioned on a workbench and are riddled manually, according to the traditional method still used by a very small number of

specialists whose know-how has been handed down from generation to generation.

Winemakers often make comments along the lines of 'when the grapes are ready, they're ready' to highlight the simplicity, random-ness, and intuitive nature of winemaking. Such techniques are compared and contrasted with the industrial production methods of other producers – the same winemakers will chastise New World winemakers for making things 'too scientific' and for 'over thinking wine' (Beverland 2005b).

Outside of wine, craft traditions are critical to the brand stories of the *Morgan* and *Rolls Royce*, toy soldier manufacturers such as *W. Britains, King and Country*, and *Imperial Productions*, small cheese and chocolate makers, fast food providers such as *Krispy Kreme* and *In-N-Out Burger*, Trappist beer producers, and haute couture fashion houses. Even hi-tech brands such as *Dyson* (who stresses the need to return to the British tradition of 'making things') and *Apple* allude to craft traditions in their myths. For example, Steven Levy's book *Insanely Great* (2000, p. 139) recalls Steve Jobs' reasons for rejecting the first Macintosh circuit board on aesthetic grounds:

> When you're a carpenter making a beautiful chest of drawers, you're not going to use a piece of plywood on the back, even though it faces the wall and nobody will ever see it. You'll know it's there, so you're going to use a beautiful piece of wood on the back. For you to sleep well at night, the aesthetic, the quality, has to be carried all the way through.

Two: I wasn't formally trained

Amateurs usually lack formal training. As mentioned earlier, Steve Jobs cannot write code, Ralph Lauren and Manolo Blahnik received no formal fashion training, and Peter Jackson was a self-taught filmmaker. Our enduring image of these innovators involves founding myths of hobbyists tinkering in their garages, often innovating through trial and error. Unlike many professional brands, authentic brands play up the fact that founders 'originally had little idea of what they were doing, just lots of passion'. Legendary model-kit maker *Airfix* was founded by Nicholas Kove, a Hungarian immigrant described as energetic and excitable, who stumbled into kit manufacturing when demand for his other products (plastic combs) dried up. The early models, although highly sought after by collectors today, were described as 'rather crude attempts at animation [that] frequently snapped' (Ward 2003, p. 19). Although this can lead to subpar results, authentic brands use such stories to enhance their aura and mystique, contrast themselves with professional brands, provide an excuse for when failures occur, and reinforce their image as innovators not bound by formal rules and mainstream thinking.

Famed shoemaker Manolo Blahnik provides an excellent example. Struggling to find a fulltime occupation that would satisfy his creative urges, Blahnik decided on shoemaking because it presented a challenge large enough to satisfy his potential (he described his choice as an accident). There was just one problem – Blahnik had no training in shoemaking. His initial forays into shoemaking were unsuccessful both commercially and creatively. Following a lucky break, Blahnik was commissioned to produce a line of shoes in 1972. The lack of training was apparent in the designs, but this also gave Blahnik's shoes a creative edge over other established makers, resulting in much buzz and press coverage. Biographer McDowell (2000, p. 52) recalls the debut collection.

> As Vogue said of his debut, 'If you're buying shoes, employ a sense of humor.' The problem with the shoes was a basic design one, in a practical rather than aesthetic sense. His collection consisted of ten models, including a green sandal with a seven-inch heel of rubber. He knew nothing about tensile strengths and, in the words of Joan Juliet Buck, current editor of French Vogue, 'Yes it bent. Not always, not at first, but eventually.' It could have been the disastrous end of a career nipped in the bud, but the shoes were so much fun that the fashion world forgave.

Blahnik's career took off quickly after this debut, particularly when he decided to get his shoes made by manufacturers with an understanding of material strengths and safe shoe design (Manolo remains heavily involved with all aspects of shoe design and manufacture to this day). Such dedication made it possible for Jessica Parker to run down the street in Blahnik's 115mm heels in episodes of *Sex and the City*. The lack of formal training also extends to business practice, with many founders noting they had little business training, little idea of marketing or branding, and little understanding of consumers, markets, or finance.

Three: We don't do marketing

> We are at No. 1 Savile Row and that's a 'fuck off' address to have. ... In the new century, it's time to go back to the real values, where you need real things, real products, where material, craftsmanship and detail is counting more than the logo, so we are reinventing Asprey as the luxury house which is no logo. The label is inside, it's not on the outside. (James Whislaw, Gieves & Hawkes, quoted in Dent 2003, p. 58)

One of the most common responses I receive upon requesting interviews with people behind authentic brands is provided in the excerpt from an email below, from *Chateau Margaux* owner, Corrine Mentzepolous.

> The sheer question of our wine being-or not-a luxury product is-weirdly enough-almost controversial for us ... yes, we have a centuries-old track record of fine wine production, and yes, we are at the top end of the wine market. Still ours is a very special situation as, to make a long story short, the quality and the resulting prestige of our wine is due at first to a very French-albeit very real-concept of 'terroir' the meaning of which, as you surely know, is a combination of soil, micro-climate, grape varieties etc. I don't need at this point to tell you about all the work that is being done to enhance even more this quite unique situation. What I am trying to say is that we do not have a true marketing approach, nor our own distribution channel for that matter. I could not even give you accurate numbers concerning our export markets!!! In view of those quick remarks, you may have some difficulties in selecting us as a typical case study. (Beverland 2005a, p. 1018)

The surprise at being considered a brand is common to many artisans and amateurs. Some, such as *Lonely Planet* co-founder Maureen Wheeler are even hostile to the term 'branding', insisting that staff never use it for fear that it will undermine creativity (Flavell 2008a). James Dyson also rails against marketing, going so far to state that his firm 'does no marketing' even though the brochures included with each of their products recount the *Dyson* legend (Carruthers 2007). Manolo Blahnik is reputed to understand his female fans intuitively even though he expresses his discomfort at meeting consumers, while champagne makers *Krug* state that consumers can take or leave their product. Perhaps *Hermès* are one of the exemplars of feigning ignorance of marketing, as detailed in Michael Tonello's (2008) amusing book *Bringing Home the Birkin*, and by *Morgan* CEO Charles Morgan.

> I watch Hermes with interest, because if you like, they're much more extreme than us. I know a bit about it, because my wife is a little fashion fanatic and she owns this business about these handbags and it's quite funny actually walking in the shop asking about it. Because they go 'oh we don't know, maybe if you go to Düsseldorf'. Why would I want to go to Düsseldorf to buy a handbag? 'Yeah you never know, but maybe not this year, next year.' They really do make it very very difficult. And it must be a game, it must be, because you couldn't possibly run their business properly like that. (Charles Morgan, Morgan Motor Company CEO)

As Michael Tonello identifies in his account of buying Hermès Birkin's for resale on *ebay*, Charles' view that it is a game is not so far from the truth. Tonello (2008) notes that gaining access to the desired *Birkin* simply involved spending a significant sum on other products up front. Amateurs and artisans do things for love, not money. In fact, research has noted how marketing taints claims of authenticity because it undermines notions of sincerity (Beverland 2005; Fine 2004). Just as the people behind authentic brands downplay their scientific expertise and formal training, so they downplay their marketing expertise and knowledge of the market. Part of this reflects their approach to innovation which is focused more on breakthrough products (which require one to reject the voice of the customer; Christensen 1997), part of it is an act, but most of all these people make these statements because they genuinely love what they do, and are therefore not primarily motivated by consumer desires or profit.

Four: I love what I do!

> Our philosophy has been to grow a small, good idea rather than an average big one. In all this time, in all these markets, we've never

adjusted our style of work. Rather, we adjusted which markets we selected to fit the work we were interested in doing. We didn't get into the fashion business to make product we weren't passionate about. To this day, what we make still lights us up. (Karen Walker, Designer of *Karen Walker Ltd*, quoted in Tischler 2006/2007, p. 39)

Central to the definition of an artisanal amateur is a love of doing (see Chapter 6). The serious leisure approach involves people effectively getting paid to pursue their hobbies (Stebbins 2007). Many authentic brands started this way. *L.L. Bean* for example was started because L. L. (a passionate outdoorsman) struggled to find equipment that suited his requirements. Surf brands such as *Quiksilver, Billabong*, and *Ripcurl* were also founded by surfers who desired gear better suited to local conditions than that available at the time. A. J. Hackett turned a passion for bungee jumping into a global brand. Likewise, *Morgan* employees are all passionate classic car enthusiasts. Consumer research also highlights the importance of staff passion and love of product to a brand's authenticity (Beverland et al. 2008; Napoli et al. forthcoming).

Dilmah Tea (named after his sons Dilhan and Malik) founder Merrill J. Fernando is passionate about tea and the art of tea drinking (Figure 4.3). As he states, 'I have devoted my life to tea.' Tired of poor-quality teas, in the 1950's Fernando devoted himself to bringing authenticity, ethics, and quality back to tea. This love has led him to pioneer the development of single origin teas packed fresh at the source. Previously tea had been picked and then sold through distributors to large firms for house blends. Not only did this result in poor returns to local communities, but it also denied tea lovers the variety that came with single plantation and varietal teas. Only absolute love of the product could drive Fernando to fight the large corporates and government officials opposed to his desire to change how tea was sold for 38 years. Love is what has powered this Sri Lankan firm into the top ten tea brands globally.

Five: Luck played a big role

The marketing team behind the *Dunlop Volley* know they got lucky. The timing couldn't have been better since the team were in the midst of revitalizing the *Volley* brand. However, had the team been more

FIGURE 4.3   **The instantly recognizable face of** *Dilmah Teas* – **Merrill J. Fernando**

'knowledgeable' about branding, more savvy and skilled, they would have exploited the shoe's cool status and immediately marketed it to the mainstream. The true lucky break resulted from distraction and ignorance. First, the team was distracted elsewhere, seeking to build a branding programme that would support the shoe with mass-retailers targeting a mainstream audience focused on performance and value. Thus the marketing team never saw the sudden cool status among teens as the 'main game'.

Second, the team admits they had no idea how they should treat this market, and therefore decided to take a wait and see approach. Effectively, they let the innovative teens call the shots. As a result, the brand regained its iconic status and earned higher margins than originally planned. And, the *Volley* avoided the fate suffered by other once hot brands such as *Tommy Hilfiger* and *Hushpuppies*. What is most fascinating about authentic brands such as *Dunlop Volley* is that the marketers behind them are so open about the role of luck in the brand's success. Surely no professional marketer wants it known that the success of the brand they cut their teeth on had little to do with them. Worse still, the success of the brand occurred in spite of their marketing knowledge.

For example, *3M*'s official history stresses that a deliberately created culture of innovation gave rise to icons such as *Post-it Notes*, even though the product resulted from an accident and it took a further 13 years for the product to find acceptance internally. While brand consultants such as Matthews and Wacker (2008) stress that the official story sounds better, I believe it is hollow, especially since its lack of truth-value is widely known. The ability to sustain such fabrications is increasingly difficult in an Internet environment where consumers can challenge official myths via blogs and through sites such as *Wikipedia*. Since luck and chance play a role in people's lives, human history, and even in the fates of great historic individuals, why downplay it when it comes to brands? Why are *Hermès* products packaged in bright orange? Certainly not because brand consultants 'focused-grouped' the colour. The reality is more interesting – during the Nazi occupation of Paris, paper was in short supply, except for some orange cardboard that was deemed so vulgar no one would want it. As Hume (2004, p. 39) notes, 'Its sunny brightness became such a beacon in tough times that the firm stuck with it after the war'.

Certainly brands can't survive on luck alone (*Motorola* has found that one lucky product does not build a sustainable business; Kelley 2008), but lucky breaks and accidents add colour to the brand's story and are often central to the development of many products.

Six: Admit failure

No one likes failures, especially not traditional marketers. Marketers are often fearful that failures may undermine perceptions of brand leadership and quality (and it is certainly true that consistent failures will do so). Given the large investment in new products, it is perhaps understandable that we celebrate successes and try to forget failures. In fact, some firms so dislike failure that they try and spin their way out of problems (witness *Microsoft*'s marketing driven response to criticisms of *Vista*). As well, many firms look for scapegoats when failures occur, often sacking the people responsible for the initiative. In contrast, artisans view every failure as a learning experience. Rather than pretending the failure didn't occur artisans focus on how much has been learnt, and use this knowledge in their next product. Such attempts become part of brand lore and are often celebrated as important milestones in the brand's history.

Most of the brands in this book have had their failures. Some of these are used to identify the dangers of straying from the brand's roots (see Chapter 5). All however are acknowledged. *Apple*'s failures throughout the non-Jobs' period in the 1990s actually contained advances that contributed to the brand's revitalization later on. Although many relate *Apple*'s comeback to the colourful and fun design of the *iMac*, this focus on outer styling ignores the increases in speed, memory, reliability, and performance that had been achieved in unloved products such as the *PowerPC* (Levy 2000). Not all of *Vespa*'s scooters were successful either (especially during the 1980s). Nevertheless all take pride of place in the brand's new museum *The Piaggio Historical Archive* (Piaggio & C. S.p.A. 2003). The same applies to *BMW*'s first failed foray into car production – the whimsical two-person *Isetta* (Kiley 2004).

Why do consumers accept that authentic brands can fail? Partly it has to do with the protective buffer that amateurism provides. Since amateurs are untrained and unprofessional it is perhaps understandable they will make a mess of things every now and again. However, the more important explanation is that we have all failed at various activities, only to pick ourselves up and try again. Notions of trial and error are so ingrained in many cultures that the very fact the firm is trying to do something difficult, and keeps doing it, is admirable. We love the honesty that comes with an open admission of failure, as well as the integrity that comes with reflecting on why things went wrong and what can be learnt from this attempt.

Seven: We just want to have fun!

It goes back to slowing down, having some original thoughts and not taking yourself too seriously. ... Our style has for the past 29 years been considered different. We have played with humour, irony, imagery and ... Real life situations. (*Camper* Founder Lorenzo Fluxa, quoted in Hall 2004, p. 44)

Want to travel to the Principality of Sealand? Lovely? The Kingdom of Elloeore? What, you've never heard of these destinations? Perhaps you need to read *Lonely Planet*'s 'Micronations', a book describing such home-made nations in the brand's authoritative style (detailing visa procedures, currencies, and populations). Why would *Lonely Planet* release such a book? Because they desire comprehensiveness, or because they want to have fun? I think the latter – after all the brand was co-founded by Terry Wheeler, a self-confessed hopeless dreamer (Flavell 2008). The founder of New Zealand's iconic *Real Groovy Records* chain Chris Hart started the business because he wanted to have access to great music, and later, great movies. For Chris, work is fun. As *Google* VP of Search Product and User Experience Marissa Mayer states:

> For me one [word that defines Google] would be 'whimsical'; we have a certain sense of whimsy around our brand with the 'I'm Feeling Lucky' function and Doodles – products where we don't take ourselves too seriously ...' [Interviewer] I'm pleasantly surprised by her choice of 'whimsy' as a brand tag; it's not one that I would inherently think of when it comes to Google as it makes the brand seem almost accidental and fanciful. (Kendall 2009, p. 20)

Authentic brands are typically irreverent. *Apple*'s advertisements poke fun at competitors, particularly *Microsoft* (much to their consternation – perhaps they should lighten up). It is a well-known myth that when surf's up, *Quiksilver* employees are out of the office and down at the beach (Jarrat 2006). The advertising team behind the *VW Beetle* regularly poked fun at their product. Founder of bungee jumping A. J. Hackett regularly uses more and more outrageous stunts to build his brand's reputation (Hackett and Aldworth 2006). Richard Branson branded a bridal chain *Virgin Brides* (Figure 4.4). Labels on *Innocent* drinks contain a range of humorous anecdotes to the joys of fruit (Simmons 2006). *Altoids* ads are full of fun including pictures of dolls with their hair standing on end after consuming the mints, while *Bruichladdich* makes fun of the British and US intelligence services with their WMD brand.

Professionals are paid to do a job and therefore must take their role seriously. This dedication to a profession often limits their ability to laugh at themselves or make fun of what they do. Not so authentic brands. Vodka brand *42 Below* was built on a series of politically incorrect advertisements that deliberately broke every New Zealand advertising code and formed part of a very successful viral marketing campaign. Legend has it that the inspiration behind the brand, Geoff Ross (former *Saatchi & Saatchi* director), used all the ideas other more professional brands rejected in their campaign for *42 Below*. Advertisements made fun of the English, Australians, and

FIGURE 4.4 **The sign says it all – *Virgin* gyms encapsulate Richard Branson's laid-back fun image (unlike all those other corporate gyms)**

Chinese, and their advertisement to the gay community concluded with the line 'in an effort to resist sexual stereotypes, this ad was run past two fags and a queer'. As marketing director Angela Barnett stated, 'We like to have a good time. That comes through in our advertising' (Rahoi-Gilchrest 2007). In contrast to market-tested, decency regulated campaigns, *42 Below*'s approach is best described as 'fuck you' marketing (and has since been copied by many less original advertising agencies). And, in contrast to the staid marketing of most vodka and gin brands, *42 Below* is a breath of fresh air, so much so that *Bacardi* brought the niche brand for $NZ138 million in 2006.

Workers often take whatever job pays well or is available and thus invest little emotion in their work, often trading off lifestyle for economic gain. These workers often try to get through the day (or week) so that the real fun can start at night (or in the weekend). In contrast, amateurs love what they do, and they do what they do because they love it. Although their irreverence should not be taken as evidence that they are not serious about their roles (they are), they do understand that they are getting paid to engage in what for them is leisure or a hobby (Stebbins 2007). Whereas many brands position themselves around 'fun' (such as *Vodafone*, New Zealand) authentic brands reflect the passion and irreverence of the amateur, often going so far as to poke fun at themselves (*ING*'s use of comedian Billy Connolly is a great example), others, and the unnecessary seriousness that characterizes this politically correct age. They get away with this precisely because they are seen as amateurs.

Eight: Not bad for no budget

Central to the myths surrounding innovation in New Zealand is the term 'number 8 wire mentality'. Since New Zealand farmers were geographically isolated, they made do with whatever materials were at hand, often developing innovations out of very basic items including number 8 fencing wire. Today this myth still holds true, with backyard amateurs such as late super-bike producer John Britten being lauded as heroes because they took on the world and won on 'the smell of an oily rag'. In fact, Britten's iconic motorbike the V1000 is given pride of place in New Zealand's National Museum, *Te Papa*. The placard under the bike highlights that Britten's very amateurism is what should be most admired about his story of innovation (Hanna 2003). This 'doing more with less' mentality is part and parcel of appearing as an artisanal amateur.

The example of *Snapple* and *Quaker* is instructive here. *Snapple* was built on word-of-mouth rather than advertising since the brand's founders had limited resources and wanted to put all their money into the product. In contrast, all the resources of *Quaker* could not improve the brand's equity – in fact arguably the brand suffered because of access to too many resources. *In-N-Out Burger*, similarly, earns some of the highest returns in the fast food industry, and has devoted customers despite limited marketing and innovation (Moon 2003). *Morgan*'s first new car in almost 40 years, the *Aero 8*, was developed at a fraction of the cost of new *Fords* and *Chryslers*. *Apple* is renowned for spending less on marketing and research and development than its competitors. And, the *Dunlop Volley* established a level of awareness and authenticity without the sponsorship and advertising budgets of *Nike* and *Adidas*. Like the New Zealand farmers with their number 8 wire part of this is born out of necessity – these firms often have limited resources and must therefore do things differently.

Of course, this is consistent with being an amateur – amateur theatre productions deliver performances of a higher standard than big budget Broadway plays (just as independent films often do better than large Hollywood blockbusters). Also, consumers respond to these stories in a variety of ways. First, achieving great results on small budgets simply highlights the creative genius of the people behind the brand. Second, this strategy reinforces our love of the underdog. Third, we love the sheer audacity of people like John Britten and the late Steve Irwin (the 'crocodile hunter') because their examples show just what is possible if one simply believes things can be done. Finally, consumers have experienced too many disappointments backed by large marketing budgets, and thus respond to brands that focused on investing time and resources into great products and services.

THE OTHER HALF OF THE STORY

Part of this chapter's title includes the word 'appearance'. Those knowledgeable about brands understand that these eight themes are just part of the story. For example, despite claims to the contrary, *Chateau Margaux* is one of the most scientifically innovative and knowledgeable wine estates in the world. The famous vineyard has been carefully mapped to ensure that best possible outcome is extracted from each part of the estate (including careful fit between location and grape type). Likewise, spiralling labour costs and union rules have seen the adoption of automated riddling machines at most Champagne Houses (Beverland 2005a). Despite its commitment to handcrafted tradition, the increased quality of the latest range of *Morgan*'s has as much to do with the adoption of Japanese Kanban systems and better production planning (all of which the company acknowledges were recommended by the late Sir John Harvey Jones in the *Troubleshooter* series; Laban 2000). Likewise, many so-called traditionalist manufacturers of food and beverages have adopted industrial production techniques to improve quality and reduce labour costs. Does this mean these brands lack sincerity? Are they simply on to a new 'anti-marketing' marketing approach?

Research reveals that authentic brands face a dilemma. Consumers demand certain standards of quality, and will desert brands that fail to deliver these. In services for example, consumers deserted small local banks in favour of larger institutions because these banks could provide a one-stop shop for customers' complex banking needs. However, in doing so, consumers lost the personalized service that came with local banks. Thus US banks such as the *Umpquaa Bank* play up their local connections and personalized service standards while downplaying their large corporate back office. This back office is necessary to provide the efficiencies and services customers demand, but is not consistent with the brand's central story of being a small local player. The brand does not deny the existence of the back office; rather it simply does not go out of its way to promote it (McCallion 2004).

I've labelled this strategy 'decoupling' (Beverland 2005a). Decoupling refers to how brand managers reinforce perceptions of authenticity through downplaying certain cues associated with professionalism, mass production, and rational scientific methods. The combination of seeming naivety with a steely eyed professionalism is central to authentic brands. For example, *Beauty Engineered Forever*'s (B.E.E.) (a brand of environment-friendly house cleaners) founder Brigid Hardy (whose business sense was developed during a stint with the *Boston Consulting Group*) equates authenticity with being naïve in one's belief that an individual can change the world, while also investing in product quality and design in order to outperform your rivals. Brigid rejects the 'hair shirt' approach of many green cleaner brands that charge higher prices for less effective products by investing heavily in research and development and scientific testing to produce cleaners that are both good for the environment, get the job done, and (can you believe it), look good too (who said FMCGs had to be boring).

As long as brands do not lie, consumers often suspend disbelief, or simply bias certain cues to create their desired story that helps them achieve self-authentication (Arnould and Price 2000; Beverland and Farrelly forthcoming; Grayson and Martinec 2004). The behind-the-scenes investment in production is important for how consumers experience the quality of the brand and informs their assessments of quality commitments and also sincerity. Although founders such as James Dyson may say they reject marketing while engaging in story-telling that enhances brand equity, this story is essentially true, reflects dominant myths, and critically, his products deliver. The same goes for the other authentic brands. These brands do not represent a triumph of style over substance – in fact, like *B.E.E*'s cleaning products, authentic brands deliver both.

CONCLUSION

Marketers are taught to revel in their professionalism and skill. The stories that inform our understanding of brand celebrate market-orientation, customer driven innovations, and careful targeting. Marketers are urged to tell stories that reinforce this view. Thus accidents, luck and failure are swept under the carpet. In contrast, authentic brands are founded and run by artisanal amateurs who celebrate their lack of professionalism, the role of luck and chance in their success, and even go so far as to focus on their failures. Far from being an act for commercial effect, such actions and stories reflect the essential amateurism of the people behind authentic brands. These activities also provide the brand with a rich history and importantly a story that reflects our own humanity and ultimate desire – to get paid for doing what we love. The very fact that such amateurs continue to marvel with innovations and products that often set the standard for quality lends them a powerful aura of authenticity similar to that held by great artists.

CHAPTER 5

STICKING TO YOUR ROOTS

By modern standards and the length of time we have advertised, our advertising has changed relatively little. This is particularly true for the first 35 years, in which advertising remained black and white, long copy print ads telling stories about the special process (charcoal mellowing) we use to make our whiskey, the people who make it and the place they live (Lynchburg, Tennessee), and the history and heritage of the brand and its founder, Jasper Newton Daniel. Much of our advertising today still tells the same story.

(Gus Griffin, Global Managing Director, *Jack Daniel's*, quoted in Drummond 2008, p. 18)

TAKING PHOTOS AT MELBOURNE AIRPORT

I'd recognize that picture anywhere – Max Schubert, legendary Australian winemaker and the inspiration behind one of the world's greatest wines, *Grange*. What intrigued me more was the story. I'd just exited the arrivals hall at Melbourne airport and was waiting for a taxi. To my surprise there was a large billboard in front of me celebrating Schubert and *Grange*. The message was simple – 'To those who do things for love, not money.' Ironic, I thought. *Penfold's* is now owned by conglomerate *Fosters*, a company that has long chastised the wine industry's poor understanding of financial returns (and one at time of writing was delivering less than stellar returns itself due to poor wine sales). However, the message was a signal – *Grange* was being returned to its roots. After years of less than stellar wines and a commercially motivated brand extension, perhaps the marketing team behind this icon was recognizing why people paid over US$300 a bottle for this brand.

The story of *Grange* is one of a passionate craftsman battling against the odds to produce something truly unique. Max Schubert (then *Penfold*'s chief winemaker) desired to produce a wine that expressed the uniqueness of Australia. Critically, he desired to produce a wine that would rightfully take its place among the great wines of the world. At the time, local wines were pale imitations of European products (often labelled as 'Burgundy' or 'Hermitage' even though they bore no relation to these wines). Schubert laboured to produce *Grange*, a dry wine style that blended the best red grapes from *Penfold*'s vineyard holdings in South Australia. Initial results were so discouraging (critics were scathing – suggesting no one in their right mind would ever drink the wine) that *Penfold*'s board ordered Schubert to cease his experiments just before the 1957 vintage. Undeterred, Schubert continued on in secret, building a false wall in the cellars to hide the maturing barrels of *Grange*.

Entered in a local wine competition in 1962 under a nondescript code, the 1955 vintage won several awards. Feeling vindicated, Schubert continued to produce *Grange* in good years, ultimately producing Australia's greatest red wine. Emboldened by this success, in the 1990s the *Penfold*'s team under new owners *Southcorp* decided it was time to exploit the franchise. Suddenly *Grange* was released every year, and a new wine – White *Grange* (or *Yattarna*) was released. In 2001 *Grange* was being discounted in bottle shops and critics were voicing concern that the wine was no longer as good as it should be. *White Grange* also initially received unfavourable reviews and was often passed in at auction.

Grange was in trouble because the marketing and winemaking teams had turned their back on its roots. Schubert desired to produce a world-class wine that was a unique expression of Australia at its best. He was not motivated by high prices or record auction prices. In contrast, the motivation behind the extension to *White Grange* was profit. Far from being a unique wine, *White Grange* was simply another expensive chardonnay. As well, changes to *Grange* had been made to appeal to the American market, thus alienating traditional fans. Now under new stewardship (*Fosters*), the brand is attempting to return to its roots, with a new marketing campaign featuring a contemplative Max Schubert and his initial experimental bottles with the tagline 'To the Renegades: Max Schubert, winemaking legend and creator of *Penfold's Grange*. To those who do things for love not money.' Hopefully, this represents more than just marketing spin.

Authentic brands stick to their roots – or as advertisements for *Chuck Taylor's* say 'Stay True'. This may seem strange given that the hurricane metaphor suggests these brands either always evolve or may radically change direction. Although the marketers behind authentic brands allow stories to attach themselves to the brand, they also contribute stories of their own that reinforce its roots. Such stories may be explicit (in terms of marketing communications) or implicit (in terms of actions). And, the marketing team never reneges on core brand-related practices and values. In contrast to those suggesting marketers should go with the flow (Wipperfürth 2005), authentic brand marketers play their part in building the brand's myth. Typically, this involves stories that represent a playing out or even a reinterpretation of the brand's roots (as identified in this chapter).

The example of *Penfold's Grange* is instructive. Many myths had grown up around the wine, most of which had been created by wine industry insiders, critics, and consumers. The *Penfold's* marketing team communicated some of these and Schubert's dedication to excellence and regional expression in its promotional activities. As well, the practice of releasing wines only in good years implicitly reinforced the brand's commitment to quality, while the original choice of old vine Shiraz at a time when this grape was out of fashion, reflected his belief that this grape was the best expression of the Australian climate. The practice of slow evolution of wine style (following Schubert's retirement and death) reinforced a commitment to the original desire to produce a truly iconic excellent wine without resort to market fashions. The actions of the *Southcorp* team breached these implicit rules, and the community surrounding the brand reacted accordingly, eventually forcing the new owners to explicitly communicate a return to the brand's roots. Time will tell if these commitments are substantive, but early indications (the newly released 2004 vintage) suggest they are.

WHAT STICKING TO YOUR ROOTS DOESN'T MEAN

Sticking to a brand's roots is not the same as simply repeating past practices or staying on message. The first will lead to obsolescence and failure while the second (a core mantra of modern branding and advertising theory; Beverland and Luxton 2005) is untenable in markets where consumers are in charge. Simply repeating past traditions in the form of products, styling, and practices is obviously dangerous as *Christian Dior* found out prior to its rebirth at the hands of John Galliano in 1996. *Vespa* suffered a similar fate in the 1980s due to emergence of high-quality low-cost Japanese products and a shift away from scooters due to increased consumer affluence (which resulted in people trading up to cars; Piaggio & C S.P.A. 2003). Brands that fail to change quickly become historical relics. As Dent (2003, p. 56) notes in her study of the rebirth of several British iconic brands:

> Essentially, a lot of the classic old British brands were run by people who did not move with the times or didn't quite know how to balance out the need to maintain their traditional core customer with expanding it into their younger customers. It's been an extremely difficult balancing act.

In contrast, authentic brands evolve. *Alessi* captures this spirit, continuing the long held tradition of applying art to everyday life, and retaining handcrafted skills by marrying them with machines (under the banner of 'mechanized craftsmanship') (Alessi 1998). Nor do the marketers of authentic brands simply repeat the same message year-on-year. Staying on message is what undermined *Rover*'s comeback attempt. Despite making award-winning cars under new owners *BMW*, the decades of previously poor-quality cars had changed the perception of *Rover* in the public's mind. *Rover*'s attempts to position the brand as an affordable luxury based on its pre-war reputation fell flat (Brady and Lorenz 2005). Likewise, continuing to promote Australian wine under 'Brand Australia' has resulted in the slow commoditization of these products because the social network surrounding wine has demanded different styles, richer stories, and more regional knowledge and expression (Ritson 2007). Rather than sticking to a line, authentic brands reflect their roots in their stories and actions (via the seven strategies below) while also allowing for the collective evolution of the brand's meaning over time.

HOW TO STICK TO YOUR ROOTS?

The brands that informed this book communicated their roots in seven different ways. The number of strategies used by each brand depended on their industry, product, history, and sociocultural context. The first means of communicating one's roots involved stylistic consistency at the product or service level. Second, firms also communicated commitment to their roots by retaining key traditions. Third, new initiatives were often communicated in terms of reflecting the original founding spirit of the brand. Fourth, commitment to roots was communicated via stories that included important moral messages. Fifth, during times of change or revitalization marketers often recommitted themselves to the brand's roots. Sixth, brand managers continued to highlight the importance of supportive communities and their traditions. Finally, the firm retained commitments to the focal activities of the brand's consumers. The sidebar entitled 'The other Dr Pepper' provides an example of the firm that has made a virtue out of sticking to its roots.

Side Bar:
THE OTHER *DR PEPPER*

There are actually two *Dr Peppers* – well almost. *Dublin Dr Pepper* is located in Dublin, Texas and the world's oldest *Dr Pepper* bottling plant. Founded by Sam Prim, the plant received informal permission to bottle *Dr Pepper* in 1891 (franchise agreements were not issued until the 1920s). In 1925 when *Dr Pepper* formalized these arrangements, Prim was asked to name his territory. Drawing a rough square around the Dublin area, Prim gained exclusive rights to bottle and sell in the 44-mile radius around Dublin. This area was chosen because Prim thought Dublin would be larger than Fort Worth and because he was not interested in biting off an area that was larger than he could service. Unlike the gimmicks used by its parent company, *Dublin Dr Pepper* remained true to its roots, making a virtue out of its vintage bottling line (the firm uses the same equipment as it did 100-years ago), vintage bottles (the company still refill traditional 6.5 and 10 ounce bottles) and logo, and critically, the brand continues to use real sugar rather than the corn syrup used in the *Dr Pepper* most of us know. During the 1970s when the price of sugar went up, *Dr Pepper* switched to corn syrup to save money, whereas *Dublin Dr Pepper* continued to use real sugar. Why? Son of plant heir William Edward Kloster states:

> The corporate office said they were going to change the formula and Dad thought corn sweetener made an inferior product which he refused the accept. He had always used sugar and he intended to continue using sugar. I don't think he gave any consideration

to the added costs. He was too stubborn to switch. (Wright 2006, p. 136)

When William's son Mark took over running *Dublin Dr Pepper*, the MBA qualified heir initially questioned the decision to use sugar. He soon realized that promoting something that cost more money was one of the reasons that attracted so many fans to the brand. This decision provides a point of difference from its rivals (which Mark admits you can't put a price on), and is why an estimated 50,000 fans visit the small factory and shop each year.

One: Stylistic consistency

If design changes are made correctly and are part of a slow evolution, then people often forget that the changes even occurred because the page becomes more of what they want. The goal of the [Google] homepage is to be focused on search, and we try to convey the sense of focus through the design. (*Google* VP Marissa Mayer quoted in Kendall 2009, p. 20)

The look and feel of authentic brands always evolves (as the quote about *Google* shows – the brand makes several changes to its ranking functions each week to improve the search engine; Kendall 2009), but always retains a historical imprint to ensure stylistic consistency. For example, given the importance of the zip fastener to *Hermès'* original travel luggage (Emile-Maurice Hermès brought the technology to France), the jagged teeth motif appears on every one of the signature brown ribbons that secures a *Hermès* purchase (Hume 2004, p. 39). Ralph Lauren famously stated, 'I offer style, not fashion' (Gross 2003) to reflect his disdain for the short-term and his desire to make a lasting contribution to how people dressed. *Tiger Balm* (see sidebar) and *Tupperware* (2005, p. 108) takes a similar view:

Resist[ing] overconsumption, the disposable culture, fashion fads, and the trivializing or commercialization of design to an impoverished definition, which goes against our point of view regarding quality, durability and human values. Over all these years, we have preserved, adapted and interpreted the Tupperware heritage to meet increasing and changing needs of the consumer.

Want to soothe a body ache? There's always been only one solution. It's still one of Singapore's top 15 most valuable brands, comes in a beautiful jar with a bronze top (recognized as a national design icon by the Designers Association of Singapore) and is called *Tiger Balm*. *Tiger Balm* was the brainchild of Chinese Imperial Court herbalist Aw Chu Kin who produced the product in the 1870s and asked his two sons Aw Boon Haw and Aw Boon Par on his deathbed to perfect the product. Aw Chu Kin's vision was to create a uniquely Chinese herbal remedy to soothe aches and pains. His two sons took *Tiger Balm* to Singapore and set about making it the household name we know today. The product range has evolved to reflect the times – as we have become increasingly stressed so too has the *Tiger Balm* range expanded from this simple jar of ointment (as the web page says 'reflecting simpler times') to multiple products in the 1990s including plasters, sprays, and lifestyle remedies. The firm remains true to Aw Chu Kin's original vision of producing a Chinese, herbal remedy that is constantly perfected to fit with the times.

Consumers regularly attribute authenticity to products that retain a sense of their original styling. Although consumers recognize updated versions of the product are just that (rather than being exact replicas of originals), authenticity is retained because of a clear connection between the original and the new product. Therefore consumers see a link between the original *VW Beetle* and the latest version, just as they can trace a link between the original *Morgan* and the new *Aero 8* and *Aeromax*, and the original and latest *Vespa*s. Likewise the innovation in special effects and the commitment to details evident in Peter Jackson's early splatter films were clearly on display in his subsequent big budget movies.

In contrast, *Harley Davidson* suffered under the management of *American Machine and Foundry Company* because of cost-cutting measures:

Under the new management, the bottom line was the bottom line, and if they could make the handlebars with thinner chrome and save 40 cents, then they made the handlebars with thinner chrome. AMF bought a line of motorized scooters and christened those Harley

Davidson's, which watered down the Harley name. As quality slid, so did sales, and by the 1970s, Japanese bikes outnumbered Harleys on the highways. (Scott 2003, p. 121)

Others brands have also suffered from the false economy of cutting quality. *Krispy Kreme* quickly lost fans when they used lower-quality ingredients to save money (Kazanjian and Joyner 2004). Likewise, *Converse* went into receivership after they used lower-quality laces, less canvas, and poorer materials in their iconic chucks as part of cost-cutting measures in the 1990s (Peterson 2007).

Returning to the *Penfold's* example above, Australian wine critics in 2000–2 chastised the company for what they perceived as changing the style of the wine. With the dotcom bubble yet to burst, newly rich tech-entrepreneurs in the US were driving up auction and release prices for *Grange*. There was a belief among traditional consumers that the wine was being made in a more 'upfront style' to appeal to the American pallet and to allow for early consumption. There was some truth to this as leadership in the winemaking team changed following a merger with *Rosemount*. *Rosemount's* chief winemaker Philip Shaw changed the winemaking philosophy of the team because he believed they were simply making *Grange* to a formula and the wine therefore risked becoming dated (Shaw 2006). Unfortunately, the market did not greet such changes positively primarily because they were poorly communicated (and even denied) and also seemed to reflect a large-scale change in direction when seen in the context of other activities (such as several resignations from the winemaking team, *White Grange*, and an espoused need for professionalizing *Southcorp*).

The nature of the wine and automotive industries means that styling evolves slowly. However, even fashion designers are aware of the importance of retaining a certain stylistic imprint. As Manolo Blahnik states below, he desires to produce shoes that have a certain timeless quality and that are instantly recognizable as his design.

My 'commercial' shoes are not really fashion in the sense of wearing a look one season and throwing it away the next. Good basic design just keeps going. My Sabrina slipper, for example, is still one of my all-time bestsellers. The customers like the classics. That's why they remain in production. My crazy and creative designs will not matter to most of my customers but I don't want it thought that I'd prefer to create for the few rather than the many. I want to see every woman in my shoes. (McDowell 2000, p. 170)

Firms retain these stylistic imprints in a number of ways. First, teams often work on new product developments within firms. Typically these teams include more experienced members as well as younger employees to ensure knowledge transfer and the retention of a stylistic imprint. Second, design teams often work in conjunction with marketers to ensure that the brand's heritage is reflected in each new innovation. Third, new employees are immersed in the history of the firm and its products. Fourth, these firms retain key creative staff (or are run by them) in an attempt to ensure consistency over time. Fifth, staff at these firms take a stewardship view to the product and are thus aware of the need to balance relevance with heritage. Sixth, firms often allow designers external outlets for their creativity (such as personal labels and collaborations). This ensures designers do not become bored with the slow evolution in style (Beverland 2005b). Finally, some of these firms adopt a two-pronged approach to innovation like Manolo Blahnik and other fashion designers, automotive manufacturers with concept cars, and wine and whisky makers with special releases.

How do they avoid falling into the trap of ignoring innovations and stylistic changes? Through a process called market immersion (see Chapter 7).

Two: Retaining tradition

Why is *Louis Vuitton* luggage so strong, yet so light? Louis Vuitton was trained as a box maker/packer (boxes were the ancient forerunner of today's luggage) in 1837. This apprenticeship forced young Louis to gain a thorough understanding of all aspects of customized box design, allowing him to understand where improvements to basic designs could be made. These ancient skills are still followed at the firm, allowing the continued tradition of innovation in travel luggage as well as the ability to respond to customized requests such as *Louis Vuitton* branded guitar cases (Pasols 2005). Advertisements for *Jack Daniel's* still use the tagline 'Jack's Still Here'. The message is simple – the spirit of the long-dead founder (still lovingly referred to as 'Mr. Jack') still watches over the direction of the company, ensuring that it will continue the traditions started in 1866 (Krass 2004). Authentic brands express commitments to their roots by retaining important traditions. The head offices of *Gucci* retain an old saddle to reflect the supposed link between the brand and its founding traditions. Manufacturers such as *Champagne Krug, Bruichladdich, Chivas Regal*, and Trappist brewery *Chimay* continue to use old production equipment, techniques, and traditions despite the adoption of modern production practices. Manufacturers such as *Morgan, Dublin Dr Pepper*, and *Imperial Productions* (NZ) make a virtue out of continuing important production traditions such as using wood in car production, sugar (instead of corn syrup) in soft drink, and spin casting collectible toy soldiers.

All brands have founding traditions, whether it is particular production practices, people, families, products, and service standards. These traditions become part of the brand's lore and enhance perceptions of authenticity through associations of quality, heritage, and sincerity (Napoli et al. forthcoming). The retention of such traditions, even if they are used only sporadically for special occasions or production runs (such as *Schwinn*'s decision in 1995 to release the *Black Phantom* – a modernized replica of their original pre-war cruiser-styled bikes; Pridmore and Hurd 2001) connects the brand back to a particular time, place, person, and culture. As well, these traditions often provide the brand and their attendant products and services with a point of difference that is difficult to copy. Giving up such traditions is dangerous and often results in brand decline.

Tradition is on display whenever one visit's an *In-N-Out Burger* store. The stores retain their old-fashioned diner look including the 1950s signage style. The menu has changed little since founding, as has the commitment to low pricing, cooking to order, hand-cutting fries (which is done in view of the customer), wax paper wrapping, packaging, friendly service, and the secret menu. The contrast with other fast food chains could not be more obvious. First, staff obviously enjoy their work and love the brand (which is why turnover remains so low in an industry renowned for retention problems). Second, the products delivered resemble those advertised. We're all familiar with the complaint that other chains advertise large, fresh, juicy burgers and then deliver shrink-wrapped, mass-produced versions to customers. In contrast, an *In-N-Out* burger is freshly made, uses quality ingredients, and doesn't need to be hidden shamefully in a box. The fries still retain some potato skin and are also freshly made. No wonder the brand leads the industry in perceptions of quality and taste.

This is not to say that brands simply repeat pass traditions without process innovations. Behind the scenes, investments in process improvements are being made continuously. And, these brands do not shy away from communicating these. For example, *Morgan* emphasizes its tradition of innovation in documentaries about the firm (see *Handmade* [1988] and *Handmade 2* [2003]), stressing the retention of traditions such as handcrafted production, the 1909 springs, live axels, and the use of wood, while also emphasizing its commitments to improved production practices and radically new innovations such as machine-blown aluminium cars (in the cases of the *Aero 8* and *Aeromax*). And, those traditions not only provide a point of difference, but also regularly connect with the *zeitgeist* of the times. So the use of wood in *Morgan* cars is now seen as a renewable resource, while the lightness of wood plus aluminium allows the firm to produce a high-performance hybrid-fuelled sports car.

For authentic brands, the more things change, the more they remain the same.

Three: The founding spirit

Part of any brand's founding myth is the original motivation or spirit of the founders. As the case of *Penfold's Grange* demonstrates, marketers breach this spirit at their peril. The decision to make an expensive chardonnay as a *Grange* brand extension was commercially motivated and ran counter to the original spirit of Max Schubert. This coupled with other changes to *Grange* traditions saw the status of the wine diminish. The *Fosters* campaign is a direct attempt to return the brand to the original spirit of invention, dedication, and love of craft. Explicitly, *Fosters* have disconnected the brand from any hint of commercial motivation. Giving up the brand's founding spirit (rather than gently reinterpreting them for the times) diminishes equity in the brand because it undermines perceptions of heritage and sincerity. Authentic brands understand this, and therefore treat their spiritual legacy with care.

During the turmoil associated with the failure of Australia's second largest airline *Ansett*, *Virgin Blue* founder Richard Branson received a generous offer from *Ansett's* parents *Air New Zealand* and *Singapore Airlines* for his airline. The purchase was aimed at reducing competition in the Australian market, thereby shoring up the aging *Ansett*.

Branson flew in to Australia and quickly announced that he had decided to take the money and run. No longer would he side with Australian consumers against entrenched players. Although the press announcement was a media stunt, Branson's carefully planned message and his playful approach contained three aspects of the brand's founding spirit – have fun, side with the consumer, and take on the big boys (Branson 2005).

This spirit was formed early on in Branson's commercial life with his decision to start-up *Student* – an edgy, relevant magazine for English school pupils. The original *Virgin Records* stores were a stark contrast to the soulless stores of the time. The signing of iconoclastic performers such as Mike Oldfield, the Sex Pistols, and the Human League further reinforced this playful spirit. Each time *Virgin* enters a new industry, be it trains, fitness, travel, space tourism, or finance, the story remains the same – consumers are poorly served by entrenched players and its time for a change. So important is the *Virgin* spirit that employees believe in it with religious-like zeal – Branson reports that staff at the *Virgin Blue* related media stunt started to cry (even thought they were going to be retained as *Ansett* employees in the supposed deal) (Branson 2005). *Virgin Blue* is now Australia's second largest domestic carrier (while the truly awful *Ansett* is long gone) and has reshaped the competitive environment and grown with the size of the market.

Four: Telling moralistic tales

When *The Body Shop*'s legal department told Anita Roddick (2008, p. 244) to stop using the word 'activist' because people might associate it with terrorism, she launched a new fragrance of the same name and supported it with in-store advertising that stated she would 'use the word whenever I can'. The lesson was clear – for the legal department, staff, consumers, and stakeholders – the brand would never sell out its roots. The great works of fiction are often morality tales (Charles Dickens' *A Christmas Tale* springs to mind). Some stories surrounding authentic brands also contain strong moral lessons (see Chapter 3). For example, *Apple*'s simple comparative advertising (Mac vs. PC) is an exemplar of this latter approach. In one advertisement PC is sorting money into a large pile – the smallest one to invest in the innovation necessary to fix the troubled *Vista* program, the largest, to be spent on a public relations campaign that pretends all is right with the program. When Mac asks whether the small pile is enough to fix all the problems with *Vista*, PC looks at him and merges the small pile with the larger one, indicating that all money is to be spent on advertising. Not so subtly, Mac indicates that the switch should be the other way around, clearly indicating the difference between the two brands.

The moral of the above story is simple – *Apple* is substance and style while PC (or *Microsoft* in this case) is all spin. *Linux* has recently run its own viral ads that mimic the *Apple* ads and present both Mac and PC as a comfortable, aging couple, with *Linux* as the truly innovative player. The *Linux* character, deliberately a sassy female, has her clothes changed in real time to reflect the latest fashions. Mac immediately exclaims how much he wishes that he could have a jacket as cool as *Linux*'s. Once again this captures *Linux*'s spirit of constant innovation. While *Apple* and *PC* are closed communities and thus slow to change, *Linux*'s open community of developers means their software is updated in real time. The ads end with a message about the growing popularity of *Linux*, which is greeted with real surprise by the two entrenched players (once again reinforcing the view that both are old, comfortable market leaders that take their consumers for granted).

Although morality tales are implicit in the stories of many authentic brands (such as the benefits of hard work, or following one's heart), they are made explicit, often in cases involving breaches of sincerity or crisis. For example, in response to legitimate criticism regarding the practice of sourcing grapes from outside the Champagne region for wines labelled 'Champagne' *Bollinger* committed itself to a Charter of Ethics forbidding such practices (Jefford 2002). This charter is on open display for all to see and is used to remind people, including their competitors in the region, of the dangers of chasing short-term profits at the expense of integrity. *Krispy Kreme* donuts had a similar experience, when they decided to change their original recipe in order to save money on ingredients. Consumers deserted the brand in droves, and the tale is now used internally as a warning against such thinking (the *New Coke* experience plays a similar role in *Coca Cola*). Undoubtedly the refusal of the brand to adopt more transparent financial reporting practices in the wake of the Enron-era will later be reinterpreted as reflecting poorly on a company dedicated to old-fashioned values and transparency (Kazanjian and Joyner 2004).

Five: Returning to or continuing roots in periods of transition

Morality tales are often told by consumers and critics during periods of transition including ownership or leadership changes to remind newcomers of the brand's roots. For example, when *LVMH* took a controlling interest in *Chateau d'Yquem*, the original owners, led by Alexandre de Lur Saluces baulked at the more commercial direction that would occur under Bernard Arnault, effectively locking the CEO out of his own business. Part of this had to do with the French establishment's view that Arnault was an upstart entrepreneur who had no understanding of France's cultural heritage. Upon winning a court case confirming his ownership, Arnault surprisingly retained the services of Alexandre de Lur Saluces because he had fought so hard to retain the integrity of the Chateau and was thus judged to be the best person to guide the estate into the future (Olney 2008).

A brand's roots are also used to interpret less than successful periods of the brand's history. *Apple* provides a compelling example. Many *Apple* enthusiasts refer to the return of Steve Jobs to run the company as 'the second coming' (Belk and Gumbat 2005). A core part of the *Apple* legend is that *Apple*'s current success is due to Jobs' returning the brand to its roots – the focus on breakthrough, consumer friendly, design-driven innovation. Prior to his return, the brand's failure was due to poor leadership that focused on convergence between *Apple* and *PC* manufacturers. Thus, although *Apple* machines were more powerful and reliable, they were largely unloved by consumers because they were simply more expensive versions of *PC*'s. The lesson is clear – mess with the brand's roots by trying to be like every other market-led company at your peril. Undoubtedly, concern about the firm's roots are central to debates (in 2009) about the fate of the company should Jobs retire due to his current health problems.

Famed toymaker *W. Britain's* suffered a similar fate. The largest toy soldier manufacturer in the world, this 100-year company suffered in between 1997–2005 due to ownership changes. Collectors of the hand-painted figures raised concerns about the quality of sculpting and painting under the ownership of *Racing Champions*. Soldiers from this period attract little interest from collectors and many collectors at the time had real concerns for the future of the iconic British company (particularly after the loss of sculptor Charles

Biggs). Happily, new owners *First Gear* have returned the company to its historic status with exciting new lines of figures, investments in standardized sizing, new moulds and better painting. As well, the company has returned to the practice of doing significant historical research into each figure to ensure accuracy. As a result collectors have returned to the brand, as have a new generation of fans (Joplin et al. 2008).

The two sets of stories above concern brands that have struggled and then recovered, thanks to a return to their roots. In each case, firms effectively rewrite their histories in moral terms in order to remind staff and management of what makes the brand special. Consumers and critics often follow suit – once again to forewarn managers not to mess with the brand's roots. Thus *Morgan's* failed +4+ reminds the firm not to chase fashions for short-term gain. While this story is part of the firm's official legend, it has also been written as an attempt to innovate, and is an example of why the firm is successful – since cars are built to order, poor performing models can be dropped quickly at little cost because there is no stock that needs to be cleared (Laban 2000). Regardless of the story, incidences concerning the brand's roots are used to convey moral stories about appropriate actions.

Six: Retaining community traditions

Many brands emerged from a particular scene or community. It's no coincidence that *Starbucks* comes from Seattle, which has a thriving coffee scene. It's also no surprise that *Starbucks* retains links to this spiritual home by keeping its first store at Pike Place in its original state. When brands break links with their founding communities and their traditions, they lose authenticity. For example, research suggests that the difficulties faced by Trappist breweries in differentiating themselves from so-called religious beers (or Abbey beers) relates to their decision to expand their reach beyond their original geographic communities. Because the Trappists failed to remind consumers of their substantive social commitments to their surrounding communities, these beers were effectively repositioned globally as 'traditional Belgian beers' or 'religious beers', thus losing key parts of their original story that gave them a genuine point of difference against larger commercial manufacturers (Beverland et al 2008). By way of contrast, *Dublin Dr Pepper's* decision to retain its links to its original sales territory is central to the brand's fans' enduring patronage.

Star Trek is one franchise that has often struggled with community traditions. For many fans or 'Trekkies', brand extensions and licensed products run counter to the original spirit of the series and founder Gene Roddenberry (Kozinets 2001). Debates about the authenticity of derivations such as the *New Generation* or *Voyager* are common, and many believe the failure of the last series *Enterprise* (and the television franchise) was due to breaches of community norms (e.g., scenes involving nudity, continuity problems). Revitalizing other dormant brands such as *Star Wars* and the *VW Beetle* has also raised the ire of their fan communities (Brown et al. 2003). The new series of *Star Wars* were seen by many fans as little more than a pale imitation of the originals. Criticism of director George Lucas was common because many believed that he was more motivated by money and licensing deals than creativity. Similar concerns have affected the latest Indiana Jones movie – *South Park* featured George Lucas and Steven Spielberg raping *Indiana Jones* in an episode entitled 'The China Problem' parodying the motives of the two directors in revisiting their back catalogue.

In each case, losing connections to founding communities undermines the roots of authentic brands. Common to much criticism is that the original spirit of the brand has been traded for short-term profit. Typical of criticism is that new versions of the brand are tired imitations of the original and reflect a lack of genuine creativity. As well, such reboots or extensions often ignore the communities that surround the brand altogether. The fact that many brand managers understand that their brands are often embedded in community traditions has resulted in increased attention being given to ethnographic research. This is especially so for lifestyle brands because these can suffer from sudden popularity.

For example, surfing and skating brands have suffered in the past because they have focused on fashion or extended into other activities at the expense of product quality. *Vans*, for example, suffered when it extended into non-skate footwear. The extensions were poorly received because of their lack of authenticity. At the same time, the lack of innovation in skate-wear opened up opportunities for other niche competitors more attuned with the skate community. Only through refocusing on skate did the brand trade out of bankruptcy (Ragas and Bueno 2002).

Seven: Engaging in focal activities

Vans' situation provides a segue into the final means by which brands reaffirm a commitment to their roots – the staff and firm remain committed to the focal founding activities of the brand. Fans of surf brand *Ripcurl* raised questions about its authenticity when the brand listed on the stock exchange. For many surfers, being owned by bankers and stockbrokers that didn't even surf was the last straw (Beverland, Farrelly and Quester forthcoming). Now driven by the need to improve quarterly earnings, *Ripcurl* expanded their retail offer beyond the beachfront. The resulting increase in staff meant that few retail salespeople had surfing experience and the brand began to lose authenticity with its core audience. A similar fate befell *L.L. Bean*. Dramatic growth meant that few staff engaged in outdoor activities. Extensions into fashion didn't help consumer perceptions either. Authenticity began to return when staff (including new CEO Leon Gorman) personally tested equipment by engaging in outdoor pursuits (Gorman 2006).

Tanya Thompson, founder of the cultish *Misery* fashion and toy label gained a following through her darkly comic artworks, many of which often took graffiti form. Despite starting a brand with global ambitions, Thompson continues as an artist, and in her self-published DVD *The Magical World of Misery* (2006) continues to engage in graffiti and clandestine tagging, much to the admiration of her fans. Continued involvement in focal activities matter to a brand's authenticity. They explain why *Virgin* managers are required to work at check-in desks regularly, why *Morgan* prefers staff that are sports car or classic car enthusiasts, why *Cooper's Brewery* requires family members to be available to consumers, why monks remain involved in the production of *Chimay* beer, and why business closes down when surf's up at *Quiksilver*.

Such involvement also helps with innovation, as covered in Chapter 7.

CONCLUSION

A brand's roots matter. Thomas Friedman (2000) coined the phrase 'The Lexus and the Olive Tree' to indicate the complexity of the post-modern age. On the one hand, we embrace the global through the purchase of the *Lexus*. On the other, we also desire to be like the olive tree – deeply rooted to place. Friedman identified the tensions between globalization and localism in his work. A brand's roots matter in the similar way. Brands gain by being open to the world, but they also lose when they become disconnected from time, place, cultures, and values because such disconnections make it difficult for consumers to achieve authentication. Thus as surf brands move into fashion at the expense of their founding community, so long-time consumers abandon the brand in favour of a more genuine partner. Without a direct connection to real surfers, fashion-oriented consumers quickly drop the brand and move on to 'the next big thing'. As a result, the brand loses.

A brand's roots matter in another (but connected) important way – they provide a point of difference against large global competitors. The roots of famous global brands are often long forgotten, usually due to deliberate marketer choice. Thus who knows where *General Motors* came from (in fact the brand name is so bland it could have been invented yesterday)? Large corporates are often little more than hollow names (such as *WorldCom* or *Enron*), and thus are often greeted in a suspicious manner or with disinterest. Hollow brand names also require marketing campaigns that try to infer points of difference and build emotional connections with consumers. Usually, these so-called points of difference are easily copied. In contrast, the uniqueness of a brand's roots provides the basis for storytelling and emotional connection. Continued commitment to one's roots also enhances the sincerity of the brand because the brand makes a virtue of refusing to compromise core values.

I started this chapter contrasting sticking to one's roots with mindlessly repeating past behaviours even when data clearly suggests such strategies are no longer relevant. However, managing the tension between roots and the need for change is difficult. One means of doing so is retaining symbolic or limited commitments to one's roots, such as a place of founding, the first store, or use of historic production techniques, while at the same time embracing the new. The second means is to recast one's roots in ideological terms. Therefore, *Virgin*'s roots are not in publishing or music, but in a set of values that can be applied across multiple sectors. Third, brands maintain substantive commitments to their roots, through direct engagement in core activities, continued family involvement in the business, commitments to place, means of production, while slowly embracing new practices that enhance the quality of output and keep the firm relevant (a process called 'market immersion' is critical here – see Chapter 7).

CHAPTER 6
LOVE THE DOING

Great technologists, great product people, people committed to innovation, develop new products and that's what causes products to succeed or fail. I'm really lucky, I get to work with really amazing, really motivated, really talented people each day and if the quality of people is any indication of the future, I think it's very bright.

(*Google* VP, Marissa Mayer quoted in Kendall 2009, p. 25)

AYN RAND AND JAMES DYSON

Ayn Rand's classic 1943 [1994] novel *The Fountainhead* involves two characters of relevance to our discussion on authentic branding. The novel tells the stories of two friends and architects – Peter Keating and Howard Roark. In the first two-thirds of the novel, Keating rises to prominence, winning large commissions, fame, fortune, and a trophy wife. However, Keating's success is an illusion – his buildings are mere copies of previous designs or those he stole and adapted from his friend Roark. His happiness is also an illusion – he gives up the love of his life twice (his painting and childhood sweetheart Katie), marries a woman who despises him, and knows in his heart he is a parasite. Rand originally titled her novel *Second Hand Lives* because Peter puts aside his own beliefs and desires and instead adapts to the views and demands of others.

Howard Roark by contrast spends most of the novel failing (in society's terms). He drops out of architecture college, chooses to work under faded star and alcoholic Henry Cameron, is hated by leading critic Ellsworth Toohey, struggles to find clients and is forced to close his business and work in a quarry, and loses his love to Keating. In contrast to the compromising Keating, Roark stands by his beliefs and (in the first two-thirds of the novel) loses (even though he retains his integrity). However, Roark slowly wins commissions for his ground breaking buildings (the character is loosely modelled on Frank Lloyd Wright), and by the novel's end has a thriving architectural practice, is recognized as a visionary, has defeated Toohey, and married his love, Dominique.

The climax of the novel involves a large-scale, low-cost housing project called Cortlandt. Keating knows only Roark can provide the winning design while Roark knows he will never gain the commission from the conservative committee. Keating, a beaten man forced to confront the meaninglessness of his life and career approaches Roark to convince him to design the project while giving him the credit. When Roark states that he might be tempted if Peter offers him enough Keating seizes his chance. He offers Roark money, fame, virtue, and even his soul. Roark is not interested in any of these. Finally Keating states that Roark should help because he'd love designing Cortlandt. Roark agrees noting he has been passionately working on the problem of affordable housing for years, examining new developments in raw materials, engineering processes, and design. Why? As Roark states:

I want you to think and tell me what made me give years to this work? Money? Fame? Charity? Altruism? Keating shook his head slowly. All right you're beginning to understand. ... I'm never concerned with my clients, only with their architectural require-ments. I consider these as part of my building's theme and problem, as my building's material – just as I consider bricks and steel. Bricks and steel are not my motive. Neither are the clients. Both are only a means of my work. Peter, before you can do things for people, you must be the kind of man who can get things done. But to get things done, you must love the doing, not the secondary consequences.

Long ago, I remember someone writing that Roark was an archetypical representation of the production orientation – an approach that might have been useful once, but that was now viewed by serious marketers as naïve. Roark dedicated many years of his life to becoming the great-est architect of his time, whereas Keating took short cuts and ended up forgotten and broken. In this sense, Roark's effort resembles that of the outliers Malcolm Gladwell catalogues in his book of the same name.

Gladwell (2008) downplays the importance of innate talent and notes that leadership in a field comes after around 10,000 dedicated hours of effort spent in honing and perfecting one's skill. Outliers aren't geniuses (although they can be); they simply love the doing more than others. Rand (who appeared on the US 33 cent stamp in 1999) herself embodied this perfectly – overcoming language barriers and publisher rejection to produce novels that still sell by the truckload today (27 years after her death).

James Dyson is the perfect embodiment of Howard Roark's spirit. Just as the architectural establishment in *The Fountainhead* copied classical building styles even though material advances offered new ways of doing things, so too did the established brands of vacuum cleaners continue to build machines based on the original patented process. Dyson challenged this. He was furious that modern vacuum cleaners performed so poorly and that companies too lazy to challenge convention were exploiting consumers. Using new materials and processes, Dyson designed the *Dual Cyclone* system. Like Roark and Rand, the established players rejected the design, giving it little hope of success – an experience typical of many authentic brands. As a last resort, Dyson founded his own company to produce the *Dual Cyclone*. The rest is history. Dyson dominates the market, continues to innovate, and importantly, continues to reject marketing as meaningless impression management (Dyson 2002). Like Roark, Dyson is a man who can get things done because he loves the doing. In order to build an authentic brand one must have some substance to sell. And to do that, one must love the doing.

WHY DO WE LOVE THE 'LOVERS OF DOING'?

Love of production is central to consumer-based brand authenticity because it enhances perceptions of quality commitments and sincerity. Since love of production involves commitment to craft and design, indirectly this habit also enhances perceptions of heritage. Authentic brands sit in contrast to the majority of brands on the market. Like Roark, the people behind these brands love the doing, and they therefore get things done (authentic brands typically outperform others in their class and/or set the standard by which others are measured). The owners and employees of authentic brands are perceived as being sincere because they are motivated by their passion for doing rather than money, fame, and many of the other outcomes that they often experience anyway (only the cynical view it the other way around). As chef Gordon Ramsay states:

> Let's be honest. Flipping burgers and dressing Caesar salads in division four cooking is a doddle. It's a piece of piss. When you decide to carve it out at three Michelin stars, and go to the very, very top, then there's a price to pay for that. You've got to live it, breathe it, push it, enhance it. (Dapin 2008, p. 28)

Ramsay's attitude sits in contrast with the employees and owners of others brands. It is not unusual for CEOs to hop from one industry to the next in search of a bigger pay packet (and to stay one step ahead of the mess they often create). Employees too focus on jumping from one project (or pay packet) to the next, switching firms to do so. These employees see each firm and activity as a commodity and focus on short-term gains. As such, few brands staffed by such employees inspire consumer loyalty. Just like Peter Keating, many of us have been told to get a practical job, instead of following our passions. Just as we secretly admire artists for having the courage to do what they love, so we admire brands that are run and staffed by true enthusiasts – people that will do whatever it takes to ensure the survival of the brand. As a result, such dedication results in innovative products that become part of history – such as the *Apple Macintosh, Britten V1000, Mathmos Lava Lamp, Leica M3, Sesame Street, Chateau Margaux, Krug, Chuck Taylor's All Stars, Sony Walkman, Chanel's* little black dress, *Dyson Cyclone, Hermès Birkin, Louis Roederer Cristal, Manolo Blahnik* shoes, the *Aston Martin DB5*, and so on.

HOW TO DEMONSTRATE A LOVE OF DOING

The people behind authentic brands demonstrate a love of doing in six key ways. In contrast to marketing theory these brands revel in their product/production orientation. Second, they allow consumers to experience production by taking them to the 'back region'. Third, leaders and senior management remain involved in production or production decisions. Fourth, stories surrounding the brand espouse a love of craft. Fifth, employees behind the brand are never satisfied with anything less than excellence (even though this can never be achieved). Finally, the firms that house these brands are design-led. Together these six practices enhance a brand's authenticity and when combined with the other habits (particularly market immersion – see Chapter 7) result in a constant stream of market defining innovations and devoted consumers.

One: Product/production orientation

Serving the customer begins with making a good product, and because it's a good product, to guarantee it longer than anybody else and to service it longer than others do. I don't care when they brought it, if they've got a point, we lean toward them and we fix it, replace it, or we give them their money back. (*Nordstrom* CEO David Oreck quoted in Rosica 2007, p. 44).

Those of us that have experienced introductory courses in marketing (usually imposingly entitled 'Marketing Principles' or 'Foundations of Marketing') know the folklore (and yes, studies have shown that this history really is myth; Fullerton 1988). First, firms made products and consumers brought them (the 'build it and they will come' approach, which curiously characterizes many authentic brands such as Steve Irwin's decision to build a crocodile arena at Australia Zoo; Irwin, T. 2005). This was labelled 'product orientation'. Then this was no longer sufficient, so attention moved to being more efficient and effective in production. This was labelled 'production orientation'. When this approach no longer worked, we focused on persuading people why they should buy our products. This was called a 'sales orientation'. The problems with these strategies were that they didn't start with the consumer. Each approach was inside out – the firms produced products they wanted without regard for the consumer. What was needed was a new mantra – market orientation, which involves designing products and services by working backwards from target market needs (or an outside-in approach) (Fullerton 1988). The current mantra even goes so far as to suggest consumers should co-design products (Vargo and Lusch 2004).

By the standards of modern marketing theory, authentic brands are relics of a dying age. Technology magazine *Wired* predicted in June 1997 that *Apple* was doomed to fail because it did not embrace licensing and open sourcing, instead preferring to go it alone – in fact the cover of the magazine showed the *Apple* logo being squeezed by barbed wire under the heading 'Pray'). *Wired* did an about-face in April 2008, in the face of overwhelming evidence to the contrary – *Apple*'s closed approach to production might not have been 'market oriented', but it did result in market leadership and increased stock prices (Kahney 2008).

Comeuppances like this are starting to occur more often. The market-driven, consumer-worshipping, marketing savvy Australian wine industry is losing margin and sales while consumers go on a waiting list to the mail order list of specialist wineries run by those espousing contempt for marketing. Major fashion brands struggle while craft production (not only through websites such as ETSY.com) is back with a vengeance. Beverage manufactures try to retain the share taken off them by fruit juice lovers such as *Innocent, Emma and Toms, Nudie, Snapple,* and *Honest Charlie's.* Just as Peter Keating found that his appeasers despised him, so too consumers are starting to treat obsequious consumer-loving brands with open disgust (Brown 2008).

At the same time, consumers flock to brands that feign disinterest in their needs. The 116th *Seinfeld* episode featured the Soup Nazi. Consumers loved his soups. But the Soup Nazi did not love consumers. To get their beloved soup, consumers needed to line up patiently and quietly, order, move two steps to the left, pay, and then pick up their order (which they were to accept without question). Those that failed to follow the rules would lose their soup for the day (repeat offenders such as Elaine were barred altogether). Only Kramer seemed to truly understand that the Soup Nazi loved his soups (he suffered for them) and imposed such harsh rules because consumers should show proper respect for his skill. Although authentic brands rarely impose rules like the Soup Nazi (although there is certainly a skill to getting a *Hermès Birkin* crocodile bag; Tonello 2008), they do not place the consumer on a pedestal. *Champagne Krug* and *Bollinger* make this clear respectively:

> Either you love it and the beginning of the love story will be Krug or you don't like it. We're not for everyone.

> I would say that we are extremely different because we are extremely wine oriented, and we only want to produce the best wine and offer the consumer this without any elaborate marketing. It's more the approach of a producer which offers the best he can to consumers and then the consumers makes their choice. You should not

appear as an old fashioned company but I don't think Bollinger wants to be a fashionable, trendy champagne brand. We really base our marketing on true values and not on invented, fake marketing values. (Beverland 2005b, p. 205)

The approaches of these two legendary Champagne Houses (and incredibly valuable brands) are derided as a product/production orientation in marketing textbooks. However, the question remains 'why have they been so successful, for so long?' If the product/production orientation is so yesterday, why does it continue to deliver value to *Apple, Bollinger, Dyson, Krug, Morgan*, and others, many of which operate in highly competitive markets full of market-driven firms? And, why do customers start to reject brands such as *Tiffany* when they are too easy to get, or too focused on appealing to as many customers as possible? Consumers respond to these product-oriented brands precisely because they make substantive commitments to quality instead of trying to sell poorly performing products with advertising campaigns (such as *Microsoft*'s *Vista*) or producing me-too products derived from focus group tests. In a world where we are told we can have anything we want, we also admire firms that have the courage to say we can take it or leave it. As one long-time consumer of *Tiffany* put it, 'People should have to travel to get to Tiffany. That's part of the thrill' (Gallagher 2002, p. 48). We admire Roark for having the courage of his convictions (regardless of the cost), just as we admire other creators who love what they do and see their vision come alive. This is the spirit that authentic brands embody.

Two: Experiencing production

Authentic brands may not worship consumers but they do know customers love the objects and services these firms provide. While disavowing a role for consumers in the development of goods and services, authentic brands allow people to see behind the scenes through experiential tours, books and documentaries, museums, factory tours, hosted events, and through stories regarding production. Long before many brands talked of supply-chain transparency, ISO quality and environmental standards, and stakeholder audits, authentic brands opened up their operations to their fans. For example, *Dublin Dr Pepper*, *Krispy Kreme*, and *In-N-Out Burger* allow consumers to see the backstage of their operations, allowing customers to confirm for themselves that the products are fresh and that claims of being handmade are in fact true. *Schwinn Bicycles* were pioneers in experiential marketing when they insisted that stores ensure that consumers could see their bicycle repair facilities. This strategy raised consumer trust in an industry suffering from dishonest operators and ensured Schwinn gained a leadership position for several decades (Pridmore and Hurd 2001).

To the horror of studio executives, Peter Jackson started a blog for fans during the filming of *King Kong*, a practice he began with the *Lord of the Rings*. As reported in the fan-developed 2005 documentary *Ringers: Lord of the Fans*, many Ringers felt this approach allowed them to share in Jackson's journey, and led to people camping outside of cinemas for days before the release of each film (something not seen since the original *Star Wars* movies). Likewise, the late Steve Irwin (*aka* the Crocodile Hunter) brought people up close with wildlife because he believed that only through close encounters with nature would people appreciate how precious animals were (Irwin, T. 2005). Irwin's low-key documentaries allowed us to share directly his sense of wonder and love for the wild.

Such practices reinforce authenticity precisely because they allow us to go 'backstage' and thus confirm that there is substance to the brand's claims (MacCannell 1976). Also, making things has always been a source of excitement. Young children (and the not so young) are enraptured by *Krispy Kreme*'s doughnut production processes – the sound of the production line, the steady march of the donuts through frying, dusting and packing, and that wonderful smell. At their larger stores one can view staff making the donut mix, cutting individual donuts, and cooking and icing them. We get to see our favourite snack food produced in front of us (by staff clearly enjoying the process) from scratch. The fresh donuts are then handed to us by smiling staff. Despite being a relatively large, publicly listed firm, this decision to open up the backstage provides a point of connection between the brand and consumer and reinforces *Krispy Kreme*'s old time, authentic positioning. Suddenly *Krispy Kreme* seems little different to the local baker of old.

Allowing consumers to experience the production processes behind the brand also reinforces the brand's aura. Many practices behind authentic brands are tacit – that is, they are difficult to explain, yet are easy to understand in practice. For example, although I had heard many winemakers talk of the importance of place (or *terroir*) to a wine's taste, I remained sceptical – surely this was just another claim used by the Europeans to denigrate the status of New World wines. My views were changed following an interview and tour at *Domaine Joseph Drouhin* in Burgundy (France). My guide, Robert Drouhin, allowed me to taste wines that were still fermenting. Although undrinkable, wines at this stage of their development are in such a raw state one can easily distinguish the character of different pieces of soil. After several tastings of wine, usually from vineyards only meters apart, I finally 'got' *terroir* or the notion of place. I instantly had a different insight into wine and Burgundy in particular, and now understood that notions of the 'best wine' were simplistic – instead (for me) wine quality (assuming no defects) should be judged on the degree to which the final product communicates a sense of place. The claim so central to Burgundian production was real.

Is this strategy a carefully scripted experience – much like that in many service encounters or retail stores? Although tourists often try and go backstage to gain an authentic experience of a particular place, research reveals that this backstage is no more real than the front stage because locals simply put on a different front, resulting in a stylized view of local life. As well, the backstage quickly becomes littered with tourist friendly amenities, resulting in a more sanitized view of local life (MacCannell 1976). Certainly many of the experiences at large firms (the tours) follow a carefully managed schedule due to large number of customers, health and safety concerns, and the desire not to impede production. But, just as ethnographers quickly blend into the background of their site (simply because people cannot keep up an act for long periods of time), so tours become part of everyday life for employees. Since work must get done, behind-the-scenes tours (even when documented in books and film) are more likely to capture some of the 'warts 'n all' nature of production and the passion for the task shown by employees.

Three: Leaders involved in production

There is an element of management that I largely underestimated and that is passion – you have to be rational as a CEO but you also have to be passionate about the product. Passion is fantastic stimulator to creativity. ... Forty per cent of my time is spent on product creation. I am eventually responsible for brand equity, so I get involved in marketing. (*Tag Heuer* CEO Jean-Christophe Babin, quoted in Rubython 2002, pp. 48–9)

How many of today's senior managers and CEOs of large corporations have been, or are involved in production decisions? Historically, managers worked their way up from the shop floor. As a result, they were often experienced in all aspects of the business prior to reaching senior leadership positions. Admittedly this didn't always work – sometimes being so immersed in the business resulted in myopic decision making and new blood was needed. However, today few senior managers have cut their teeth in the core aspects of the business. Instead, CEOs often have a strong background in finance, an inherently conservative discipline (lest you're wondering the author is a trained accountant who works with finance professors). Similarly, the trend of chief marketing officers becoming CEOs continues the tradition of disconnection between the leader and core business practices. In contrast, senior managers behind authentic brands remain heavily involved in their core activities.

The people behind authentic brands embody Roark's spirit. Authentic brands are staffed with people passionate about the product/service and run by leaders heavily involved in all aspects of production. Charles Morgan continues to race *Morgan*s at *Le Mans* and other events. The firm is staffed with classic motoring enthusiasts, many of whom restore and race their own cars. Despite several health problems, Steve Irwin continued to make wildlife documentaries up until his untimely death (from a stingray barb). *Real Groovy Records* is run by, and for, music lovers – it is not uncommon for staff to spend a third of their pay at the store on music and movies. When the chain required recapitalisation after some of the founders retired, legions of fans rallied around the brand with several leading lights in the New Zealand music industry (who had often got their first break at *Real Groovy*) providing funding. Richard Branson requires all management staff to front airline check-in counters regularly, to keep in touch with the main job at hand. Ralph Lauren is known for walking the floors of *Bloomingdales*, to ensure his clothes are presented just right.

Development teams at Apple regularly face questions from CEO Steve Jobs about new innovations. Jobs has often intervened to ensure products meet his exacting standards, live up to the expectations of *Apple*'s fans, and remain user friendly. As Grossman (2005, p. 41) states 'Jobs has a great native sense of design and knack for hiring geniuses, but above all, what he has is a willingness to be a pain in the neck about what matters to him'. Peter Jackson loves the art of film-making so much that no detail is too small. For example, in the opening battle scene of the *Fellowship of the Ring*, an alliance of Dwarves, Elves, and Humans desperately fight the armies of darkness. The scene is set thousands of years before the formation of the Fellowship. *Weta's* design team were aware that over time (in Middle Earth) technologies would change and evil creatures such as Orcs and Goblins would also evolve. As such, there are subtle differences in the features and technology (such as weapons and armour) of the different races (Sibley 2006). Many filmmakers would have reused the same props to save on time and budget. They would have rationalized that most people wouldn't know. Not Jackson – he would know, as would the fans.

Four: Espoused love of craft

When Richard Branson sold *Virgin Records* in 1992 to help fund his airline many of his friends advised him to slow down, retire from business, and have fun. Branson found this amusing because he had been having fun ever since he started up his first business *Student*. Branson could no more give up business than stop breathing – he simply loved running businesses. Just as Roark painstakingly spent years learning about low-cost housing (even though he knew he would never get to see his ideas in practice) because of his love for problem solving and building, the love staff have for authentic brands is obvious to their consumers. Such love partly explains why *Virgin Blue* staff broke down in tears when (jokingly) Branson announced to the Australian media that he was selling the company in 2001. Staff view their craft in terms of a mission – whether it is to shake up competition in a monopolistic industry, produce handmade cars, save endangered wildlife, change women's fashion, bring great novels to life on screen, make beautiful machines, and produce high-quality food.

Authentic brands espouse their love of craft by identifying that behind the brand is a passionate creator, or team of individuals who love what they do. For example, three friends who loved fruit founded *Innocent*, staff at *The Body Shop* are passionate about their products and the social causes the brand champions, and *Morgan* and *Apple* are inundated with job applications from people passionate about their craft. Once iconic New Zealand winery *Martinborough Vineyards* gained its status through the efforts of winemaker and CEO Larry McKenna (dubbed the 'Prince of Pinot Noir'). In 1999, Larry was asked to stand down from his role as CEO and focus solely on winemaking. One criticism at the time was Larry was too easily distracted from leading the small company because he was only too happy to talk to small groups of consumers about the wonders of Pinot Noir. Larry has moved on to his new vineyard, *Escarpment*, and *Martinborough Vineyard*'s wines continue to improve under a new team, but the brand no longer commands the press attention and iconic status it once did. Why? The move to a more professional management structure might have been part of the problem.

The love of craft can be seen in toy soldier maker *W. Britain*'s 2009 Delhi Durbar range. The beautiful Jaipur elephant (Figure 6.1) was premiered in December 2008 at the London Collectors Club event (attended by yours truly) and caused a sensation among long-time fans of the brand. The team behind the range researched old photos and pictures of the 1903 Durbar to ensure that the resulting figures were accurate representations of the event. Reviewing the collection

FIGURE 6.1 **Eagerly awaited by collectors, *W. Britain's* return to the Delhi Durbar range kicks off with this lovingly crafted, and carefully researched, Jaipur elephant**

in club magazine *The Standard,* club member 1621, Nick Spenceley (2009), identified that the *Britain*'s team had used impeccable sources – the paintings of artist Mortimer Menpes who was commissioned by the illustrated *London News* to cover the 1903 Durbar and published a subsequent book on the Durbar – when crafting the Durbar range. Spenceley noted the new Durbar range was likely to become the brand's Jewel in the Crown, in reference to the Imperial view that India was the Jewel of the British Empire. Subsequent interest and pre-orders bear this prediction out.

During Industrialization jobs where split up into small tasks to ensure efficiency and standardization. Under the guise of scientific management, this system led to massive increases in output and lower costs, but it also created a backlash by those desiring a return to more traditional methods of production. Today, online craft markets such as ETSY.com are thriving because of a renewed interest in hand-made, unique items. Just as many consumers are buying from farmers' markets because of a desire to meet the people who produce their food, so the renewed interested in craft reflects a desire to connect with passionate creators behind brands and objects. As part of this desire to connect with passionate craftspeople, designers are now accorded superstar status, fans of *Apple* line up for hours to gain tickets to see Steve Jobs talk at *MacWorld*, skilled chefs such as Gordon Ramsay and Ferran Adrià sell tickets faster than the Rolling Stones, and thousands of excited fans attend *World of Warcraft Conventions* to meet members of the game's design team. We engage with such people for two other reasons – their love reflects our own passion for the brand and our desire to be creative.

Five: The quest for excellence

I have to get to the bottom of things. I have to try to understand something ... the world we live in suffers terribly from a sort of trademark-ism where everybody thinks they can find these simple keys to things and then fit everything in. The truth of everything is in the detail. (Vivienne Westwood, quoted in Turner 2004, p. 18)

Just as Jobs and Jackson delayed the release of products they felt were not quite perfect, so staff at authentic brands describe their jobs in terms of an elusive quest for excellence or perfection – a characteristic typical of many designers (Beverland 2005b). These brands are often at the forefront of quality and performance because employees are never satisfied with sitting still and resting on their laurels. *Apple* continues to enhance their *iPod*, often deliberately killing off versions that are still in the growth phase of their lifecycle. Dyson adopts a similar approach, releasing newer improved versions of their *Cyclone* vacuum well before earlier releases have entered the maturity phase. In fact, Dyson, Jobs, and Branson share this passion for improving performance standards in their products and in sectors they have yet to enter. For example, *Apple* desired to improve conditions for music consumers and artists with *iTunes* (who pay greater royalties than recording companies do), Dyson has sought to improve standards in clothes washing with the *Contrarotator* and in hand drying with the *Airblade*, and Branson regularly enters industries with an eye to upping service standards.

Despite being seen as purveyors of tradition *Chateau Margaux* and *Morgan* never stop making small adjustments to their products. Every vintage (built to order Morgan's are vintage dated like wines) represents a furthering of the design team's skill. Whereas consumers of fine wines used to accept that only one vintage in four years would be exceptional due to variable weather conditions, now the fine wine estates have become noticeably better at producing very high-quality wines in diffi-cult years. For example, Port Houses such as *Churchill's, Cockburn's, Sand-eman, Taylor's,* and others are allowed to release wines labelled 'Vintage Port' three times in a decade. These wines represent the pinnacle of port production and the term was restricted to only the very best of vintages (which usually reflected weather conditions in the Douro Valley). Now, the winemaking teams have become so proficient in managing adverse weather conditions that they have been forced to release Vintage Style, Vintage Character, and single vineyard Vintage-style Ports to get around the restrictions of the three-in-ten years tradition.

What impresses consumers and other stakeholders about authentic brands is their attention to detail. As Champagne Deutz Fabrice Rosset states, 'The art of making Champagne is like a Byzantine fresco, where it takes many small parts to make the grand picture. The picture is, indeed, grand, but we have to look out for the small pieces to make it great' (Farmer 2005–6, p. 36). Alessi's Richard Sapper stated the best designers by definition are very familiar with the technology with which he works (Alessi, 1998, p. 29) 'because of the innumerable, hard to execute details which constitute his projects'. The loving care with which Peter Jackson puts together movies may be obvious on first viewing, but what is fascinating is how many more details one notices on further viewings, not to mention ones that are only brought to our attention when reading his blogs.

Reidel glassware provides another example. In order to enhance the drinking experience, Georg Reidel and his team spend an enormous amount of time researching the nature of different beverage aromas and tastes before they produce their range of specialized glasses. Anyone attending Georg's entertaining tastings cannot help but be impressed at how the design of a glass can enhance or destroy the experience of a particular wine, beer, or spirit. *Reidel*'s glasses are designed to work in tandem with different wine styles. For example, a narrow glass enhances the experience of a Sauvignon Blanc because it concentrates the aroma and the taste of the wine on the front palette. In contrast, a chardonnay glass is fuller, because the nose is more complex and subtle, and the wine must coat the entire mouth so one appreciates its full-bodied taste across the front, mid, and back palate. Such differences only come from an understanding of how small details come together to produce the overall experience.

This understanding of the importance of attending to details is what sets authentic brands apart from others. As Chandler Burr (2002, pp. 145–6) writes in the *Emperor of Scent* about Chanel's approach to perfume:

> These perfume people – their obsession is what's so terrific. They get a flight to Rome, connection to Palermo, and the supplier, who basically greets them on bended knee, says, 'Here's our new citrus for this year, and they smell it, and it's the best, the best in the entire world, and they snap it up. At Chanel, when they have to dilute the perfume with ethanol – Jesus, ethanol! It costs nothing, and it *smells* of nothing! – Chanel gets ten competitors from Europe to bid for it, they put all the samples in wineglasses, everyone is standing around smelling this stuff, and then they decide OK, this Spanish guy is going to supply us with ethanol for *Chanel No. 19*. This is the kind of obsessional *mania* that makes great perfume. You *have* to be this obsessed.

Claudia Kotchka of *P&G* intuitively understands this in her discussion of why the 'P&G effect' would ruin the authenticity of *Altoids* mints. It's why *Chateau Margaux* Estate Manager Paul Pontallier refuses to adopt the New World practice of eliminating 'underperforming' parts of the vineyard. Pontallier understands that although such underperforming areas may seem poor in isolation, they also contribute something unique to the final blend that bears the *Chateau Margaux* name. This love of details and intricacies reminds us of the work of great artists and the artisanal products of old. Great paintings, concertos, pop songs, and designs are richly layered – no detail is deemed insignificant and the greatness of the work derives from the synergy of small parts.

In contrast, other brands make trade-offs. *Qantas Airways* (regularly voted the worst airline by Australian flyers) employed market researchers to design its cabin for the new Airbus A380. These researchers employed conjoint analysis to understand the trade-off between legroom and customer satisfaction. In contrast, other airlines such as *Virgin Atlantic* simply add more amenities such as bars and better seats.

Six: Being design-led

Much of the appeal comes from the fact that Lamborghini has always pushed the limits of design. The legendary Countach sat impossibly low and looked as if it had just zipped in from another planet. At any moment, you expected it to lift off the ground, fold its wheels away and quickly hit Warp 9. (Eisenstein 2002, p. 98)

Authentic brands place a great deal of emphasis on design thinking. In contrast, other firms often apply design as an afterthought. This approach is called 'styling' by designers and is usually associated with making a product look nice for consumers. Design thinking in contrast requires a different orientation to business. Research suggests design-led firms have a culture that embeds design thinking throughout the firm – this thinking informs decisions such as product and service innovation *a priori*. Central to design-leadership is a culture of curiosity (Beverland and Farrelly 2007) – an approach reflected in Roark's approach to materials and building. Curious cultures focus on constantly questioning past practices. As Anita Roddick (2008, p. 41) stated, 'I think you have to ask questions of everyone, and never stop asking questions, and knock on doors to seek as many different opinions as exist. Then you have to make up your own mind and plough your own furrow.' These can result in major breakthroughs that shape the market such as *Dyson's Dual Cyclone* vacuum, or a series of small component or process improvements that enhance performance or the customer experience such as the improvement made to *Leica*'s famous M-series range of cameras or *Louis Vuitton* luggage.

Design is central to the positioning of America's *Umpqua Bank*. CEO Ray Davis notes that design was the only means by which this bank could compete with larger banks such as *Wachovia*. *Umpqua* decided that banking should be much like retailing and that banks should therefore be 'stores'. *Umpqua's* Pearl Store concept blends aspects of boutique hotels, retail, and banking to create a more personal banking experience. Rather than hiding behind imposing security counters or closed offices, *Umpqua* staff man hotel-style desks that allow close interaction with customers and also subtly provide privacy (McCallion 2004). Such a design-led approach resulted in a radical transformation of the concept of a bank, increased revenues, and importantly, gave customers a reason to come into the store (where they can browse different product options). Because of its focus on design and the customer experience *Umpqua* bank is often viewed as the 'women's bank'. Since women inform or make the vast majority of financial decisions, this is quite an advantage.

Design has also been at the forefront of *Seiko*'s strategy to build on its heritage of innovation to enter the high-end watch market. *Seiko*'s spring drive movement outperforms every other movement on the market, but its watch designs have left a lot to be desired. Desiring to live up to its fine engineering, the company has invested in design and even gone as far to change its brand line to 'Design your time'. The results so far are impressive, as watch specialist Bani McSpedden (2008, p. 30) notes, 'Now the spring drive is appearing in watches that reflect the edginess you'd expect from streetwise young Tokyo-istas. At this year's Basel watch fair, *Seiko* showed a monster chronograph called the *iZul*, which came dangerously close to eclipsing everything in the vicinity'. *Seiko* Australia managing director, Shunji Tanaka, comments: 'The importance of (pure) timekeeping will be reduced – we are investing and developing "emotional technology" to appeal to individual customers ... we want to be a brand to be *chosen*.' In investing in design that reflects its sense of place (rather than copying Swiss designs), *Seiko* is following in the footsteps of *Sony*, *Mazda*, and *Honda*, and like those brands, is likely to be seen as an industry leader in the years to come.

Design is at the forefront of debates about authenticity (Postrel 2003). Well-designed products intuitively seem to work. Certainly, they cause us to stop and think. *Morgan*'s controversial *Aero 8* shocked many long-time fans of the car with its radically modern styling (even though the car is unmistakably a *Morgan*). Although the design stopped many people in its tracks when it was released, marketing manager Matthew Parkin noted people kept returning to gaze at the new design (which quickly continued Morgan's tradition of success). Well-designed products and services are the physical manifestation of the brand (Beverland and Farrelly 2007). More importantly, products and services often implicitly communicate that the brand intuitively understands the consumer, their desired identity, and life world.

CONCLUSION

What drives the people behind authentic brands? As the passage from Ayn Rand's novel noted, not the customer, fame, money, or feelings of duty. These people simply love their craft, be it providing great service, growing businesses, or producing great products. In an age where the connection between the product and the people who produced it is usually described in terms of geographic location (e.g., outsourced to Asia or China), being able to identify directly with individuals who love their craft helps us reconnect with the pre-industrial skilled-artisan tradition. We can identify with these employees because their love for craft reflects our own level of passion and deep-seated desire to get paid for doing what we love. The love workers exude for their craft reinforces perceptions of sincerity and brings the brand to life.

As we mentioned earlier, Roark's approach is seen in terms of a product orientation. Also, stories of creative self-indulgence are legendary (especially when it comes to designers, marketers, and advertising creatives). Passion is not always enough – as the experience of legendary toy retailer *FAO Schwarz* demonstrates. Despite featuring in the film *Big* and being renowned for their passionate, child friendly staff, the firm filed for bankruptcy in 2003. Part of the problem related to price competition from *Wal-Mart*, but the bigger issue was that traditional *FAO* products such *Steiff Bears* no longer excited children. Children may have played at *FAO Schwarz* but the toys they wanted were sold through *Toys R Us* (London's *Hamley's* provides a counter example with their up-to-date products, great aesthetics, sharp pricing, and fantastic staff). Thankfully *FAO Schwarz* has returned, but how can they avoid further problems without selling their soul? They need to live in their consumers' life world – the subject of Chapter 7.

CHAPTER 7

MARKET IMMERSION

RIGHT WING CUSTOMERS

Want to question someone's sincerity? Just say their work or ideas are 'focus-group tested'. Authentic brands never ask customers about innovations. After all what would they know? As one designer said, 'How would customers know how to use an iPod if their only experiences were with CD players? If *Apple* had asked customers about an iPod prototype, customers would have wondered, "How do I load songs onto it? Where are my CD covers with the words on them? How will I know what songs are coming up?" They would've been bamboozled by the iPod, but now everyone can't imagine life without one' (Beverland and Farrelly 2007, p. 10). As academia's best marketing writer puts it (referring to the decrease in spontaneity in the later *Harry Potter* books):

> Most mainstream marketers, admittedly, will maintain that the customer is always right, that the sales figures speak for themselves, that the public gets what the public wants. This may be so, but it's also true to say that the customer is always right wing – conservative, reactionary, stuck-in-the-mud – that sales figures don't always speak the truth, and that the public shouldn't always get what the public wants. (Brown 2007, pp. 189–90)

As Charles Morgan says, 'customers always have a viewpoint, but they're often wrong. In fact many old-time customers think we lost the plot when we added a fourth wheel to the car back in the 1930's'. Some of the greatest product failures of all time were the outcome of rigorous market testing – the *Ford Edsel*, *New Coke*, and *McDonald's Arch*

Deluxe (Brown, 2008). In contrast, some of the greatest brands seem to reject market testing. *Apple's* Steve Jobs was referred to as 'The man who always seems to know what's next' on the front cover of *Time Magazine* in 2005 (October 24) – but *Apple* conducts no formal market research and also spends less than its competitors on research and development, yet no one can deny the firm's ability to successfully launch a stream of breakthrough products that redefine the competitive landscape. Top selling LVMH-sponsored perfume *J'adore* failed to excite focus group participants (Wetlaufer 2001). *Leica, Louis Vuitton, Hermès, Morgan, In-N-Out Burger, Chanel,* and *Chateau Margaux* openly reject any role for the customer in product development yet continue to launch beautiful products that set the standard in their respective fields. James Dyson echoes Jobs in talking about his mentor, designer Jeremy Fry:

> Jeremy never did market research, he just did things his way. I adopted this lesson at my company. Sure, we do some market research, but we don't listen to it slavishly. There are times when you have to bravely step forward. A true innovator takes risks. (Hatch 2006, p. 16)

For the company's 1989 collection Muccia Prada broke with tradition and adopted conventional market research techniques. The result? Critical and commercial failure. *New Yorker* writer Ingrid Sischy commented, 'The clothes were overdesigned, and it seemed commercial considerations and self-consciousness and not the usual articulation of her unconscious, were leading her'. As Prada stated, 'I hated all the people around me, and I told them it was the last time others would push me to do what I didn't want' (quoted in Peters 1994, p. 108). What had made the *Prada* brand so special – Muccia's imagination and her ability to capture the *zeitgeist* of the times, were missing. Prada noted the tension between her creative desires and the marketplace – she wanted to develop a huge brand while also continuing to make what she desired.

> This is where I really suffer. Because there are three basic questions I have to ask myself: Do I like the clothes? Will they sell? And are they new? They are very different questions, and I can almost never seem to match them up. From a selling point, I know perfectly well what people will want. If I try to turn this into something that is possibly

nice to wear, it will come out banal. Because usually what's nice to wear is banal. And this is my problem. Do I make clothing people want or the clothing I think they ought to wear? (Specter 2004, p. 104)

Tom Peters suggests that focus-group driven firms produce products 'of' the market – products that generally represent more of the same. As innovation guru Clayton Christensen (1997) notes, the last people you should listen to for breakthrough ideas are your current customers. In contrast, firms like *Prada* are 'in' the market – they gain inspiration from their surroundings to inspire breakthrough innovations. I call this market immersion. Market immersion allows firms to ensure they create breakthrough innovations that address real customer concerns or problems – that is, they are relevant (see the sidebar on *Tata Motor's Ace*). This overcomes concerns that the only alternative to market testing is designer intuition and luck, which too often results in creative self-indulgence and continued failure (Beverland 2004).

Side Bar:
TATA MOTORS

Understanding the life world of the consumer was essential to the success of the *Tata Ace* (affectionately referred to by people as the 'Chinna Annai' or little elephant), *Tata's* unique small four-wheeled vehicle. Three-wheelers are the mainstay of many small business operations in India because of their relatively low cost (when compared to four-wheel vehicles). However, three-wheelers also reflect one's social status, resulting in less marriage proposals and diminished social standing of the driver and their business. The development team gained these insights through visits to villages where the *Ace* was most likely to be used. Once there, they talked to businesspeople, spouses, listened in on conversations, and became part of village life. These ethnographic insights resulted in a vehicle that has taken India by storm (Palepu and Srinivasan 2007).

The biggest pay-off from market immersion is that it reinforces brand authenticity. Because the products or service breakthroughs that characterize authentic brands are derived from 'informal' research, designers can swear with hand on heart that their creations derive from intuition, inspiration, or the creative spirit – powerful markers of authenticity. In contrast, market tested products will always be tainted by commercially motivated compromise, just as artists lose authenticity when they overtly adopt marketing techniques (Fine 2004). One can imagine what would have happened if *Apple* had used focus groups prior to developing the *iPod*. We would have got a mini disc player with more functions and better battery life – and consumers wouldn't have bought it. In fact history shows this to be the case – one company's response to the *Sony Walkman* was the *Audio Technica AT-727 Sound Burger* – a portable record player that could be worn over your shoulder. It failed miserably (and also ruined records in the process).

HOW TO BE IMMERSED IN YOUR MARKET

Being in the market sounds great, but just what does it involve? I was asked just that question when I co-wrote an article on design-led firms (see Beverland and Farrelly 2007). I believe five tactics underpin this habit. First, behind authentic brands are employees that more often than not are also customers or fans. Many firms simply test drive their prototypes or ideas with employees who represent their target customer base. Second, in various ways, staff live in the marketplace – they are part of consumption communities, engage in activities that bring them in touch with consumers, lead and continue to participate in industry events and read widely on a range of trends and changes for inspiration. Third, these staff 'trust their gut'. They give preference to qualitative data, observation, experience, conversations, and outliers. Fourth, employees are often encouraged or even required to dabble in various activities that may provide spin-offs for the brand. Finally, these firms seed the fan base through conversations, rumour and stories.

One: Employ your customers

Seen a yummy mummy lately? Chances are she is pushing the baby around in an inline buggy designed by *Phil and Ted's* in Wellington, New Zealand. As *Phil and Ted's* marketing manager Richard Shirtcliffe states, 'we think a lot in terms of creating a category first rather than going to the market and saying "Oh, what looks good out there, let's try and create something similar to that but somehow better and different."' How do they know if they're on the right track? They turn to their workforce, most of whom are parents. For example:

> Campbell Gower (CEO): 'We're all parents too and so there's enough people in the business, different ages and stages, that know a lot about parenting and so we can draw internally and act on what we feel and for us it's good enough.'

> Richard Shirtcliffe (Marketing Manager): 'There is a habit for companies to think "Ok, we need to simply create a brand story about ourselves that galvanizes the attention of consumers." We say, "Listen, we've got parenting experience; we've got great ideas that stem from that parenting experience that enable us to live dynamic lives with kids, and we're focused on helping new parents to do the same". Since that's actually what we're trying to do, there's an authenticity and integrity to the message, and our products deliver against that. That flows through all our marketing. But also behind the scenes, we're saying to the designers when they come to us with a product idea, "Is it adaptable or does it help parents adapt some part of their life," and if the answer's no we say, "Well this isn't true to what we're trying to do here."'

Employees who are not parents also play an important role in the evolution of *Phil and Ted's* products (Figure 7.1) – they often ask those

FIGURE 7.1 *Phil and Ted's* **Inline Buggy – a product improved through direct feedback from staff-as-parents**

seemingly stupid or naïve questions that result in important changes (see Chapter 9 for how firms encourage employees to make such suggestions). Many other companies adopt *Phil and Ted's* approach. *Tupperware* recruited its most enthusiastic customers to be product demonstrators. Why? Because these demonstrators were also housewives who were able to empathize directly with customers. The result was consumers were more honest in their feedback abut *Tupperware* products to demonstrators. And, demonstrators were best placed to make sense of housewives' feedback, resulting in more sensitive innovations at lower cost (Tupperware 2005).

People who loved music, people who were always looking for something new, founded *Virgin Music*. As a result, the label was able to pick up artists such as Mike Oldfield, the Human League, and Japan long before they became mainstream – this avoided expensive bidding wars, reinforced that the firm was at the cutting edge of music, and paid off when these bands eventually hit the big time – especially when the Human League's third album *Dare* broke through and literally saved the struggling company (Branson had personally stepped in to ensure the band remained on the roster). *Nike* is much the same – eschewing conventional research in favour of on-the-ground insights gained from employees engaged in amateur or professional sports (Hollister 2008). As David J. Taylor (2007) notes in his amusing brand book *Never Mind the Sizzle, Where's the Sausage? Branding Based on Substance not Spin*, *Nike* doesn't have to find the consumer because their staff are the consumer. Other firms do the same – *Morgan* employs classic car enthusiasts and amateur racers, *Quiksilver* surfers, *Vans* skaters, *Leica* photographers, *Weta* movie and game lovers, and *Vespa* scooter riders.

Many years ago over lunch with a friend who helped market *Chateau Musar* (a great family-run winery in Lebanon) I asked why he did not drink wine with meals. He stated that he wanted to remain objective when approaching the business and was worried that drinking wine would (no pun intended) 'cloud his judgment'. For some reason this position always bothered me – isn't success in business due to being close to the product? Babich winery in New Zealand thought so when they aimed to turn around their tired brand. Shocked that many of their sales representatives and distributors didn't even like wine, they quickly sought out new agencies that reflected their own passion for the product. How else could they communicate to the customer and understand feedback from the market (or evaluate competitors)? As Anita Roddick (2005) says, 'Business is personal!'

Using employees as customers has one other benefit – you can use them and their families as guinea pigs for prototypes. *Quiksilver* gains feedback on prototypes from the children of their staff. *Quiksilver* employees are given products for their children on the condition they give honest feedback on the performance and desirability of surf-products. Sustainable fashion designer *Untouched World* (recognized by the UN for their commitment to social causes) does the same thing – using staff and their families as real life models for new innovations. This approach often provides a timely reminder to the design team to temper their personal preferences, as the following quote from designer Emily Drysdale shows:

Mike: Do they influence what you do in terms of product?

'I think everybody really influences what I do and I'm not sure they understand quite how they influence, like it just can be conversations around the office and it'll sink in. And like our marketing coordinator loves pink. She absolutely loves it and for 6 months all she talked about was pink and then all of a sudden we're going to have a lot more pink in the collection. I think an Irish lady who was very out there. And the both of them were really into pink. And it seemed like you couldn't go wrong if you did pink. And when you stop and back up and think, "Now how did I get to that point where I decided I've got pink in the collection for three seasons in a row, and now the retail operations manager is saying, 'Please no pink'". I test-drive things on people just around the office too, I quite often hit up our CFO – he's just a bloke and he's into mountain biking and he's got a family and he's a number cruncher and he really doesn't care about fashion and he just wants something that works, thanks very much, and I quite often hit him up for his opinion on things, and he'll be like, "Why are you asking me? I don't know what I'm talking about". It's just good to get that perspective outside you know, sometimes when you're right inside you can't see it.'

By employing your customers, firms can get honest and real time feedback about innovations without alerting competitors and investing in formal research, and still have time to make improvements before launch. No wonder these firms have a convention-defying track record of breakthrough products.

Two: Live in the market

One benefit of employing your customers is that they live in the same space as the consumer and as such have tacit knowledge of their life world. This is partly the reason that firms such as *L.L. Bean* encourage employees to continue brand relevant pursuits such as hiking, fishing and hunting. Since staff are also fans of the product, they can easily be motivated to expand their knowledge of the consumer's life world, the broader sociocultural context the brand is embedded in, and immerse themselves in developments in the macro-environment that may improve the brand's performance. *Li Ning* has become synonymous with Chinese sporting prowess in its homeland because staff immersed themselves in the world of running and found that most brands did not comfortably fit Chinese feet. Working in partnership with a local university, *Li Ning* developed inner soles uniquely adapted to Chinese feet and have started to take share from brands such as *Nike* and *Adidas* (Wathieu, Wang, and Samant 2007). Thierry Mugler noted during the Australian launch of his fragrance *Alien* that his design influences come from everywhere:

> I am inspired exactly when I'm not looking for it. It's like a puzzle. I travel and I'm a photographer. (Fox 2006, p. 10)

As well as employing customers as staff, authentic brands are staffed by people who are encouraged to live in the marketplace. Bernard Arnault, CEO of *LVMH*, encourages his designers to travel widely.

> Not long ago I said to one of our designers, 'why don't you take a trip to Japan and see what the teenage girls are wearing on the streets at night?' These girls are very leading edge in fashion; they create trends years before they hit the mainstream, like with those very high shoes, and it makes good sense to watch them. I did not say to the designer, 'go and see what kinds of shoes they are wearing and copy them', although I was hoping he'd notice their shoes. I just suggested, 'go look'. And in fact, he came back home very inspired. (Wetlaufer 2001 p. 119)

Arnault's policy of encouraging designers to travel for inspiration perfectly encapsulates the 'in the market' or 'market immersion' approach. Arnault has identified a source of trendsetting (Japanese girls) who are critical to the company's success (Japan is a huge market for luxury goods). He is hoping that designers such as John Galliano will find some form of inspiration they can then merge into *LVMH*'s brands. *Louis Vuitton* in particular has had a history of always being in step with the times – and Arnault's approach partly explains why. By identifying trend makers early, new innovations often arrive just when the marketplace is ready for them. The brand's famed graffiti monogram bag arrived as edgy street art was gaining acceptance, giving the upscale brand instant street credibility. Like Emily Drysdale above, Marc Jacobs had effectively absorbed the New York street culture that he was surrounded by and created the iconic bag.

It's not just high fashion brands that benefit from this approach. Lisa S. Roberts' (2006) book *Antiques of the Future* identifies a number of everyday mass-market products likely to gain iconic status within the design community in years to come. One product listed is *Click Clack's Airtight Canister* (produced for *Target*). How did a plastic manufacturer from a rural hub in New Zealand produce products that take their place alongside those of Philippe Starck? Recently retired *Click Clack* designer and CEO John Heng identifies how he has consistently developed products that provide low-cost stylish design-driven solutions to American consumers: 'To design a product for the United States you have to be part of the US, which is why I'm out of the office seven months of the year. I'm a US resident, I'm into it everyday, I watch CBS News, Fox News, CNN, ABC, just to become part of what happens.'

In each case, innovations are derived by absorbing the culture surrounding the product. This results in products that are relevant yet radically different from competitors. One result of this is that designers seem to intuitively understand consumers without having to ever ask them what they want. Another means by which authentic brands retain relevance is through encouraging staff to take lead roles in industry events, forums, and lobbying groups. This gives them access to market information, emerging trends and challenges, and competitor information. For example, although many famed winemakers claim to ignore competitors and consumers when creating their wine, they are often in direct touch with emerging stylistic trends and practices because they act as judges in wine tasting competitions. For example, famed Australian winemaker Rick Kinzbrunner from

Giaconda (producer of some of the country's most sought after wines) is a regular judge of wine because it 'helps keep my palate impartial and open, to what's going on around the world and in Australia' (Beverland 2005b, p. 204).

These staff also live the market in another way – they are deeply immersed in their field. Howard Roark (see Chapter 6) developed great architectural breakthroughs in low-cost housing by constantly being on the lookout for innovations in a wide range of fields – from materials, to process, to design. The *Sony Walkman* and *Fisher & Paykel Dish Drawer* dishwasher were similarly developed. In the case of the *Walkman, Sony* designers blended consumer desire for privacy and portability with the development of cassette tapes, batteries, and advances in miniaturization (Nathan 2001). The *Dish Drawer* was developed by mixing staff observations of people stacking dishes, with trends towards living in smaller houses, and developments in engine technology in other parts of the firm (Davies 2004). *Vivienne Westwood's* signature punk clothes (including her famous 'bondage pants') came from immersing herself in the world of fetish:

> The whole punk thing came out of the fact that I got so intrigued – when I started to make clothes in rubber-wear for SEX [the name of Westwood's shop] – by all those fetish people and the motives behind what they did, that I really went into the whole research of it. I wasn't content with thinking: 'Oh, I'll just do something that looks a bit like what they wear.' I wanted to make exactly what they wore. ... That's where all the straps and things came from. (Turner 2004, p. 18)

Westwood is famous for her independence (stating 'I have contempt for popular opinion' Turner 2004, p. 19), while her continuing relevance cannot be denied. She rejects market research or any hint of customer orientation in favour of following her own interests. The sidebar on Hans Beck and *Playmobil* provides another example of this process.

Side Bar:
HANS BECK AND *PLAYMOBIL*

At the time of his death, over 2.2 billion of Hans Beck's *Playmobil* figures had been sold. Beck's success is one of the great stories of the toy business. His approach to design is typical of authentic brands. Eschewing

FIGURE 7.2   **Hans Beck's *Playmobil* figures were developed after observing how children draw faces and figures. Original uploader: AndreasPraefcke at de.wikipedia. Photographed by Andreas Praefcke, 2004, http://commons. wikimedia.org/wiki/File:Playmobil_Buegeln.jpg**
With kind permission of Geobra Brandstätter GmbH & Co. K G, Germany. PLAYMOBIL is a registered trademark of Geobra Brandstätter GmbH & Co. K G, for which also the displayed PLAYMOBIL toy figures are protected.

short-term trends, violence, and horror, Beck sought to develop toys appropriate for young children (Figure 7.2). Beck described his approach to design using a German word 'Fingerspitzengfuhl' which translates to 'instinctive feeling'. The figure's distinctive head and facial features were developed after Beck had observed how children draw people – 'children invariably draw a head with exaggerated proportions, and while the eyes and mouth are always present, the nose is often omitted' (Anonymous March 30, 2009, p. 10). Such observations, coupled with Beck's gut feeling and management support helped create an icon of the global toy industry that endures to this day.

Three: Trust your gut

> The ability to stand out from the crowd because entrepreneurs act *instinctively* on what they see, think and feel. And remember there is always truth in [gut] reactions. (Anita Roddick 2008, p. 40)

Music stores in the 1970s were not attractive to music lovers like Richard Branson. Stores could and should be better. The first *Virgin* store in many ways represented the original third place retail concept. To outside observers and commentators, many of Richard Branson's decisions are irrational. Contrary to accepted wisdom, the *Virgin* brand is extended across a range of seemingly disconnected business categories. The only thing that connects these categories is Branson's belief that each new category provides the perfect context to implement the *Virgin* brand promise. Oh, and Branson's sheer passion for improving consumer's lives. Each time *Virgin* fails (e.g., *Virgin Cola*) critics engage in another round of *schadenfreude*, which simply tells us more about their own cynicism than anything else. If only Branson was more professional he'd enjoy the same level of success and respect of others say the critics, leaving aside the fact that so-called professional business models (many of which are arbitrary constructions) have a much poorer track record of success than *Virgin*. And, it ignores the fact that behind every Branson move is a thorough business case of the *Virgin* brand's potential for success (Branson 2005).

Just as artisans are seen as authentic because they are guided by non-rational sources of knowledge such as emotion, intuition, and personal insight (Sennett 2008), so too authentic brands gain their stature because they are staffed with people who do not ignore gut feeling. Although like Branson they may subject their gut feeling to wider scrutiny, they do not privilege formal market research over feeling, observation of outliers, small snippets of conversation gained accidentally, and personal experience. Employees are encouraged to collate these ideas – through memory or using notebooks – and then reflect on them privately and publicly in order to synthesize these into deeper insights about consumers and innovations.

Dyson's Contrarotator washing machine (Figure 7.3) was developed this way. Just as vacuum-cleaning technology had not changed from the original design (resulting in continued poor performance), so too modern washing machines continue to operate on principles unchanged since their original invention. Clothes are still soaked in water and chemicals for 45 minutes to an hour. This process requires a lot of power and water. Just as old vacuum technology failed to really clean carpets and floors, so too the soaking method is relatively ineffective when compared to traditional hand washing. In fact, it was Dyson's observation of women hand washing clothes that got him thinking about how to design a more effective washing machine. Hand washing clothes involved working soap into the fibers of clothes, thus resulting in better cleaning with much less water and power in less

FIGURE 7.3 **Dyson married cutting edge technology and design with tradition in the firm's new take on the washing machine – the *Contrarotator***

time. Dyson sought to replicate hand-washing techniques mechanically with the radical *Contrarotator* (Dyson 2002).

The results were impressive – a machine that cleaned clothes more effectively than traditional washers; used less water, power, chemicals; and only took 15 minutes. The *Contrarotator* was a major advance, especially in light of environmental concerns. Unfortunately the *Contrarotator* suffered from three problems. First, it was expensive, much more so than a traditional washer. Second, its core benefit was difficult for consumers to grasp – unlike the easy-to-view cyclone action. Third, the product was in many ways ahead of its time – environmental concerns had not yet penetrated the mainstream. Nevertheless the product was likely to return in some form, as it just was too good not to. Dyson's observational approach also resulted in the far more successful *Airblade* hand dryer, which is fast becoming standard technology in the world's airports (Figure 7.4). The same issue was involved – traditional hand dryers took too long and were too energy hungry and ineffective. Yet, hand drying is a critical health issue. The *Airblade* solves this, taking a few seconds to truly dry your hands (Carruthers 2007).

These firms develop a form of peripheral vision – that is, they institutionalize practices that focus on noticing outliers, capturing snippets of information, and casual observation – and turning these

FIGURE 7.4 **Now a staple of kitchens and airports, the Dyson Airblade is another example of how the firm constantly challenges traditional thinking in designs**

into innovations. They often do this through locating themselves in particular spaces and acting as amateur ethnographers – such as *Click Clack's* John Heng. Heng could not identify exactly what he was looking for, he just sensed that being there would pay-off. Once in the US, Heng was insatiable in absorbing local culture – watching television, reading magazines, talking to retailers, observing shoppers, trade-shows, lifestyles events, and so on. The story behind the development of the *Sony Walkman* was a similar trust-your-gut exercise based on simple observations and a sense that a small portable music device could be a winner. As Anita Roddick (2005, p. 50) stated:

> Be opportunistic. Successful entrepreneurs don't work within systems, they hate hierarchies and structures, and try to destroy them. They have an inherent creativity and wildness that is very difficult to capture. But they have antennae in their heads. I can walk down the street anywhere in the world and I have always got my antennae out, evaluating how what I am seeing can relate back to The Body Shop, whether it be packaging, a word, a poem, even something in a completely different business. I find myself saying: 'How could this relate to us, how could this work for us?'

Roddick's constant curiosity about the world has resulted in countless innovations including using products like raw sourdough mixture as a body scrub (derived from a trip to San Francisco, home of sourdough bread) and balsamic vinegar in shampoo, and stainless steel packaging (gained from observations of water carriers in India). The sidebar on Alessi shows what happens when designers ignore their gut.

Side Bar:
ALESSI

Alessi is another company that exemplifies market immersion. Seeking to marry craftsmanship with design the firm has produced one iconic product after another (e.g., the 9091, kettle by Richard Sapper, Philippe Starck's Juicy Salif and Michael Graves' 9093 Kettle) without the help of market research. *Alessi*'s 4060 Coffee Service was a fiasco, failing to achieve the success of its earlier products. Why? Marketing gave the designer a tight brief to produce the 4060 series for the catering industry. As Richard Sapper (who was in charge of marketing at the time) stated, 'I learnt that it's very difficult to make him [i.e., the designer] work on too specific a brief, it's better to let him go free-wheeling after having found a subject of common interest [between the brand and the designer]' (Alessi 1998, p. 29). In contrast the company's famous Neapolitan Coffeemaker (designed by Riccaro Dalisi) went through the longest gestation process in *Alessi*'s history. Eight years of anthropological research was conducted that examined how coffee makers were perceived and used in small Neapolitan towns (Alessi 1998).

Four: Allow employees to dabble

Google engineers have 20 per cent of their time set aside for them to pursue individual projects. *Google* sets no limits on what engineers can work on and has no set expectations for success. By providing creative staff with this 'headspace time' *Google* has benefited enormously, including the development of *Google News* (Kendall 2009, p. 19). *Louis Vuitton* allows its designers to develop their own branded lines (e.g., *Marc Jacobs*) so they create outside of the confines of the brand. *Weta Works* staff are also allowed to develop their own lines of products – *King Kong* dinosaur designer Gary Hunt developed his own range of collectible fantasy and historical figures, while other employees were instrumental in developing the cult comic series *The Red Star*. This strategy allows designers and creative staff to explore new styles that may not fit with their host brand's style. By being allowed to innovate, craftspeople and designers are also likely to identify new ways of doing things that can be applied to the host brand.

In many cases these products reinforce the host's brand reputation and often provide the basis for new lines of products. Importantly however, this institutionalized dabbling keeps staff creative, open to new ideas, and often further embeds them in the marketplace. For example, Gary Hunt's (*Weta*) move into collectible figures indirectly keeps the *Weta* brand alive in consumers' minds (important during movie production downtime) and requires him to engage directly with fans of fantasy and the retail networks that supply them. This implicitly takes Weta into a growing part of the fantasy market they do not yet occupy and forces Hunt to engage with different consumers, learn new techniques, observe fan norms, and gain an understanding of competitors and trends. All of this can then be used by *Weta* to enhance their own line of collectibles, move into new territory such as fantasy figures, role-playing and computer games, and keep track of new trends.

Winemakers in the great wine estates are often free to pursue their own interests once their vintage duties are over. Typically this involves moving between the Northern or Southern hemispheres. For Northern hemisphere winemakers, the chance to take part in Southern hemisphere vintage allows them to gain experience in less restricted industries and try out new things in younger winemaking cultures. For Southern hemisphere winemakers and staff, the chance to work in the Northern Hemisphere immerses them in different traditions and has resulted in greater respect being shown for the role of place in winemaking and for reducing winemaker heavy-handedness in production. Such approaches have resulted in subtle evolutionary changes to production practices, vineyard management, wine style, and marketing, resulting in enhanced authenticity for all.

Cloudy Bay's oak-aged Sauvignon Blanc *Te Koko* developed out of this institutionalized dabbling – a wine that divides opinion among consumers and critics but that also reinforces the view that the now *LVMH*-owned brand remains open to new ideas. Since the wine was truly experimental, the team was encouraged to break with precon-ceived ideas about producing wine. One practice that differed was the choice to age the wine for some years before release. At the time most New Zealand wines were released relatively early – after a few months of harvest for whites and a year for reds. The *Te Koko* practice forced the winemaking team to question this practice for their other wines, resulting in more delayed releases for some wines so that they were at their best for consumers. Legendary *W. Britain*'s toy soldier sculptor Charles Biggs was encouraged to develop his own range of limited edition World War I soldiers under the *Premier* label. These figures have since become highly collectible and also reminded fans and staff of what the company was capable of producing at a time when quality standards were falling (Joplin et al. 2008).

The *World of Warcraft* team were encouraged to play around with game lore, including recasting races in good or bad terms. As detailed in the behind-the-scenes DVD *World of Warcraft: The Burning Crusade* (2006), previously noble elves became blood elves after aligning with evil in order to feed their addiction to magic and rescue their crumbling empire. No longer allied with other good races, Blood elves look after themselves and although not evil, they certainly have a dark side. By recasting this character, the creative team added a grey element to the game (the team notes they want fans to take away a sense of uncertainty about the Blood elves' identity – given the average age of the fan base this uncertainty reflects young consumers' own search for identity), increasing the mystique of the game world and providing the basis for new stories among gamers. And, this decision meant the *World of Warcraft* setting continually evolves. Recasting the Draenoi as heroic had a similar effect. Such dabbling resulted in a new game *The Burning Crusade* – which sold over 2.4 million copies on the first day of release (16 January 2007).

Perhaps *Leica* provides the greatest example of being allowed to dabble. Inventor of the portable camera Oskar Barnack was encouraged to pursue his idea to revolutionize camera design by Ernst Leitz, owner of an optical business of the same name. Barnack gained Leitz's support because his boss respected his carefully selected employees, and trusted their judgement. At the time, Leitz had nothing to go with other than Barnack's desire and his belief that a hand-held camera was possible (the company did not at this stage produce cameras). Barnack drew on his knowledge of optics, his experiences with movie cameras and the expertise of other *Leitz* staff to produce the *Ur-Leica* – the world's first hand-held camera (Pasi 2003). Like Branson, Phil Knight of *Nike*, Peter and Charles Morgan, Coco Chanel, Steve Jobs, *Sony*, Ignaz Schwinn's bicycle innovations, and Dyson, the *Leica* was also dismissed by the establishment (as Lane notes, 'To many of the old photographers it looked like a toy designed for a lady's handbag'; 2007, p. 166), while being embraced by professional and amateur photographers and changing the marketplace. Thankfully Barnack and *Leica* never stopped tweaking their original design as it is hard to imagine key events of the twentieth century without photographs taken on *Leica's*.

Five: Seed the fan base

Officially, consumers have little role in shaping new innovations. Unofficially, authentic brands go out of their way to seed the fan base. Such activities are designed to create a sense of expectation and excitement, but also to test the waters, and gain unmediated feedback and insights from lead users about planned innovations. Technical experts (often media based writers) are also courted for insights and reaction to new ideas (and of course for favourable publicity). The best proponent of this is Steve Jobs. Jobs' annual speech at *MacWorld* is treated as a religious event by Mac fans given that new innovations are always highlighted. Even though many are years away from release, immediate feedback is gained, from technical writers, critics, competitors, and fans. And buzz is created. Although *Apple* conducts no formal market research, Jobs is not averse to dipping his toe in the water early to gauge interest in new product ideas and gain invaluable insights on likely problems and issues.

During the filming of the *Lord of the Rings*, Peter Jackson constantly explained to fans the difficult decisions he had to make, and the technical reasons for differences between the book and the films. During this period, Jackson and his team were also gaining direct feedback from the lead users about their decisions. This approach was formalized during the filming *of King Kong* where Jackson started a blog detailing his decisions and keeping fans up to date on the project. Part of this process also involved providing early snippets of the sumptuous retelling of the 1930s classic. This approach has built even stronger bonds between *Weta* and their fans, increasing sales of merchandise as well as new lines such as *Dr Grordbort's Rayguns*.

The desire to seed the fan base also explains why authentic brands are keen to develop or support fan communities. *Morgan* gains direct feedback on quality problems (as well as solutions) from the *Morgan Owners Club* magazine *Miscellany*. Likewise *Harley Davidson* keeps in touch with its diverse customer base by sponsoring various community and sub-community events. This keeps the brand in touch with old-time consumers concerned at the erosion of the brand's authenticity, while also reaching out to new consumers attracted to the lifestyle the brand embodies. Finally, brands such as *Apple, Bruichladdich, Chateau Margaux, Dunhill*, and *Louis Vuitton* cultivate critical feedback from journalistic authorities partly to ease the launch of new products, but also because both parties share an interest in each other's survival. Thus feedback may be private and discrete, but also brutally honest.

CONCLUSION

Authentic brands are paradoxical in many ways. In this chapter I've identified one major paradox – how these brands lead the marketplace with innovations while maintaining they never do market research or seek consumer input into new products/services. Authenticity has always been derived from the intuition of the artist. While other brands suffer the tyranny of the served market or the blandness that comes from focus groups, authentic brands innovate by drawing on data absorbed by staff deeply immersed in the marketplace. Although these innovations may not be generated from formal market research, they are influenced and informed by consumer trends and lifestyles, although the data used is gained *in situ*, represents unmediated consumer comment and experience, and is broad ranging (rather than focused on a narrow set of questions and alternatives). The results are often breakthrough innovations that change the way we live, failed experiments that provide useful insights for future innovations, and enhanced brand authenticity because leaders can swear that such products and services reflect the creativity of the firm.

One means of market immersion involves embedding oneself within communities – a subject I take up further in Chapter 8. The discussion of immersion also identifies the importance of creating an environment where employees feel free to explore new ideas – a subject addressed in Chapter 9.

CHAPTER 8

BE AT ONE WITH THE COMMUNITY

Only some brands become icons. Revered by their core customers, icons have the power to maintain a firm hold in the marketplace for many years. Icons succeed because they forge a deep connection with the prevailing culture.

(Douglas Holt quoted in Drummond 2008, p. 18)

CHATEAU MARGAUX'S COWS

One can't help but be entranced by *Chateau Margaux*. The estate grounds and signature building are simply stunning. The walk (or drive) down the tree-lined driveway is simply romantic. And the wine – well if you can get it, it's to die for. The wine itself is a product of place – both of the area 'Margaux', the unique topography of the estate itself, and centuries of estate and Bordeaux winemaking tradition. The brand is much more than this. No discussion of wine history can be had without mentioning the wines of Bordeaux, the *1855 Bordeaux Classification* (which gave *Chateau Margaux* Grand Cru status), the Grand Cru Estates (of which *Margaux* is one of just five), and the wines themselves. Quite simply, for wine lovers, it is impossible to imagine a wine world without *Chateau Margaux* given that the estate is so embedded in the shared history of the wine trade. Much of the authenticity of the brand comes from its connection to time, place, and culture.

Chateau Margaux takes its connection to place more seriously than many other wineries. Estate manager Paul Pontallier and his staff intimately know the potential and challenges of each part of the vineyard. The vineyard itself has been scientifically mapped so the winemaking team can gain the very best from the estate even in difficult years. When one tours the estate or reads interviews with Pontallier in the press, the synergy between the land, the Bordeaux culture of wine-making, the creative team, and the history of the wine is made very clear. *Margaux* is a 'complex' wine that takes time to show its considerable charms (much like the development of the 600-year brand itself). Although many in the wine world remain cynical about the link between place and wine style, you cannot doubt the integrity of *Chateau Margaux*'s commitment to place given they even have their own herd of cows to ensure even the fertilizer is local.

AUTHENTICITY IS LOCAL (EVEN WHEN THE BRAND IS GLOBAL)

> I think there are big cultural issues there that are just not well understood. For example the Americans think everyone has a zip code [...] they were a little late in entering and then they launched in US dollars. (Sam Morgan, founder of *TradeMe*, quoted in MacManus 2006)

One of the successes of the Internet boom of the 1990s is *eBay*. The electronic marketplace has spread from the US to encompass many parts of the globe. And in most cases, *eBay* has become the dominant (or only) site of its kind in each country in which it is based (although the site would seem to be placeless for consumers, users understand that there are separate sites for different countries). One place where *eBay* barely registers is New Zealand. Despite being early adopters of e-technology and avid traders, New Zealanders have spurned global *eBay* for local *TradeMe*. Part of this success can be attributed to *TradeMe*'s first mover advantage. However, much of the brand's success is because it's local. While *eBay* New Zealand insists locals use US dollars, *TradeMe* allows Kiwis to use their own currency (avoiding excessive bank charges and problems associated with the regular swings in the US/NZ exchange rate) and is based on direct debits into bank accounts. Seller listing fees are negligible when compared to *eBay* and the site is easier to use.

Although these advantages were crucial to the early success of the brand, *TradeMe*'s local status has become more symbolic over time. Local wiz-kid entrepreneur Sam Morgan founded the firm during the Internet boom. New Zealand has a history of using technological innovation to compete in the marketplace and Sam Morgan's convention challenging David and Goliath story fits well with this tradition. As well, the firm's success has become part of a wider national debate about branded forms of value creation at a time when a new generation of New Zealanders are challenging the country's traditional: reliance on low-value commodities and backyard inventions (whose true value is often only identified by foreigners). Morgan's decision to sell the company in 2006 to Australia's *Fairfax* for NZ$750 million, was greeted with a heavy sigh among many New Zealanders as it represented another loved brand falling to international ownership, restarting a conversation about New Zealand made and owned versus New Zealand created. Morgan himself plans to use his funds to create new businesses locally, placing him in a new class of entrepreneurs along with the creators of *42 Below* vodka who have a similar story.

The *TradeMe* example identifies the importance of being part of a wider community to brand authenticity (and equity). *eBay's* refusal to allow New Zealanders (who are very parochial) to use their own currency ensured the brand would gain little traction in a market full of wheelers and dealers. As such, the brand never gained the legitimacy necessary to access this community and play a role in bringing buyers and sellers together. Given that first mover advantages are often crucial in this form of business, it is unlikely *eBay* will gain a foothold in this wealthy market. Authentic brands (of which *eBay* is one in many markets) play up connections to local communities, places, and/or spaces, even when they are global. Typically they do so by playing up their continued connection to their home place or space (like *Chateau Margaux*) while also providing the basis for local conversations (Charles Morgan's quote about French fans in Chapter 3 is one example).

Why is connection to place (in its many forms) crucial to consumer judgements of brand authenticity? The notion of putting down roots is central to our identity. As we travel through life, we form connections with multiple communities including schools, sports teams, fan communities, family, cultures, religions, and local places. Even when we move on from these places, social networking sites such as *Facebook* allow us to stay connected with friends and family. At some point in our life we give consideration to our legacy, our family heritage and roots, and also putting down some permanent roots in a community (rather than moving from one place to next). To reaffirm our connection to place (even when we are no longer physically connected to it) we may continue traditional rituals, buy traditional products, and decorate homes and office space with reminders of our place of origin (Arnould and Price 2000).

As part of this goal of building individual and social identity, consumers draw on brands (Beverland and Farrelly forthcoming). Authentic brand partners provide the basis for consumers to connect locally and reconnect spiritually to their home. Whereas the (now questioned) holy grail of branding, the truly global borderless brand, ignores local roots for efficiency reasons, authentic brands play up their local heritage both in terms of their factual roots to their home space, and in the new roots they put down in far-off lands. Since globalization, deterritorialization, and hyperreality have resulted in a crisis of authenticity in the postmodern market, brands that have built, or allow for, connections to physical place and cultural space (including history) provide consumers with the means of authentication.

In Chapter 1 I noted that the *Morgan Car Company* is celebrating its centenary this year. The brand itself remains connected to its place of founding – Malvern Link. The brand also continues to reflect the English sports car tradition with its unique styling, independent ownership, craft production, and involvement in motor racing. During 2009, centenary events will attract owners and their cars from around the globe (including the US, Australia, New Zealand, Japan, India, the Middle East, and Europe). An entire global diaspora of *Morgan* clubs will descend on the tiny town of Malvern Link to celebrate the brand that has brought them together, catch up with friends that often acted as local hosts during international club tours, and form new bonds with communities of owners. As New Zealand's first owner of an *Aero 8* Grant said to me at a club organized dinner, 'one of the best things about buying this car [a blue *Aero 8*] that I never imagined before, was that I was suddenly part of a group of people, many of whom are now very dear friends, that I would ever have met otherwise'. John Lancaster, a historian of *Morgan*'s in New Zealand contacts new car owners and states:

> The Morgan is really the member of the club. If you happen to own the Morgan at the time, then you're a member of the club because of that, not the other way around – you don't join the club because you've got a Morgan, the Morgan brings you in as a member of the club.

John's statement clearly expresses the importance of the brand in connecting people. Without a *Morgan*, membership is unavailable – should you sell the car, membership goes with it. The brand clearly is a gateway to community, and explains why the firm invests resources in community creation (the new *Aero 8* owners club) and ongoing development (through hosted events). Through embedding the brand in communal history, the brand comes to be viewed as an institution or part of the wider environment. In many cases, it is difficult to imagine cultures, subcultures, industries, or history without these brands. For example, try thinking of France with Champagne, Italy without *Ferrari*, fashion without *Prada*, photography without *Leica*, childhood (in some commonwealth countries) without *Cadbury*, computing without *Apple*, surfing without *Quiksilver*, skateboarding without *Vans*, cycling without *Schwinn*, basketball without *Chucks*, America without *Harley Davidson*, and so on. Try also imaging the opposite. Authentic brands build links to communities and over time become synonymous with them.

HOW TO BE AT ONE WITH COMMUNITY

Authentic brands habitually build links to community using five different strategies. First, they embed themselves within images of the national culture, often by drawing on cultural resources, reflecting important traditions and even stereotypes, and through appeals to nationalism. Second, authentic brands often build links to their place of origin, or to regions in which they operate. This can include physical as well as symbolic connections. Third, authentic brands embed themselves within their industry, often through stories that identify the important role the brand or individuals behind it have played in the creation, growth, or survival of the industry, production techniques, or product-class as a whole. Fourth, authentic brands embed themselves within cultures, often through co-opting cultural myths and stories, or through images and stories that reflect cultural stereotypes. Finally, authentic brands connect to subcultural space by being active and sincere members of subcultures.

One: Nation

When people mention *Audi*, *BMW*, and *Mercedes*, we automatically think of 'German engineering' or 'Teutonic styling'. Why? Firstly, Germany's manufacturing success is world renowned. Second, these brands benefit from the fact they are representatives of a cultural stereotype – that German design is ruthlessly efficient, mechanical, cold, and elegant. There are many reasons for this, not to mention our belief that Germans are somewhat aloof and stand-offish, that their designers across a range of industries converge on a certain style reflective of this stereotype, a tradition of rationalistic philosophy, steely flinty Riesling wines, through to pioneering minimalist electronic music acts such as Kraftwerk. Third, Germany uses these brands as examples of the success of its economic policies and societal model.

Of course these are stereotypes – one only needs to travel to Germany to understand that its people are warm and engaging (and in some cases stand-offish and arrogant), their design styles range from cold modernist, wildly postmodern, through to kitschy traditional, and their art forms are as diverse as any nation's. Finally, not all of their products are well designed, engineered, or reliable. Nevertheless authentic brands such as *BMW*, *Mercedes*, and *Leica* benefit from (or in some cases are hindered by) these national associations even when they are often no longer produced in Germany. When someone mentions a German brand, we can easily form a picture of what that brand should look like.

Authentic brands build connections to the nation in others ways. Entrepreneurs such as James Dyson attempt to revitalize national energies when they stress the importance of making things rather than just selling them. Dyson is attempting to restore Britain's manufacturing prowess by example. Part of his message is the desire to create an industrial base so that young people see manufacturing as a desirable and sustainable career (Dyson 2002). In the same vein many brands in more traditional industries attempt to identify their continued existence as being central to the nation's cultural heritage. Many European agricultural producers (as well as US carmakers) make this claim in arguing for protectionism or ownership over the use of certain terms. For example, French cheese makers have gained restrictions on the use of the term 'Camembert', even though historians argue that modern products using this name bear no relation to the original (Boisard 2003). The same is true of traditional beer producers in Belgium (Beverland, Lindgreen, and Vink 2008) and French chocolate producers (Terrio 2000).

Finally, authentic brands place themselves within the national narrative by emphasizing their role in the nation's development. *Vespa*, for example, is forever associated with Italy's post-war recovery and modernization (as are *Sony* and *Honda* with Japan's). *Vespa* represented an affordable, reliable, and practical means of travelling for upper-lower and emerging middle class Italians. Importantly, the brand became a champion for women through its Riders Clubs programme. These clubs encouraged women to be more independent through the sponsorship of riding tours. These tours also helped bring Italians closer together as they allowed previously provincial locals to access parts of the country not accessible by train (Piaggio & C. S.p.A 2003). The same approach is used by New Zealand company *Edmonds* (a producer of baking products) who gives every newlywed woman a copy of the famous *Edmond's Cookbook* (McCloy 2008). The brand is therefore able to locate itself in a national narrative – in this case, the traditional favourites and changing tastes (including the recent maturing and championing of local produce and traditions) of New Zealanders.

Two: Region

As well as locating themselves within a wider national narrative, authentic brands also put down roots locally. Rosica (2007, p. 57) recommends that brands try and own their region before expanding (what he calls geo-branding) – thus brands such as *Burt's Bees* became ubiquitous in Maine before expanding to the rest of the US (and beyond). Such strategies ensure that 'you are *the* brand in your area' and help build a connection between the brand, the consumer, place, and a perceived way of life. *Dunlop Volley*, long associated with Australian sporting prowess (especially in tennis and cycling) reinvigorated its brand through localized sponsorship. Unable (and unwilling) to compete with large international brands in sponsoring mainstream sporting events and high profile stars, *Dunlop Volley* began sponsoring local, school-age sporting events. This approach started with the sponsorship of the weekend sporting results sections in local newspapers. Since children, parents, and teachers read these results after each weekend's activities, *Dunlop* gained profile in the community and re-established the emotional bond locals had with the iconic shoe (Beverland and Ewing 2005).

Krispy Kreme doughnuts also reinforce local connections as part of a strategy to enhance the brand's authenticity and ensure ongoing commitment to the brand. The brand receives many applications from wannabe franchisees but selects only those with deep roots in the local community. This reinforces the old-time feel of the brand (which promotes itself as a purveyor of small town service) and also ensures that franchisees will put their heart and soul into developing and growing the business. Since the main promotion strategy for the brand is through handing out free doughnuts to visitors and local workers, having locals running the business reinforces the sincerity of the brand. And, locals have a greater chance at gaining and keeping customers because in many cases they're serving people they know (Kazanjian and Joyner 2004).

Another way of building connections to region is through promoting the special properties of particular places. Firms producing products whose style or characteristics are affected by natural conditions often use this approach. *Chateau Margaux* is an arch example of this strategy, as are other wine producers. Burgundian legend *Domaine Romaneé Conti* (the world's most sought after and expensive wine) has the greatest advantage in this sense, since it owns the entire appellation of *Romaneé Conti* (France's smallest at just 4.5 acres) (Olney 1991). Likewise, water producers such as *Antipodes* in New Zealand have taken greater control over their links to place by buying the source of their water outright in order to ensure their message is sincere. The motivation behind *Dilmah Tea* was purely regional – founder Merrill Fernando desired to retain the unique characters of single estate tea rather than have them smothered in a blend (such a strategy would also enhance the fortunes of the regional economy).

Many fashion houses often use similar strategies, particularly when they specialize in natural fibres. *Icebreaker* draw connections between the harshness and purity of New Zealand's South Island high country, the Merino sheep that inhabit this environment, and the brand image and performance features (durability, warmth, style). Other firms may also draw links to local conditions, by identifying a link between the unique features of a region and the character of its people. Thus, *L.L. Bean* identifies how Maine breeds tough, no-nonsense, outdoors types in its brand stories. The message is simple – the people of Maine know what quality is and the products have been tested in the toughest conditions. Brands from rural or isolated areas often identify how the harsh conditions and isolation played a role in the character of the brand and people behind it. Clothing brand *66 Degrees North* emphasizes the extreme weather conditions, isolation, and independence of character of Iceland and Icelanders in its brand story. As such, these products are a unique representation of place, therefore enhancing their authenticity.

Finally, connections with regions may simply be enhanced through locating. Miramar – a suburb in New Zealand's capital Wellington is simply named 'Middle Earth' since it houses *Weta Digital* and *Weta Workshop*. Likewise, Birmingham remains the home of *Cadbury*, while *Jack Daniel's* retains its link to Lynchburg Tennessee. *Apple* is forever associated with Cupertino, Silicon Valley in California. These links with place provide the brand with a real spiritual home (even if as with *Cadbury* the local home is not the original birthplace of the brand) that people can connect too. The brand benefits because it gains from the unique characteristics of the region, tourists travelling through, and regional publicity. Likewise, the region and local communities benefit from active regional players. As a result, these brands further embed themselves in the local landscape, all of which enhances their authenticity.

Three: Industry

Authentic brands are often deeply connected to the emergence of whole industries – the histories of the computing, wine, travel, motoring, photography, and fashion industries would be significantly different if *Apple, Chateau Mouton Rothschild, Louis Vuitton, Mercedes-Benz, Leica,* and *Chanel* did not exist. Each of these brands has played a significant role in the emergence and development of their respective industries, resulting in a lasting imprint on the business community involved. These brands were not necessarily the most innovative or enjoyed a first-mover advantage, but nevertheless their lasting impact on their respective fields has often been driven by their desire to do something different. The result of this approach is shaping and driving new markets – *Leica's* invention of the hand-held camera brought photography to the masses, *Apple's* championing of ease-of-use brought computing to the masses, *Louis Vuitton's* design innovations made travelling easier and more secure, while *Chanel's* free-flowing designs literally allowed women to look good while moving freely.

Why does this matter? Ignoring the basic brand benefits (i.e., heritage and quality), these brands' historical status means they are part of relatively recent sociocultural history – these brands have played a role in shaping consumer society. While the names of kings, revolutionaries, and explorers may fade into obscurity because most consumers have little context with which to connect to these long-distant events in far-off lands, we can connect with the history of industries and brands because of our status as consumers, employees, fans, owners, critics, and other members of a networked economy. Just as links between a brand and the nation or region allow us to form connections to time, place, and culture, links to industry allow us to place ourselves in a historical narrative that includes but also transcends national and regional identity. We may not have lived in Cupertino or be American, but we can relate to the creative spirit and history of the computing industry through using an *Apple*.

As mentioned above, first mover advantages or inventing new technologies is not sufficient to form ongoing connections to an industry narrative. There were plenty of automotive brands that were innovative but have long since fallen by the wayside. Likewise, with computing – how many people remember *Sinclair* or *Commodore*? These were truly inventive companies that industry insiders know have had an impact on the industry, but their stories and role are not part of the popular history of the field. Authentic brands are inventive, but through market immersion their role in the industry is an ongoing one – thus they are active members in the ongoing evolution of the industry story. That is, these brands have roots in the history of the industry but are not historical footnotes or relics – their role as industry shapers continues to this day.

Leica, Dunhill, and *Tata Motors* provide examples of moving beyond invention to shape the history of their respective industries – photography and personal and professional travel. Although *Leica* invented the first hand-held camera, photography was an activity that only a few professionals engaged in (and early cameras are far more complicated to use than today's point and shoot varieties – such as the *Leica's C-Lux 2*). In diffusion terms, *Leica's* camera appealed to innovators, but was unlikely to cross the chasm and appeal to early adopters and the early majority (critical for achieving profitable mainstream success) (Gladwell 2002). *Leica* understood this problem and gave their cameras away to high-profile photographers. The company supported these photographers' early 'how to' publications and helped further the profile of these artists. As a result, awareness of the benefits and joy of photography were raised – and consumers now had a range of easy-to-use how-to manuals (the *Dummies Manuals* of their day). (Chuck Taylor built his brand in a similar way, writing books of basketball strategy – all of which became required reading for coaches and players; Peterson 2007.) By the 1920s photography had come to the masses and *Leica* was viewed as the camera of choice for professionals and serious amateurs, a status they retain to this day (Pasi 2003).

Alfred Dunhill played a similar role in the early days of up-market travel. Realizing that the automobile was going to reshape how people travelled, he developed a range of luxury products to enhance the driving experience. *Dunhill* was the first automobile accessory provider, developing branded headlights, horns, speedometers, clocks, and luggage to enhance the experience for passionate motorists like himself and for the wealthy who found early motorcars uncomfortable, noisy, and a far cry from the luxury of their horse-drawn carriages. Like *Leica*, *Dunhill* played a role in expanding the market for cars (in the UK and Europe). Although he targeted the up-market consumer, his efforts increased car use among the wealthy and influential, who could demand improvements in roads and laws, and whose championing of the car spelled the end of the belief in the superiority of horse-drawn transport. These early adopters also influenced the aspirations of the middle classes (in class-ridden Britain), resulting in increased demand for automobiles as well as *Dunhill* accessories such as cigarette lighters, cases, and fashion (luxury branded sunglasses and perfumes play the same role today). *Dunhill* has continued to develop products that reflect the changing nature of travel and travel consumption, ensuring their continued relevance (Foulkes 2005).

Finally, *Tata Motors* focused on providing free training to rural mechanics in order to increase sales of the *Tata Ace*. Like *Leica's* support of professional photographers, *Tata* knew that the success of their innovative cheap four-wheeler vehicle required the support of professionals. To keep costs low, the company chose to avoid developing an expensive network of dealerships and instead improve the level of mechanical skills in rural villages most likely to benefit from adopting the *Ace*. Mechanics were provided with free training, free tools, and a mobile workshop that provided parts. By developing this network, sales of this product among poorer rural Indians has skyrocketed, resulting in improved business opportunities, decreased accidents, increased status, and more marriage proposals (and less worried spouses) (Palepu and Srinivasan 2007). Tata created the category of cheap four-wheel vehicles in India and through immersing themselves in the wider industry network, are likely to own it for some time.

Four: Culture

In late 2008, *Starbucks* announced mass closures and redundancies in Australia. This decision came as no surprise to coffee lovers or many commentators since the brand had never gained the desired traction with Australian consumers (its original plans had long been scaled back because of poor sales). There were many reasons for *Starbucks* troubles, including relatively poor quality coffee, the existence of an established coffee culture that was focused around small, personalized cafés, slow impersonalized service, the emergence of the slow food and fair trade movement, cafes crowded with students doing work, and entrenched competitor chains. However, one explanation captured the essence of the problem. Unlike America, *Starbucks* had no special meaning to Australians – it was just another coffee chain. Stripped from its cultural and historical context *Starbucks* was just another provider. While in the US, the chain embodied the spirit of the 1990s, including the Internet boom, networking, freelancing, and casualization, and played a key role in getting Americans to restart a love affair with coffee, none of these associations were relevant to Australia or New Zealand (where it also failed). The few stores that survive tend to target international students who enjoy the large sweeter flavoured coffees hated by so many locals.

Authentic brands not only become embedded in time and place, they also embed themselves culturally. Luxury brands like *Cartier* and *Hermès* publications locate their designs and designers within a wider context that celebrates innovation and creativity (often taking time to highlight the works of competitors and unknown artists along the way). Authentic brands reflect cultural symbols and stories in their communications and stories – the image of *Tic Tac*'s latest campaign (under the heading 'Fresh Since '76') provides one example. The latest advertisement for the mint that punches above in diminutive stature reflects symbols of the 1970s (when it was founded) through to the present day – instead of mints being in the iconic container, we see images of VW Combi vans, peace and flower power symbols, disco mirror balls, platform shoes, roller skates and boards, and the word 'far-out'. The message is easy to understand – *Tic Tac* was formed in a cultural milieu and remains a free spirit today. Authentic brands can embody culture in many ways. Like *Tic Tac* they can co-opt symbols of a certain era or spirit. Others may try and capture a certain sense of life of a particular people, time, and/or place.

When one thinks of the 1960s one image that comes to mind is the *VW Beetle*. The classic minimalist advertisement that launched the car in the US captured the spirit of the times. In contrast to the large, gas guzzling, chromed, and winged vehicles of the time, the *Beetle* reflected the desire on behalf of many consumers to return to a simpler, less-image conscious, authentic time. No longer would cars be objects of social status; rather cars were utilitarian vehicles for the masses to get from A to B with the minimum fuss (Patton 2002). No wonder the hippy and counterculture movement fell in love with the people's car. The low cost, reliability, and humanistic design were also perfect for young Californian surfers, an association the brand was quick to capitalize on. Although the new version of the *Beetle* was priced far higher than the original and had far more features, the updated design and fake flower fixture on the dashboard reflected a desire to reconnect to cultural milieu that adopted the brand.

Teenagers (wearing their *chucks*) in Southern California undoubtedly drove their *VW Beetles* to *In-N-Out Burger*. This brand enhances its authenticity by continuing the practices that were shaped by the spirit of 1960s Southern Californian beach culture. As teenagers of the day sought freedom from conformity (often referred to as 'The Man') in surfing, music, nature, and love so *In-N-Out Burger* continues to buck industry trends towards mass production, low pay and poor service, frozen, processed ingredients, warming trays, increasing prices, advertising, and lack of flexibility (ever tried to get a *McDonald's* burger without something?) in their practice. The brand has developed a cult following among fast food lovers with its cheap, high-quality fresh handmade products, secret menu, friendly staff, old-styled diners, without advertising that usually over-promises and under-delivers.

The success of *42 Below* can be attributed to its direct referencing of, and lampooning of, culture. In a series of controversial viral advertisements the marketing team play on a range of cultural stereotypes that make fun of Australians, Britons, Canadians, Chinese, and New Zealanders (among many others). The first campaign entitled *Story of 42 Below* established the brand globally (in conjunction with an award-winning product) even though the ads many cultural references were so localized and temporal (to Generation X New Zealanders) that they would have gone over the head of most. The campaign draws directly on local symbolism including noting that New Zealand is part of Australia, the vats are made out of Kauri wood, the vodka is sailed down the Shotover river in America's Cup yachts, traded by the white man with the fierce All Black tribe (the national rugby team) for muskets and blankets (a reference to the original land trades between the English and Maori), and references to Peter Jackson, Billy T. James, *Once Were Warriors*, and the *Buzzy Bee*, among many others. Later campaigns drew on other cultural references, all of which required some degree of insider knowledge, and all of which became stars on *YouTube*.

Not only does this cultural referencing create a humorous connection between the brand and the spirit of a generation, they are also reflective of the so-called no-nonsense, fun-loving Kiwi spirit. The brand often plays up its country of origin in internationally based communications that focus on the quality of the vodka (usually along the lines of 'where did the highest awarded vodka come from? Russia? Finland ...? Actually none of these, it came from New Zealand'). But in its lampooning of other nations, its lack of political correctness, and its 'let the product do the talking' attitude, the brand team reflect a mostly true image of New Zealanders as non-nonsense pragmatists that get the job done well. The best exposition of this fun loving, no bullshit attitude is reflected in an advertisement that was taken out by the team in response to complaints about the accuracy of one of *42 Below*'s ads regarding its success in an international vodka competition. *42 Below*'s response directly reflects the spirit of Generation X Kiwis and all those who revile the pettiness of big brands and bureaucrats.

Five: Subculture

The revitalization of *Dunlop Volley* was initiated by Melbourne teenage rave (dance) culture. This subculture had its own norms and definitions of authenticity. Authentic brands were those that published in the many short-lived (usually amateur-produced) street magazines that represent the rave world. Authentic brands avoided mainstream retailers and consumers, and even shopping hot spots such as Melbourne fashionista capital Chapel Street, in favour of the many back alleys and laneways that make up Melbourne's thriving youth, design, and alternative cultures. *Dunlop Volley* avoided sponsorship and overtly commercial acts, instead providing products to street artists to use in sculptures or designs such as the *Volley chandelier* or the *stiletto-Volley*. Authentic brands respected the views of the culture, never seeking to disassociate them from members' self-expression even if it would be offensive to the mainstream (*Volley* celebrated the efforts of many teens who had spray painted their shoes with designs, many of which would gain an R-rating).

While brands embed themselves in broad cultures, it is at the subcultural level that many brands gain their authenticity. Research has examined a number of subcultures of consumption, consumption communities, or brand communities (see Arnould and Thompson 2005 for review). The underlying logic is that these communities share similar values (or 'consciousness in kind'; McAlexander, Schouten, and Koenig 2003) and this spills over to choices about brands and debates regarding authenticity. Consumption communities are often the most extreme version of this subculture because the community is centred on a single brand. *The Star Trek* subculture provides a perfect example – a diverse group of people commune around a single brand and its extensions. Debates rage about the nature of authenticity (e.g., are offshoots not written by Gene Roddenberry really authentic and part of the *Star Trek* 'canon'?) including the status of merchandise, extensions, the increased playing up of female characters' sexuality (who can forget Jeri Ryan as Seven-of-Nine and those tight fitting outfits), and even plotlines (fans were enraged when Vulcan character T-Pol [played by Jolene Blalock] appeared naked in *Enterprise* because it was the first time overtly sexual acts had appeared in the show). *Star Trek* feeds the community by providing stories, but it also feeds off the community – particularly in times of strife (fan pressure has resulted in the new movie franchise).

Subcultures of consumption are centred on a shared consciousness or values (Kates 2002). Rather than celebrating a particular brand, these subcultures apply a litmus test to brands to judge their authenticity. This is evident in the North American gay community, extreme sports subcultures, and groups such as the Slow Food community. Kates' study of brand legitimacy was based on several years of ethnographic research in the North American gay community (specifically centred around Toronto). Kates found that brands such as *Levi's* and *Absolut* gained legitimacy or authenticity because of their sincere commitments to gay rights. Both brands advertised in gay publications at a time when homosexuality was heavily stigmatized. *Levi's* even used 'buff' male models when marketing to straight consumers – ads gays reinterpreted and appreciated as being homoerotic (many gays thought the joke was on straights) (Kates 2002). *Levi's* also extended employee benefits to same-sex couples (a practice that is still uncommon) long before the issue because a cause *celebre* among mainstream gays. *Tupperware's* practice of hiring transvestites in the conservative 1950s (jokingly named 'Tupperware Queens') also lends the brand legitimacy with the gay community.

In contrast, other brands lacked authenticity. *Coors* in particular was a target for gay anger and boycott behaviour. *Coors* only marketed to gays and targeted gay bars when the market became mainstream and it was seen as safe to do so. This cynical strategy was made worse when it was found out that the conservative owners of *Coors* supported anti-gay rights think-tanks such as the *Heritage Foundation*. When the Conservative-led Canadian government refused to support equality for gays, brands such as *Coors* became the target of gay resentment and as such were removed from gay bars and nightclubs. Other brands had to pass stricter litmus tests during this time – no longer was being gay-friendly enough, brands had to openly support the gay community and not engage in activities that threatened the community's rights. As a result, *Levi's* ended its relationship with the American Boy Scouts because of that organization's ban on gay scout leaders (Kates 2004).

Extreme sports subcultures such as skateboarding provides another example. One of the brands associated with the founding days and anti-establishment spirit of skateboarding is *Vans*. Skaters adopted *Vans* shoes because they were light, hardwearing, cheap, and importantly had a rubble sole that offered plenty of grip. Skaters engage in their sport because they are not bound by rules that come with most official or mainstream sports. Skaters are highly individual and antiauthoritarian – even the tricks skaters perform are largely done for personal satisfaction and are an expression of individual skill, creativity, and daring (Beverland, Farrelly, and Quester, forthcoming). As a result, skaters' love the fact that they can get *Vans* made to order, using any fabric of their choosing. *Vans* started to lose authenticity when they branched out into mainstream sports. Eventually the situation was so dire the firm was declared bankrupt in 1987. Only by returning to a singular focus on skating and by sponsoring documentaries that acknowledged the brand's debt to the subculture (*Dog Town and Z-Boys* featured famous skaters doing their thing – the firm made no attempt at product placement out of fear that would undermine the film's sincerity – a strategy that paid off handsomely) did the brand return to profitability (Schmitt, Rogen, and Vrotsos 2004).

CONCLUSION

Authentic brands are not disconnected from time, place, and cultural space – in fact they draw significant energy from being deeply immersed in them (not the least of which are the benefits gained from market immersion – see Chapter 7). At a time when many global brands attempt to strip themselves of vestiges of place and culture, authentic brands play up their relationship to nation, region, industry, culture, and subcultures. However, this is not a mere strategy of impression management – the people behind these brands care deeply about communities and therefore sensitively immerse themselves in them (even when advised not too). At a time when consumers find that traditional markers of identity make less and less sense in a globalised, borderless, multicultural world, brands that allow them to connect to national traditions and identity (even if they are stereotypes), regional place and traditions, industry, and cultural ideals and subcultures are critical for achieving self-authentication in the marketplace. Authentic brands may operate globally, but they never forget the local.

CHAPTER 9

INDOCTRINATE STAFF INTO THE BRAND CULT

GORDON RAMSAY

Mention the name Gordon Ramsay to a group of people and you're guaranteed to provoke an emotional response – there is no middle ground on Ramsay, you either love or hate him. The major source of complaint relates to how Ramsay treats his staff – he swears, bullies, manhandles, throws things, fires/demotes them on the spot, denigrates their efforts, and demands nothing less than perfection. To those of us brought up in a politically correct environment where schools and universities focus on enhancing student's self-esteem rather than providing honest feedback about performance, where harassment laws result in us tiptoeing around each other for fear of giving offence, and parents are encouraged to indulge children's tantrums, Ramsay's behaviour seems outrageous and even immoral. Except that is to his staff – Ramsay has retained 80 per cent of his staff over the past ten years.

Many members of the staff that were with him at the beginning (and who bore the brunt of his anger on the *Boiling Point* series) have gone on to senior positions within the Ramsay empire (who he now refers to as 'partners', Dapin 2008). Although not all leaders of authentic brands are overbearing and difficult, research reveals that staff love leaders like Ramsay because they push them to achieve their best and they get rid of poor performers (Smith 2008). Ramsay has been called 'the Kerry Packer of chefs' (Anonymous, March 23, 2008) in reference to the iconic and independent Australian entrepreneur, who although reviled by many, was seen as representative of the Australian can-do spirit. We may bristle at the personal imperfection of Coco Chanel, Ralph Lauren, Gordon Ramsay, and Steve Jobs, but no one can deny their passion for their craft, or their desire to see staff stretch them and perform to their best. So much so that firms such as *Apple* receive hundreds (even thousands) of applications from highly qualified candidates who are often prepared to take significant pay cuts just to work at their flagship stores.

HOW TO INDOCTRINATE YOUR STAFF INTO THE BRAND CULT

The term 'indoctrinate' may surprise some given the focus on building authenticity – surely being authentic involves being true to oneself rather than a mindless 'true believer'? However, the brands covered here are backed by staff that can best be described as fanatics or devotees. The firms also immerse their staff in the values of the brand to encourage innovation and high performance. The flip side of this is that firms support staff in the pursuit of their interests and actively encourage critical thinking, risk taking, questioning, and curiosity – hardly hallmarks of typical cults. So authentic brands gain the outcomes of cults – devoted staff passionate about their cause – while at the same time ensuring an openness to new ways of thinking and doing. And, while leaders such as Jobs, Roddick, Branson, and Dyson may have 'god-like' status among their many fans, these people go out of their way to encourage staff expression, including those different to their own.

How do firms create this level of passion among staff and ensure employees live the values of the brand? Although I do not claim to be a human resources expert, an analysis of authentic brands reveals seven key practices relating to employees. First, these firms select employees carefully, often inviting other staff to comment on their suitability after a short trial period. Second, these firms look after the welfare of their staff. Third, as part of the brand effort, these firms celebrate individual staff stories in order to publicly recognize their efforts. Fourth, as the Introduction notes, these firms manage performance, and in particular, remove poor performers early. Fifth, these firms create an environment that encourages risk taking and creativity. Sixth, new hires are immersed in the brand's culture. Finally, leaders lead by example.

One: Select carefully

At Hermès you are obsessed to do well. At Hermès we try and recruit people who are interested in doing well, not in doing quick and profitable. It's a very big difference. (Executive vice-president, *Hermès* International Christian Blanckaert, quoted in Meagher 2005, p. 67)

When the newly formed *Southwest Airlines* came to hire pilots they wanted to make sure they got staff who were prepared to help out with all aspects of the business in order to ensure high service at low cost. Hiring took place in a non air-conditioned aircraft hangar on a particularly hot day. The heat was sweltering, particularly for applicants who, like all pilots, were dressed in dark blue formal suits. *Southwest* staff invited the applicants to put on a pair of shorts (which they provided) to feel more comfortable in the heat. Several pilots did so, while many didn't. Those that did, were invited back for another interview because they were willing to put aside convention to get the job done – although they may have looked stupid, these pilots were practical. If they could put aside their uniform when circumstances demanded it, it was highly likely they would help load bags onto the plane to ensure the aircraft left on time.

Virgin is another organization that forces potential new hires to get out of their comfort zone. Several current affairs shows in Australia have often run segments featuring disgruntled applicants who felt they had the necessary technical skills but were passed over (usually, they claim, for younger, more attractive applicants). Yet these disgruntled people miss the point when they question the relevance of requests to sing, perform, mime, or dance. *Virgin* desires people who will go the extra mile to get the job done and to satisfy customers even when things go against them (such as flight delays). By asking applicants to engage in spontaneous actions that may make them uncomfortable, the hiring panels are looking for staff that will live up to the brand – the technical skills can always be developed or improved with training, while attitudes are much harder to change.

Poor selection was one of the major reasons for *The Body Shop*'s American difficulties in the mid-1990s. As founder Anita Roddick (2005, p. 152) stated:

In fact some business student should write a case study on our unerring ability to consistently employ the wrong people. We didn't know how to look for signals of bullying, the signals of verbal violence, the signals of indifference to our reputation or mediocrity.

We didn't even know how to detect indifference to retailing. And it was simply because we no longer practiced due diligence in checking out behaviour, as we used to do initially. By then we were leaving that to consultants.

In contrast to their previous approach that selected people based on their passion for the brand and genuine business ability (Roddick believed in hiring people better than herself – quite a contrast to today's insecure managers who surround themselves with weak people), franchisee and employee selection in the US focused on potential employees' music and film tastes, esoteric views regarding life and death, and political awareness. As the brutally honest Roddick (2005) noted, although charmingly innocent, such an approach was naïve and resulted in the hiring of people seriously out of their depth, and who undermined the authenticity of a brand totally reliant on the passion of their staff for survival and dedicated to caring for people. Only after Roddick stepped in and scaled back the operation did the brand return to profitability in the graveyard of European retailers, the USA. The message is simple – the right people matter and you don't get them by accident.

Two: Look after their welfare

Many of the original industrialists took a paternalistic interest in employees' welfare. Often towns were built around the main factory to house employees, school their children, and monitor their morals. Towns such as Hershey in the US (named after the chocolate brand) were built out of a belief that a happy workforce was a productive one. Authentic brands take care of their employees – perhaps not to the extent of the early industrialists such as *Hershey*, *Cadbury* and the like – but they never forget to value their staff. This does not mean that authentic brands pay their staff more than their competitors (although sometimes they do as in the case of *In-N-Out Burger* in the US). In fact, often they pay less while engendering higher rates of loyalty because employees simply enjoy working there. In fact, paying increasingly more to employees in order to discourage them from switching is simply delaying the inevitable – disgruntled or bored staff won't stay simply because of high salaries. A common refrain is 'the pay was great but I was bored out of my mind'.

Examples of taking care of staff abound. They may be small, such as the *Morgan* factory's decision in 2007 to raffle off a car to help pay for the costs of an employee's cancer treatment. They may be large, such as the initiatives of Australia's *Peters Ice Cream* to accept lower profits during the Great Depression in order to retain all their staff – in fact the firm actually increased employment during the 1930s. The brand, which at the time was positioned as 'The Health of the Nation' reinforced the sincerity of its pledge by ensuring that children contin- ued to be fed, educated, and medicated (Harden 2006). *The Body Shop* opened a childhood development centre for staff in 1990 (at the cost of one million pounds) as part of a comprehensive family care policy. *Google* staff enjoy full maternity pay and parental leave, health insur- ance, stock options, retirement plans, tuition reimbursement, childcare support, on-site medical care, massages, gyms, sports facilities, and transport. It's no coincidence that *Google* was named destination of choice for graduates in 2007 and 2008 in *Fortune* (Kendall 2009). India's *Atlas Bicycles* and *Tata* are leaders in working conditions and pay, with *Atlas Bicycles* winning an award for industrial relations and *Tata* paying 25 per cent above market rates.

Cadbury has long been identified as an enlightened employer. Disgusted at what they saw as shameful employment practices in nineteenth-century Birmingham, the firm built a town around their Bourneville works that housed its employees, provided free health care and education, a magazine, and sporting facilities among others things (Bradley 2008). While such practices are often derided as paternalistic by many writers today, I believe they were fundamental in building lasting brand value because they ensured loyalty, performance, and a constant stream of talent, all of which were critical to producing great products and services. *Louis Vuitton* is in many ways the modern day bearer of this nineteenth-century legacy. The brand's leather goods ateliers (or factories) are built in country areas, away from the pres- sures of big cities to provide a high quality environment in which to contemplate and work. Out of a desire to retain an artisan spirit, each workshop houses just 25 employees. Attached to this workshop are employee lounges, gardens, and a restaurant. Workshops are designed to maximize natural light and provide craftspeople with a desirable work environment to carry out their work (Pasols 2005).

Many of the brands examined here have been leaders in other ways. *Levi's* extended benefits to same-sex couples (a practice that is unfor- tunately still rare), *Louis Vuitton* provides beautiful workspaces that reflect their respect for their craftspeople, *Cadbury* provided their own Pension and Savings Fund during the 1920s to soften the impact of necessary layoffs due to the Great Depression, *Dilmah Tea* gambled on demand for single estate teas to provide better income and livelihoods for their people, *Tupperware* allowed women to work around family commitments (such as their children's exam periods), and *The Body Shop* worked closely with its all important suppliers of raw materials to ensure they got a fair deal. Why do such actions, and their modern equivalents, resonate so powerfully with consumers? First, although such actions have spillover benefits for the firm, they are often done out of a genuine desire to improve people's lives. Second, since consumers connect with the people who produce the product, they want to know that employees are treated well because the continued quality of products and services depends on it. Third, since consumers use these brands to build their identity, they hold these brands to higher account, expecting values to be more than just espoused marketing spin. This partly explains why *Nike* got into trouble over its poor labour practices – consumers wondered how a brand that professed to be about the pursuit of excellence could treat workers so poorly (Beverland and Farrelly forthcoming).

Three: Tell their stories

It is common for many CEOs to thank their staff for all their efforts over the years. I don't want to question the sincerity of these managers, but many authentic brands go beyond such pronouncements, directly tying brand stories to those of their staff. *Bruichladdich* and Australasian winemakers *Yalumba* and *Palliser Estate* directly reference their staff (or their pets) in their brands. Compulsive storytellers *Bruichladdich* feature staff that contribute to the production of whisky in the *Port Charlotte* labelled products. Each release features pictures and stories of key staff that have played a role in the history and revitalization of the *Port Charlotte* distillery including surviving members of the original workforce (1929), whisky-maker Jim McEwan, and other production staff and owners critical to rebuilding the independent whisky trade on Islay.

One of 160-year old Australian winery *Yalumba's* most eagerly awaited releases is entitled *The Signature* (a blended red wine). *The Signature* is special because it is signed by the staff member judged to have contributed the most to the firm. No honour is more prized by *Yalumba* staff. As well as being signed by the contributor, the label and advertising then tells the story of the signatory – from the first day on the job through to their current efforts. Over the Tasman, New Zealand winery *Palliser Estate*'s most prized *Pinot Noirs* are named after staff pets that have sadly passed away. Each wine is a tribute to the pet (and their owner) that has brought so much joy to winery staff over the years of their life. To date three wines have been released – *Great George*, *Great Harry*, and *Great Bear* (all names of Labradors). Whether it is *PC*, *The Signature*, or the *Great* wines, these are very public cele-brations of those staff (and their animal companions) that have best embodied the spirit of the brand.

Why do these stories matter? Firstly, because they are stories – each time a brand publicly recognizes employees in its brand communica-tions they add another layer of richness to the brand's mythology. Second, because they reflect the personal efforts and experiences of staff, they are truly different, and they are 'real'. Third, they connect consumers in a very personal way to the history of the brand, thus reinforcing perceptions of heritage. Fourth, these stories reject the conceit of many others that great leaders drive firm success. Although leaders matter (even for authentic brands), we all understand (because we're employees too) that without workers, nothing would get done. The deliberate acknowledgement of staff reinforces this essential truth of branding. This also explains why many brands such as *The Body Shop*, *Cadbury*, *Dilmah*, and *Hermès* even tell stories about their suppliers of raw materials in their brand communications. Given the reliance of these brands on these suppliers for high quality raw materials, telling their stories provides a further point of difference in an age when many firms simply buy on the open market or outsource 'off shore'.

Four: Manage non-performance early

This chapter started with Gordon Ramsay – a hot-tempered chef known for his intolerance of poor performance and lack of effort. While many of us bristle at Ramsay's approach, the removal of poor performers in a high-pressure team environment like fine dining is critical for contin-ued success at the highest level. If one reviews *Ramsay's Boiling Point*, one will see that much of his outbursts are driven by the downstream problems faced by the whole team consisting of one poor performer. If a junior chef fails to produce high-quality work in a timely manner, the rest of the team have to cover for him or her, or worse, start again, which then increases the pressure on the cooking staff and service staff (who must deal with unhappy customers). It is not just fine dining that suffers in this way. *Prêt-a-Manger*, the UK-based sandwich provider, ensures the elimination of poor performers that will undermine team performance, by allowing employees to vote on whether to retain or remove trainees after the end of a short probation period (Milligan and Smith 2002). *Hermès* trainees only achieve employee status after years of training and passing a critical test – making a perfect *Birkin Bag* from scratch in less than 15 hours (Hume 2004).

All Australians smile with affection when they hear the name *Peters Ice Cream* (now *Nestlé Peters*). This iconic brand (which is over 100-years old) was part of every Australian's childhood. The company has gained a reputation for being a great place to work – as long as one works hard. Firm biographer Michael Harden recounts one example from the 1930s that captures the reciprocity expected of employees:

> Every morning during his visit [to the Brisbane plant], Fred Peters [founder and CEO] would station himself where all the workers were arriving to punch in for the day, bidding them good morning, passing on words of encouragement and asking after the families of the men he knew. On the first morning he had stern words for one young man who arrived ten minutes late for work. The next day, when this same man came in late again Fred Peters asked him how he was going to like his next boss. The next day the young fella punched in ten minutes early. (Harden 2006, pp. 81–2)

Speaking from personal experience, nothing is more frustrating than bosses that tolerate poor performers. Research reveals that the leaders that inspire the most loyalty are those that root out non-performance early (Smith 2008). These decisions are hard to take because they involve people's lives and livelihoods, but poor performers undermine the quality of the team, and ultimately undermine the brand. This trait explains the Gordon Ramsay paradox – how a seemingly intolerant boss attains high levels of loyalty among highly talented staff. Leaders of many authentic brands such as Steve Jobs, Coco Chanel, Ralph Lauren, Richard Branson, Bernard Arnault, Ignaz Schwinn, James Dyson, and Ernst Leitz (and the *Leica* CEOs that followed) are known for being tough, demanding, and in some cases, obnoxious during tense periods (much like consumers), and they undoubtedly receive more than their fair share of credit from the press when things go well. However, it is also clear these leaders are passionate about their staff and creativity, which is why they so often take time out to give credit where it is due, apologize for their bad behaviour (Ramsay's father-in-law regularly forces him to apologize to staff publicly when his antics go too far and undermine team morale), and shoulder the public blame when things go wrong.

Brands gain authenticity from this tough but fair behaviour for three reasons. First, in an age when people studiously avoid decisions that make them out to be the 'bad guy (or girl)' the tough, gut-retching decision to remove poor performers reminds us that they are in fact leaders, not popularity seekers. Second, we've all experienced the effects poor performers have at our own workforce, or studies, or sports etc., and are tired of seeing these people mollycoddled. Third, under the seeming tough exterior of these leaders are passionate people that put themselves and their livelihood (and that of their families) on the line everyday to create something amazing. Consumers recognize in these leaders the very passion they themselves have for their own goals (of which these brands are often a part) and projects. Just as we seek out like-minded people to share our dreams, so too the Gordon Ramsays of the world seek out passionate employees and partners to make their dreams come true.

Five: Encourage creativity

[Steve] Jobs doesn't care just about winning. He's willing to lose. He's just not willing to be lame, and that may, increasingly, be the winning approach. (Grossman 2005, p. 42)

Imagine the scene – an employee comes to you with a loosely formed idea that will take the company into new territory (away from its currently successful niche business), that might be successful assuming the execution is even possible, and that will result in a new-to-the-world product radically different from that which exists. Oh, and no obvious market exists for the product. Most of us know the likely response. Had Ernst Leitz been any modern CEO, we would probably have no reason to remember his name or his company. Fortunately we do have cause to remember him and his company *Leica*. The same goes for Ignaz Schwinn and his ideas for bicycles – without the support of senior managers thousands of American children would not know the name *Schwinn*. In contrast, every single vacuum manufacturer turned James Dyson away, to their ever-lasting regret. Similarly when even *Dior* judged Jean Paul Gaultier too high risk, *Hermès* placed their brand's future in his hands; a strategy that continues to pay handsomely (Hume 2004).

Playmobil management were sceptical of late toymaker Hans Beck's new designs but they backed him anyway, resulting in a range of children's toys that had sold 2.2 billion at the time of Beck's death (Anonymous, 30 March 2009, p. 10). Similarly, firms such as *Apple* and *Sony* would be very different (assuming they even remained) had they not encouraged staff to pursue ideas that resulted in hardware and software advances, *iPod*, *Walkman*, *Playstation*, and wireless computing. In contrast to *Penfold's*, which ordered Max Schubert to cease development of *Grange* (fortunately for the firm Schubert carried on), authentic brands support staff creativity. As *Hermès* Executive Vice-President Christian Blanckaert states (echoing Bernard Arnault – see Chapter 7):

> If you think and act like a typical manager around creative people with rules, policies, data on customer preferences and so forth, you will quickly kill their talent. Our whole business is based on giving our artists and designers complete freedom to invent without limits. (Meagher 2005, p. 67)

Before suggestion boxes, quality circles, or brainstorming became popular, *Cadbury* was soliciting suggestions from its employees for new ideas to take the company forward. In 1899, the company instituted a suggestion scheme to gain the best ideas from its staff. Unlike the triumph of symbolism over substance of today's suggestion box or email group employed by many Western firms, *Cadbury* genuinely desired staff input, no matter how hard the criticism. George Cadbury Jr's innovation was to make all suggestions received by the final review committee anonymous (suggestions were first filed and recorded at an office and then transcribed onto a report form to ensure anonymity). The committee that reviewed these suggestions was thus forced to judge each on its merits rather than source (critical in the heavily class-based workforce in nineteenth/twentieth-century England), since any one suggestion could come from George himself. Much like academic peer review (at its best), committees acknowledged receipt of the suggestion from the worker, provided reasons as to why some suggestions were not taken up (in the *Works Magazine*), identified those that would be and reported on their progress. Rewards were given for suggestions based on the size of the benefit derived. English workers had never before been asked for suggestions (based on the belief that they had little to offer). By 1929, *Cadbury* had received 141,000 – five for every single employee. Some of the suggestions included the development of bite size rectangular chunks for the famous *Milk Bar* – an innovation that is still with us to this day (Bradley 2008).

Providing a supportive environment for risk taking and free thinking has long been essential to creating lasting brand value. In fact, the further firms moved away from this principle – as the difficulties faced by many Western firms in the 1970s and 1980s attests – the greater the disconnect between the consumer and the brand. Why? Because ultimately the consumer bonds with a product or service, and the failure to create an innovative culture leads to dated products, tired service environments, or staff who are unsure about their responsibilities (such as the ability to satisfy a customer's request rather than pass them along to a higher manager). The need for an innovative environment that encourages employee curiosity is obvious in the campus-like environments of *Google*, *Yahoo*, and *Facebook*, design agencies such as *IDEO*, in the deliberate efforts of manufacturers such as *Dyson*, *Phil and Ted's*, and *Fisher and Paykel* to break down functional barriers, and in Bernard Arnault's long-term support for up-and-coming designers, many of whom take years to achieve market success.

Six: Immerse staff in the brand's culture

A brand lives only if all staff (not just those in the marketing department) understands and loves it. Authentic brands immerse their staff and stakeholders in the culture of the brand in order to build a corporate brand memory (Neumeier 2003) – as Anita Roddick (2008, p. 86) stated: 'We needed to learn more from our own story-tellers within the company because the penalty for failing to listen to stories is to lose our history and the values we strive to promote.' A colleague of mine, Professor Mark Ritson (of MIT and Melbourne Business School), recounted his first experience with the *Louis Vuitton* organization (for which he consults on marketing issues). Invited to visit Paris (from

London), Mark was picked up at the train station and taken to Louis Vuitton's original residence (which has been lovingly restored by *LVMH*). Ritson was dropped off, told to explore and make use of the facilities.

As Mark tells it, he played a few games of pool (or billiards), smoked a few cigarettes, and looked around the house. A few hours later he was picked up, dropped off at the train station, and somewhat baffled, returned to the UK. Why would a firm invite him out at full consulting rates to sit in a house for a day? Had it been some form of test? Had he passed? The next day, he was rung with an invitation to return and engage with them as a consultant. The initial visit to the house of the brand's founder was something *LVMH* did with all Anglo-consultants and senior employees, to immerse them in the world of the brand, and indicate to them just what was at stake (in terms of heritage and status).

Other brands also seek to immerse new staff in the brand's heritage and values. *The Body Shop* codified its core values (with input from all its staff) in their 1994 *Values & Vision* statement to ensure staff lived the brand's values everyday (Roddick 2008). Brands such as *Vespa*, *BMW*, *Mercedes*, and *Porsche* have built brand museums for just this purpose. *Hermès* nurtures retired workers (called *Les Anciens*), inviting them back for a free lunch every month where they share their experience with younger staff (Hume 2004). Such a strategy is also critical in times of crisis (as the example from *The Body Shop* shows in the next section) because staff share a common value-base with which to evaluate new ideas. While some brands have official histories (such as *Virgin*), others immerse staff in the brand's tradition through teamwork. For example, Port and Champagne houses such as *Cockburn's* and *Deutz* pair new winemakers up with older ones in an apprentice style system to ensure continued traditions as well as stylistic evolution and innovation (Beverland 2005b). *Louis Vuitton* and *Morgan* run a similar apprentice system that ensures time honoured skills are passed on to, and influenced by, the next generation.

The notion that employees should 'live the brand' is common in many service organizations. Writers on corporate reputation in particular emphasize the importance of organization culture and induction processes for the delivery of brand promises (Hatch and Schultz 2008). Authentic brands have long taken this view to heart, immersing staff in the culture, history, and practices underpinning the brand. Such strategies have many benefits. First, consumers pick up on the obvious love employees have for the brand (see Chapter 6), enhancing perceptions of sincerity. Second, consumers do meet staff that embody the values of the brand, resulting in a more authentic experience because staff effectively live up to expectations. Both outcomes enhance perceptions of sincerity.

Third, employees acts as stewards for the brand, being careful not to undermine core values, while simultaneously being aware of their obligation to live up to the brand's legacy by innovating. Fourth, workers often find the inspiration for innovations in the brand's history (it is not unusual for staff at *Louis Vuitton* and *Bruichladdich* to find inspiration for new releases in past traditions). Both of these outcomes result in enhanced perceptions of heritage and quality commitments. Finally, such immersion builds a shared culture (breaking down functional barriers) and helps transmit important tacit knowledge to new staff.

Seven: Lead by example

Remember Dave Thomas – the founder and CEO of *Wendy's Old Fashioned Hamburgers*? Dave was a tireless salesman for freshly made burgers, and was critical to the brand's success (since his death, the brand seems to have lost the plot somewhat). Victor Kiam loved *Remington Razors* so much he brought the company (Rosica 2007). How often do we see leaders encouraging their staff to 'do as I say, not do as I do'? *The Public Relations Society of America's* National Credibility Index ranked 'company founders' as the most credible of all professions (above teachers) (Rosica 2007). The leaders of authentic brands play a very visible role in the firm's day-to-day activities. All too often, leaders are disconnected not only from their staff, but also from the focal activities and values of the brand. As *L.L. Bean* found in the 1970s, how could they connect with their customer base when even their then CEO had ceased engaging in outdoor pursuits? Likewise, when high-profile consultant the late Sir John Harvey Jones arrived in a chauffeured car at *Morgan* as part of the *BBC's Troubleshooter* series, staff were heard commenting 'you'd think that someone coming to tell a car company how to run its business would at least be able to drive a car himself' (Laban 2000, p. 257). Such disconnections influence consumers because they signal insincerity. For example, consumers have often questioned the authenticity of brands such as *Ripcurl* and *Billabong* following listing on the stock exchange because many of their owners don't even surf (Beverland, Farrelly, and Quester forth-coming). In contrast, leaders that walk the walk as well as talk the talk lead authentic brands.

Founder of *The Body Shop*, the late Anita Roddick, regularly took part in protest campaigns, regardless of criticism from institutional investors and marketing staff. During the 1999 WTO protests in Seattle, Roddick was tear-gassed by police, something that few CEOs of firms with corporate social responsibility programmes can claim. Roddick even put her tenure as CEO on the line during the first Gulf War. When she sponsored an anti-war campaign, her marketing team removed signs and posters and suggested the campaign cease because it might harm the brand given the popular support for the war at the time. Given the positioning of *The Body Shop* brand and her belief in free speech, Roddick believed it was critical for her to speak out against what she saw as an unjust war. Consistent with her beliefs, rather than imposing them on unwilling staff, she allowed employees to debate the issue in a public forum. Had she lost, Roddick would have stepped down as CEO. Fortunately, *The Body Shop* employees were immersed in the values of the brand (a policy initiated by Roddick), and Anita carried the day (with the help of some Falkland's veterans who spoke passionately about the horrors of war) (Roddick 2005).

Leading by example is what motivates Richard Branson to insist that all managers staff check-in counters or front line service positions regularly. Branson is passionate about serving customers more effec-tively and treating them with respect. Since service firms all too often lose their authenticity because managers make decisions divorced from front line reality, Branson's policy ensures senior staff never forget what business they are in. Other leaders are similarly engaged. For example, bungee-jumping founder and legend A. J. Hackett continues to push the boundaries with ever more daring jumps, Manolo Blahnik contin-ues to be involved in all aspects of shoe production, the four members of the *Krug* family remain involved in all aspects of their Champagne House (Henri makes the wine, Caroline sells it, Rémi markets it, and Olivier works in the vineyard), Charles Morgan continues to race cars, and Gordon Ramsay (who hates the term 'celebrity chef' because he views himself as a 'serious chef'; Meagher 2008) continues to cook and receive criticism from Michelin and other rating agencies, and puts himself on the line in programmes such as *Ramsay's Kitchen* where he allows the public to judge whether his dishes are as good as celebrity guests.

I thrive on pressure. Without any pressure, I'm the worst cook in the world – not interested. Under pressure, then, you know, I'm one of the best. When I've got my jacket on, I take it seriously. Kitchen Nightmares gives me jeopardy. Three Michelin stars gives me pressure. I'm a bit of an adrenaline junkie, I think. (Dapin 2008, p. 30)

Such activities may come at a cost – as the late Steve Irwin found when he was tragically killed while filming stingrays. The global outpouring of grief and accolades attest to Irwin's authenticity, as does his legacy of highlighting the value and plight of wildlife (leading uncompromising anti-whaling group *Sea Shepard* to name their new ship Steve Irwin and the Australian government to purchase a vast track of untouched wilderness filled with crocodiles and name it the Steve Irwin Wilderness Reserve in tribute).

CONCLUSION

Behind authentic brands are dedicated people, led by passionate, imperfect leaders. Writers on branding are only beginning to recognize the importance of people policies in the development of brand equity. History reveals that authentic brands have long understood this relationship, taking care of employees' welfare, taking leadership positions on important workplace policies (such as paternity leave and same-sex health cover), creating an atmosphere of mutual respect, and encouraging employees to question, challenge, and innovate. And, while researchers talk about employment branding, authentic brands give their employees a starring role in the brand's mythology. Since consumers desire connections with people as passionate as they, building personal connections between the staff behind the brand and the brand's story is a critical way of enhancing authenticity and providing an important point of differentiation. In days when firms talk up their desire for staff to connect with customers, authentic brands provide the basis for shared storytelling, understanding, and respect by using the stories of their staff as a conversation piece.

Importantly, leaders who just seem more 'real' run authentic brands. Love them or hate them (and importantly these leaders do evoke extreme emotional reactions because they hit a nerve), these leaders seem more like us than the disconnected (from the task, their staff, and communities) CEOs of failed financial institutions who receive ever larger bonuses for non-performance while at the same time disrupting communities, shifting jobs offshore, and making large numbers of people redundant (and in some cases flying to Washington in private jets to beg for tax-payer bailouts to fund 'performance' bonuses). In contrast, despite their rock-star like status, we can relate to Gordon Ramsay, Richard Branson, Steve Irwin, Steve Jobs, and Anita Roddick because of their very humanity. Like us, they get angry, make mistakes, say the wrong thing, and are less than morally perfect. Unlike other CEOs however, they are brutally honest about their failings, and the first to apologize for losing their temper with their good staff or for making mistakes. This 'warts 'n all' approach to leadership enhances the authenticity of the brand.

CHAPTER 10

WHAT CAN YOU DO?

You always knew where you stood with Jack, he was the real deal, there
was no pretence.

(Gus Griffin, global managing director, *Jack Daniel's*, quoted in
Drummond 2008, 18).

FAKING IT IS HARD

Imagine having to live a lie. Every second of every day you would have
to consciously be on your guard, ensuring you said the right thing, in
the right way, all to present an image that isn't true. The time spent,
the emotional cost, and the likelihood of eventually getting caught
means such a strategy is impractical (even the worse serial killers get
found out, and they are often loners not burdened with regular social
interaction) and frankly, undesirable. *Intel* found this out with their
Pentium chip in 1994. The 'floating point problem' eventually cost the
company US$500 million. Since denying there was a problem just
made things worse, Andy Grove asked his management team, 'what
would we do if we walked out the door and came back to the problem
without the baggage?' The answer was to admit there was a problem,
recall the chip, and move on (Jackson 1998). To their credit *Intel* did,
and their subsequent success (the brand is rated as one of the world's
most valuable) has been attributed to their response to this problem
and their *Intel Inside* campaign.

Being true to yourself seems so much easier. One of my dearest
friends Lizzy Donnelly is finding this out with her own fledgling enterprise *Eardrops*. Liz produces CDs that teach young children sounds

(e.g., *Sounds of City* provides a link between a sound and a word). Early on, Liz (a writer of children's television programmes) focused on psychological theories and pedagogical benefits in telling her brand story. Although sales occurred, it was word-of-mouth that really drove sales – the product is wonderful, unique, and effective. However, word-of-mouth sales were slow, Liz's limited advertising had only a small impact on sales, and she wondered whether she was making the best use of the public relations activities that came her way (i.e., free editorial). Since Liz and I went way back, my advice could be brutally honest. The motivation for *Eardrops* had been her first child, Tommy, who developed glue ear at a very young age, and thus had missed out on the normal experiences of sounds. Liz originally developed *Eardrops* as a way of teaching her own son about sounds. This to me is a perfect start for an authentic brand story. Nothing is as compelling (to other mums) as a struggling first-time mother making do with what she has to help her child. A second child has recently slowed business plans, but sales have improved (without six-figure investments in 'professional marketing').

As I said, being authentic should be the easiest thing in the world. We encourage our children and friends to follow their dreams and be true to themselves, so why don't we encourage brand managers to do the same? Why is it that when it comes to branding, firms are advised to fake it? Why do employees have to put on a front to customers – pretending to be emotionally engaged with their work when they are not? More importantly, why do brand managers continue faking it when they know consumers see through the hype? If you quickly think about the last few chapters, doesn't building brand authenticity seem to be so much easier? Think about it. Authentic brands don't try to fake it. Unlike *3M* they don't try and turn lucky accidents into stories about creative cultures (although they do put themselves in a position to create and take advantage of lucky breaks). Authentic brands focus on telling their story, rather than paying an agency to invent one. Authentic brands don't hide their mistakes, or deny them, or pay spin-doctors to try and convince consumers that a sow's ear is a silk purse. Neither Richard Branson, Gordon Ramsay nor Anita Roddick (and others) hide their mistakes – they admit them, learn from them, and move on. As a result, when authentic brands do wrong, they know to apologize and make things right.

Being authentic (just like faking it) is a mindset. The term 'habit' was not chosen lightly. Habitual behaviours are reflective of deeply held values. These values are not the sort that appear in emotionally empty mission statements or brand mantras. Instead they are lived everyday. For those marketers seeking to enhance the authenticity of their brand, this chapter identifies some starting points or foundational values and strategies that can help. Rereading the seven habits, I believe there are several do's and don'ts for brand managers who aim to build authentic brands. Collectively they may require a change in the ways things are done, but they also transform the quality of a company's brand strategy and its ability to deliver exceptional results over the long term.

DON'T JUST SAY IT, SHOW IT!

Drama coach Stella Adler often told her students. 'Don't act. Behave.' Living brands are not a stylistic veneer but a pattern of behavior that grows out of character. When the external actions of a company align with its internal culture, the brand resonates authenticity. If a brand looks like a duck, quacks like a duck, walks like a duck, and swims like a duck, then it must be a duck. If it swims like a dog, however, people start to wonder. (Neumeier 2003, p. 138)

One of the things that set the likes of Richard Branson and Anita Roddick apart from their professional contemporaries is that they get things done. Instead of talking about great service, Branson makes it happen. Consumers and critics often complain that brands talk a great game, but fail to deliver (remember green washing?). As Ann Mack (5 January 2009, p. 10) notes in *Brandweek* 'Given that "Authentic" has become such a misused and overused label, brands will need to work harder to show they are authentic.' As Roxanne Quimby of *Burt's Bees* states:

We don't just talk about saving the environment, we actually help protect it! For starters, we are passionate in our efforts to stay on the forefront of the sustainable, recyclable, and reusable packaging technologies. Around the office, we recycle our toner cartridges, print on both sides of our printer paper, turn lights off when leaving the room, and always make sure that our trash cans are much less full than the recycle bin! It's the small things that make a difference; every bee knows that. (Rosica 2007, p. 43)

Making products based on beeswax demands that Quimby and her employees take care of the environment. It's why the brand was a key sponsor in protecting open spaces in nature (after all, bees need fields full of flowers to do their work), took a lead role in educating people about colony collapse disorder (where bee colonies are disbanding, with dramatic effects on food production and human life), donating five percent of all gift set profits to research on the disorder, encouraging people to plant wildflowers (they've given away 95,000 seed packets to date), and funding public service announcements outlining the actions people can take to save bee colonies (this also ran as a lead-in to the animated film *Bee Movie*).

Instead of having a corporate social responsibility programme, Anita Roddick (and her staff) march in the street, campaign for the release of political prisoners, work with local indigenous communities to better their standard of living, and campaign for a better world everyday. To critics, Branson's decisions to enter wildly different industries are irrational, while Roddick's campaigns were seen as immature (to fix falling sales critics often noted how it was time for *The Body Shop* to grow up; Roddick 2002). However, experience eventually reveals that consumers love these brands because of their actions. Often, as in the case of *The Body Shop*, declining sales are due to other problems (like a lack of innovation, poor store locations, or poor hiring practices). Authentic brands like these never mention the word authenticity while marketing because they don't have to.

When brand managers and marketers talk of engaging in an authentic brand strategy they miss the point. Authenticity is not like nostalgia or retro – it is not another fashionable marketing strategy that provides a short-term edge (nor can it be faked like nostalgia). You cannot tell consumers that your brand is authentic – you have to show them. Consumer research reveals that overt claims of authenticity are viewed as marketing hype. Worse, such claims may render genuinely authentic brands fake (Beverland et al. 2008). Just as consumers may wonder whether something is wrong when brands talk constantly about quality, saying you're authentic may confuse consumers who believe that if you're authentic you shouldn't need to say so. To project authenticity, brands can draw on a number of attributes including historical associations, relationship to place or subcultural space, non-commercial values, and the creative process.

The *Penfolds* campaign to return the brand to its roots provides a good example of this approach. Through drawing on the sincerity and authority of Max Schubert, and emphasizing love over money, this advertisement provides a very public circuit breaker for a brand many thought to be in decline. *Penfolds* could have talked about returning to their roots, the technical skill of their winemaking team, their medals and awards, their heritage. They could have legitimately marketed themselves as 'authentically Australian' with images of other local pioneers to emphasize that *Grange* was a product of the same spirit that made the country great. Gladly they didn't. In a few well-chosen words, coupled with a picture of a thoughtful Schubert, we gain a sense that the brand will become great again. In fact, communications for authentic brands (when they do occur) are more known for what they don't say – *Coca Cola*'s (a line-up of Coke bottles since founding under the banner 'Original Taste since 1886' conveys the brand's heritage and the notion that is has stuck to its roots) and *Tic Tac*'s (see Chapter 8) recent billboard advertising provide good examples.

EMBRACE THE TENSION AT THE HEART OF AUTHENTIC BRANDS

The mantra of modern brand management has always been consistency of message. Marketers are urged to engage in practices such as 'reinforcement', 'staying on message', or to adopt a 'one look, one voice' approach to communication (Beverland and Luxton 2005). In fact, when the core message no longer resonates, some urge marketers to retire the brand altogether, and simply invent a new one (Ries and Trout 2000). However, when researchers examine how great brands are actually managed over time, they rarely find consistency of message. In fact, brands such as *Nike*, *Harley Davidson*, *Coke*, *Mountain Dew*, and *Corona* regularly shift their story to reflect the changing *zeitgeist* of the time, often adopting messages in direct conflict with their historical positioning. And, they have done so in order to ensure long-term success (Holt 2004). In fact, so-called best practice brand management models often suffer from a lack of empirical validation or testing (Holt 2005).

Collins and Porras' classic book *Built to Last* (2004) identifies that long-term firm success involves balancing contradictions or living with paradox. Authentic brands embody this principle too. The world's great wines are made by firms seemingly mired in tradition but forever at the forefront of innovation and tastes. Luxury brands such as

Burberry, Dunhill, Louis Vuitton, and *Prada* play up their scarcity value while at the same time carefully managing growth through the use of entry-level accessories like sunglasses. *Morgan* is seen as a maker of modern day vintage cars that meet modern emissions, safety and performance standards. *Apple* has married beauty with functionality and power, a seemingly impossible goal in personal computing. *Dyson* is up-market but mass-market. *Dr Marten's* are worn by racist skinheads and anti-racism campaigners (and are a boot for the working classes that was adopted by wealthy teens; Roach 1999). And so the list goes on.

Authentic brands are laden with contradictions – they are old and forever relevant, up to date but timeless, they are commercially successful yet deny their commercial prowess and motives, and sometimes even committed to overthrowing capitalism while also stressing bottom line performance. The managers of authentic brands need to become experts at managing these tensions. They must accept that muddling through is often all there is, that the best plans will often be wrong or incomplete, and that messiness often provides the basis for innovation. Instead of masking inconsistency, they must deal with the many paradoxes associated with authentic brands and effectively operate two parallel systems – one focused externally on communicating a sincere story about the brand, one focused behind the scenes counterbalancing relevancy with timelessness.

PRODUCT, PRODUCT, PRODUCT (OR SERVICE, SERVICE, SERVICE – OR BOTH)

Leica M-series, Art of Shaving, Neiman Marcus, Chateau Margaux, The Birkin, Krug, Pixar, Aeromax, iPod, Cyclone, Mini, Bruichladdich, Tiger Balm, Lord of the Rings, Chucks, Dilmah, and *Upper Class.* All great products and services, many of which need no further introduction. These products and services have a devoted fan base (both on and offline), and in some cases small libraries of publications devoted to examining every detail of these extraordinary things. Check out your local bookstore's magazine rack – you will see titles devoted to *Apple,* watches, sports cars, car brands such as *BMW, Mercedes,* and *Jaguar,* photography, fashion, food, wine, cigars, and so on. Only a handful of titles are deliberately devoted to the process of branding or marketing.

At the end of the day, your brand is only as good as the products and services behind it. As research shows, ultimately consumers connect directly with products, indirectly with brands. All of the brands covered here have found their greatest fans ignore poor products, regardless of previous loyalties. Just as no craftsperson can produce great things with poor materials, so products trump brands when it comes to engaging consumers. Of course, most readers already know this, right? If only this were true. As mentioned earlier (see Chapter 6), modern marketing theory denigrates product and production orienta- tion in favour of consumer worship. The problem is that this approach more often than not results in mundane poor quality products that fail to excite or address consumer problems that are difficult to articulate in focus groups and surveys. Authenticity comes from a great product/ service, regardless of whether it is a wine, car, trip to the bank, airplane journey, or movie.

James Dyson is right – Western countries (and indeed any advanced economy) need to start believing they can design and make real things, not just provide support services such as advertising, banking, insurance, and accounting. Firms need to go against the dominant logic of the day, which proposes that manufacturing is a sunset indus- try and that advanced economies are experiential or image dominated, and connect with their nation's tradition of production. Businesses need to start investing in research and development, innovation and importantly, craft and design. Even service firms need to rediscover the soul of true service, rather than the script driven and increasingly automated service encounters of today (or experiential strategies that emphasize process (i.e., store design) over outcome (great products and service)). To do so requires the development of an organizational culture supportive of innovation, risk, and curiosity.

BE PART OF THE CONSUMERS' WORLD

Think of the extraordinary effort that most firms undergo to understand the consumers' world. They engage in all forms of market research including surveys, experiments, focus groups, depth interviews, obser- vations, and ethnographic techniques (and now, brain scanning). Firms attempt to track purchase patterns and behaviour through loyalty schemes. The more enlightened set up brand communities and invite commentary from consumers via websites (and even brand hate sites). These firms devote extraordinary levels of resource to get closer to the customer. Although all of these methods have their value, one wonders whether firms wouldn't be better off if they immersed themselves in the customer's world. And, how easy is it to get close to customers when you share nothing in common with them – including the core activity that your brand is supposed to be involved with? Like winemakers that don't like wine, CEOs of surf brands that don't surf, leaders of advocate brands that don't protest, and managers of service firms that never meet customers, most marketers today rarely engage with the consumer's world. In contrast authentic brands are at one with their consumers.

Immersion is actually a very easy and cheap way to build authenticity. Immersion is why many authentic brands have a great track record of successful innovations despite relatively lower levels of investment in research and development and supportive marketing activities than others. As the example of *Phil and Teds* showed (see Chapter 7), the easiest way to appeal to your customers is to hire them. By hiring your customers as employees and living in their world you can learn the rules of engagement with consumers – the rituals, language, norms, and values that were so crucial to *Dunlop's* revitalization in Australia. Why hire ethnographers and cool hunters when you can do this yourself? Why seek impartial, external advice when what you want is a partial, close to the action view of the consumers' world? To build authenticity, marketers need to put down the latest consumer report, and start living in and engaging with the consumer's world.

To ensure this strategy has the best effect, firms need to overcome their bias towards outliers. All too often, firms view qualitative information as less useful and certainly less valid. However, even quantitative information is subjective. And, it is unlikely that the source of innovative breakthrough products and services will be found in the convergence that is represented by the averages of survey research (the consensus of the focus group). Many of the innovations covered in this book, both in terms of product, service, and practice (including marketing), were generated from individual insights, or collections of small, seemingly random observations. While not all firms rejected formal market research techniques, they did not give precedence to this form of information: small details or one-off experiences were accorded equal or greater value than brand-tracking research or focus groups. For example, *Quiksilver* management routinely asks their staff (and staff ask their children) what they think about the latest surf fashion lines, as their decision to buy (or not to) is considered a crucial litmus test.

Marketers of authentic brands need to encourage direct observation gained during staff travel and information gained via personal experience with the products, and place great weight on the much-maligned 'gut feel'. Importantly, they need to seek information gained via immersion in the market or through membership of a subculture rather than formalized research with specific demographics. Ideas that inform the practices of such brands should come from *in situ* experiences, tangential sources (viewing other cultures), and involvement in industry-specific forums.

AVOID THE TEMPTATION TO EXPLOIT YOUR BRAND FOR COMMERCIAL GAIN

Dr Pepper has put their authenticity at risk with a campaign that promised a free can of drink to every American if rock band *Guns N' Roses* delivered their long delayed album *Chinese Democracy* before the end of 2008. The band defied expectations and released the album in October of that year. *Dr Pepper* immediately found itself having to deliver on its promise (at substantial cost). Realizing it had a public relations disaster on its hands when it tried to wriggle out of its commitment, the brand did itself no favours by requiring consumers to download coupons (the website crashed repeatedly) in a very narrow timeframe (Hein 2009). It was clear to everyone that the brand was trying to get out of a mess of their own making (i.e., they were trying to 'welch on a bet'). As a lover of *Dr Pepper* I am more shocked as to why a brand of this stature would make such a bet in the first place? What was to be gained if *Guns N' Roses* didn't deliver? Why make fun of an artist desperately trying to create an album that lived up to the band's legacy? Why would a brand seek to take pleasure in someone else's struggles? (Please note I am no fan of *Guns N' Roses*).

The short term is the enemy of authenticity. Gimmicks like that used by *Dr Pepper* only diminish the brand. What seemed like a good idea to gain free press coverage against a backdrop of decreased marketing budgets and decreasingly advertising effectiveness turned into a disaster that could have major repercussions for the brand. Authenticity has always involved a sense that one has paid their dues (Caves 2000). Artists often take years to gain the respect of critics and art lovers. Music lovers believe all great bands started small – having to earn their stripes in small venues playing to hostile audiences. It is not uncommon for great filmmakers (or authors) to take years to produce their great work. Importantly, selling out, or pandering to short-term fashions for commercial gain diminishes authenticity in art.

Branding is no different. Authenticity takes time to build, but can be lost in an instant (as *Dr Pepper* is finding out). Being authentic also places limitations on how far a brand can be stretched. The jury is out on *Ralph Lauren Paint, Prada Socket Sets,* the *Porsche Cayenne,* or *Piper Heidsieck's Baby Piper.* Consumers I spoke with were often ambivalent about extensions. Some thought that surf brands extending into other sports diluted the brand's authenticity, while others were happy as long as the brand continued to maintain product leadership in surfing. Likewise, second and third tier quality labels of fine wines often reinforced the brand's position because they represented even greater selectivity in raw material. What marketers of authentic brands must remember is that any extension must appear non-commercially driven and reinforce, rather than dilute, the authenticity of the original.

EMPLOY A BRAND HISTORIAN

In 1998 I was contacted by *Norman's Winery* to write their history. *Norman's* was an old medium-sized winery that specialized in low-priced wines. Like all medium sized firms they had neither the size nor economies of scale to compete with larger players, nor the credibility and quality to compete with niche producers. *Norman's* also had a perception problem – wine buyers and critics thought the brand constantly underperformed given the quality of the vineyards it had (the wines often won bronze medals, which are given to wines that have no technical faults but often also have no special merits either). Although the wines were cheap, they were so because the company had been forced to discount to maintain shelf space. *Norman's* desired to reposition through investing in quality, marketing, and importantly, capitalizing on its heritage.

When I arrived, I was presented with some tantalizing evidence suggesting *Norman's* was Australia's oldest winery. However, the firm's subsequent investigations had revealed a blank – they could not verify the founding date of the vineyard, nor account for around 100 years of history. They had a range of founding dates and then nothing. After several weeks of scouring libraries, shipping records, and specialist wine libraries, I managed to flesh out the brand's history to ten pages.

However, although I could provide a more accurate estimate of the firm's founding year, I could not identify a first vintage, or account for much of the lost 100 years. In effect, the brand had no history, and certainly no special claim to fame that could be defended in court (being the oldest or first in wine is critical, especially when one comes from a relatively young nation). Despite massive improvements in quality, the launch of an up-market wine named *Peacock* (after the maiden name of the founder's wife), the company eventually declared bankruptcy in 2001.

Authentic brands use their history to their advantage (which is why Australian brewer *Hahn* employed academic beer historian David Hughes as a brand advisor; Hall 2004). Spanish shoe manufacturer *Camper* draws directly on its history – the founder's (Lorenzo Fluxa) family have made shoes on Majorca since 1877. The name 'Camper' is Spanish slang for peasant or farmer, so most *Camper* advertisements focus on everyday pictures of Majorcan life. As James Hall (2004, p. 45) notes, 'That's where Camper works. One way [to achieve authenticity] is to look back at the history of the brand.' Consumers desire heritage (although brands do not have to be that old) because they seek identity in the past. As the *Norman's* example shows, without your history, you are nothing special.

Brand managers should view their brands as historical documents and retain every record, every press clipping (good and bad), and regularly engage writers to provide a historical record (if only for internal training purposes – *Bally* and *Hermès* developed historical archives to inspire their designers). The *Zippo Visitors Centre* (Figure 10.1) was opened in 1997 and attracts thousands of fans per year. *Vespa* has developed a *Piaggio Historical Archive*, which contains more than 150,000 documents from the company's past. *VW* and *Jack Daniel's* have done likewise.

DON'T BE AFRAID OF LETTING CONSUMERS IN

To Apple users it was a socio-political statement. ... Stickers are a marketing coup for Apple. It's almost guaranteed that proud owners of new Macs will affix a decal on their car, boat, bike, skateboard, or shop window. In fact, an Apple sticker is often the first thing people stick on a new car. Owners often peel stickers from their old vehicles and transfer them to new ones. (Kahney, 2004b, p. 71)

FIGURE 10.1 **Thousands visit the *Zippo Visitors Centre* every year**

In my postgraduate Brand Management class I'm often surprised by how many of my Generation Y students think marketers should try to control how consumers use the brand, and importantly, seek to clamp down on consumer-generated activities not consistent with the official brand manual. I mention Generation Y because it is this generation that laughs at old-fashioned brand managers seeking to limit what consumers say about their brand online (Flavell 2009). Charles Morgan's approach in France truly horrifies my students. In fact, it is the older members of my class that smile knowingly at their younger colleagues when they hear Charles' quote. Experience has taught them that consumers will do with your brand as they please, and the best marketers can do is respectfully listen, respond (where appropriate) in a genuine manner, and try their hardest to play a part in consumers' lives.

Footwear brands such as *Chuck Taylor's*, *Dr Martin*, and *Dunlop Volley* have never patronized customers. When *Chuck Taylor's* were no longer a basketball shoe, musicians, artists, rebellious teens, actors, and the counterculture adopted the brand as an identity statement. These groups of people provided a range of associations previously unavailable to the brand, such as links with rock and roll, punk rock, teen angst, and the peace movement. As a result, the brand often featured in movies (*Chucks* have appeared in over 500 films and television series including the recent *Dr Who* series and even a website dedicated to *Chucks* in movies [chucksconnection]), advertisements targeting teens (such as those by *Levi's*), and *MTV* music videos. The design team drew on these associations when developing new shoe styles (featuring the peace symbol, multicultural colours, rock bands etc). If this isn't enough, consumers can also design their own shoes. *Harley Davidson* takes a similar approach, never turning away any group of people that wants to adopt the brand, nor denigrating their reasons for doing so. *Harley*'s first step is to ask what they can provide these fans in return for their patronage instead of worrying about concerns of other 'demographics'.

Although the owners of authentic brands may not worship the customers' viewpoint when developing new innovations, they do welcome customers into the cult. And, they respect customer concerns about their brand. On the outside, *In-N-Out Burger* appears unchanged since founding, avoiding demand for chicken and vegetarian burgers as well as salads and larger burgers. However, *In-N-Out Burger* also has a secret menu. After customers started asking for Neapolitan milkshakes (a mix of chocolate, strawberry, and vanilla), burgers without buns (the so called 'Flying Dutchman'), fires topped with cheese, and grilled onions and special sauce ('Animal-style fries'), the owners rekeyed all the firm's cash machines to allow for these innovations. Although no four-four burger is offered on the menu (four patties and four slices of cheese – there are pictures of what I estimate to be a gut busting 24–24 on *Google Image*), in the know consumers can ask for it, while service staff can process such requests without problems (Moon 2003). (*In-N-Out Burger*'s secret menu is now a 'not so secret menu' as it is advertised on their webpage). The lesson is clear, the brand is partly owned by the consumer so respect their views even if you disagree with them.

BE OPEN AND HONEST

By this stage, this last point should seem obvious. I know some readers will undoubtedly groan at this seemingly trite statement (and my response), but consumers are demanding greater honesty, openness to alternative views, and transparency than ever before. Here it comes – business, and brands in particular, could benefit from more honesty. In examining the many brands that I have, I am always struck by how practical honesty is. Honesty is easy – in branding terms it involves simply telling things how they are – something consumers actually desire (as *Dove* found out when they were accused of retouching the photos of their real women in their campaign for real beauty; Kemp-Robertson 2008). Honesty avoids the need for expensive (and ineffective) public relations exercises, or strategies that attempt to take the focus off the issue or transfer blame to another party. Honesty is more than just efficient or cheap; honesty is also necessary for innovation and business success. *Apple* is right – no amount of advertising will fix *Microsoft's Vista* (just as award winning advertisements didn't increase sales of the *Lisa* and *Newton*). Consumers realize this, just as they understand things can go wrong and mistakes can be made – which is why they are forgiving of firms that admit their mistakes and then get on with the job of fixing them (such as *Intel* and *Zippo*). Honesty forces one to confront the reality of poor product/service performance, poor practices, poor moral behaviour, and then do something about it.

Honesty also means acknowledging the role of luck, chance, and others in your brand story. *Pacific Brand's* marketing team got lucky when teens started wearing the *Volley*. They were even luckier because their inexperience with this market made them cautious in respond-ing to the *Volley's* sudden change of status. Authentic brands make the most of these lucky breaks. The marketing team behind Islay based whisky brand *Bruichladdich* are master storytellers. Their famous *WMD* whisky arose from a misunderstanding due to government paranoia, and their *Flirtation* (see Chapter 3) a product of experimentation gone nicely wrong. The creation of champagne (as told in the legion of *Dom Pérignon*), sweet wines such as those made at *Chateau d'Yquem*, and the timeless wines of Madeira were all products of accident. Rather than spin this into stories of innovation, authentic brands admit the truth. Just as consumers know that it is not luck *per se* but what one does with it (and to create it) that counts, so authentic brands weave accounts of lucky breaks with those of entrepreneurship into rich stories that set them apart from competitors.

Honesty also requires openness. Just as authentic brands do not deny their mistakes, neither do they believe they have all the answers. Thus authentic brands are more respectful of the views of outsid-ers (after all they themselves try to go against the mainstream). As a result, they are more likely to take the time to understand who their stakeholders are, what impacts their activities have on communities (at home and abroad), and see stakeholders as potential allies rather than threats. Openness has its benefits, including the generation of new ideas and approaches, and protection from unfounded criticism or industry scandals. As consumers increasingly demand information

WHAT CAN YOU DO?

about offshore labour standards, environmental impact, fair trade, community impact, and product ingredients, firms will simply have to provide such information publicly. And, they will need to make genuine commitments in these areas otherwise authenticity will be undermined when consumers and critics compare espoused brand statements with the reality of operation and find them wanting.

WHAT ABOUT B2B?

Can business-to-business (B2B) brands build authenticity? I believe so. As consumers become more interested in the origin of product ingredients and demand greater transparency over supply chain issues, B2B organizations can benefit from brand authenticity. *Intel* for example is already one of the world' most powerful brands, largely due to the integrity of the *Intel Inside* campaign, the response to the floating point scandal, and the actions and profile of co-founder Andy Grove. Other categories can also benefit. Winemakers and other agricultural producers have already begun to include their growers in their stories. From coffee to skin care ingredients through to cigars, the stories of suppliers add further dimensions to the authenticity of the buyers' brand (as *The Body Shop* has found).

Take cigars. The cigar industry has been dominated by the *Oliva Tobacco Co*, founded by Angel Oliva and now run by his son, John. During the firm's six decades in business they have never signed contracts with their customers, instead preferring the old world handshake deal. Admired for their integrity and honour by their customers, Angel and John are recognized as quality leaders in their field, carefully selecting tobacco from their multiple Central and South American holdings to ensure product consistency for their customers – never sacrificing taste and flavour for aesthetic appeal (as John says, 'I think the people that spend money, that know how to smoke, I don't think they're smoking with their eyes' (Savona 2002, p. 165).

Authenticity can also benefit agricultural cooperatives. *Merino NZ* – the cooperative responsible for marketing New Zealand's high-quality Merino wool crop – has led the industry in terms of product quality, environmental purity, and storytelling, breaking traditional commodity cycles and building sustainable returns for their members. While competitors call for ongoing state support and protections, *Merino NZ* worked closely with its entire chain (including business buyers) to develop new products including *Denimwool* (wool and denim), *Opossumwool*, and *Zealander* (a high-quality wool cloth developed in conjunction with *Loro Piana*). Rather than sell wool in large undifferentiated bales, *Merino NZ* developed technology to accurately test the quality of each fleece. As a result, customers can select wool from particular farmers, parts of the country, or even individual sheep to fit their specific requirements. As well, *Merino NZ* regularly conducts tours of historical sheep stations in New Zealand's high country, strengthening ties between the product, place, and producer. The cooperative's public relations activities have encouraged consumers to select garments labelled (on the inside) with the *Merino NZ* tag.

CONCLUSION

The search for authenticity is an enduring theme in Western thought. The desire for authenticity has now crossed into the brand arena as many consumers look for alternatives to mass-marketed, overly commercialized, and meaningless brands. Authentic brands may stumble, but our fascination with them remains unabated. Even when abused and devalued, their latent equity continues to appeal. Despite appearances, their owners manage these brands very carefully, but often not in accordance with the traditional marketing dictum. Creating an authentic brand represents a challenge to modern marketers and brand managers who revel in their marketing skills, constant updating, customer service, and scientific understanding of the marketplace.

To commercialize, authentic brands must develop open-ended and rich stories rather than mere positioning statements. They must espouse enduring values, become part of the cultural landscape, emphasize their love for the product/service, and develop a powerful organizational memory that acts as a repository for their enduring brand story. Being authentic also requires managing the tension between commercial imperatives and the espoused values of the brand. Authentic brands solve this tension by building powerful images of authenticity while immersing themselves in the marketplace to gain inspiration for innovations. The brands presented here are brands that have lasted the test of time (some trace their lineage back 600 years). Although authenticity takes years to build, starting is actually very simple – all you have to do is be true to yourself – which should be the easiest thing in the world.

BIBLIOGRAPHY

Alessi (1998), *Alessi: The Design Factory*. Academy Editions: London.

Anonymous (2008), 'Gordon Ramsay Heading Down Under', *The Sunday Telegraph*, 23 March. www.news.com.au. Accessed 23 March 2008.

Anonymous (2009), 'Top Toymaker Steered by Children's Drawings', *The Age*, 30 March 30 p. 10.

Arnould, Eric J. and Linda L. Price (1993), 'River Magic: Extraordinary Experience and the Service Encounter', *Journal of Consumer Research*, 20 (June), 24–46.

——. (2000), 'Authenticating Acts and Authoritative Performances: Questing for Self and Community', in *The Why of Consumption: Contemporary Perspectives on Consumer Motives, Goals, and Desires*, ed. S. Ratneshwar, David Glen Mick and Cynthia Huffman, London: Routledge, 140–63.

——. and Craig J. Thompson (2005), Consumer Culture Theory (CCT): Twenty Years of Research', *Journal of Consumer Research*, 31 (March), 868–82.

Barnes, John (1998), *Made in Shepparton: The History of J. Furphy & Sons 1873–1998*. Prominent Press: Shepparton.

Berger, Peter (1973), 'Sincerity and Authenticity in Modern Society', *Public Interest* 31, 81–90.

Belk, Russell W. and Gulnur Tumbat (2005), 'The Cult of Macintosh', *Consumption, Markets & Culture*, 8 (3), 205–17.

Beverland, M. B. (2002), 'A Grounded Model of Organisational Development and Change: Evolution in the Australian and New Zealand Wine Industries', unpublished PhD Thesis, University of South Australia.

——. (2004) 'Wither Haute Couture: Emergent Change and Future Value Creation in Luxury Fashion Markets', *Business Horizons* 47 (2), 63–70.

——. (2005a), 'Crafting Brand Authenticity: The Case of Luxury Wine', *Journal of Management Studies*, 42 (5), 1003–29.

——. (2005b) 'Managing the Design-Innovation Marketing Interface: Resolving the Tension between Artistic Creation and Commercial Imperatives', *Journal of Product Innovation Management*, 22, 193–207.

191

——. (2006), 'The "Real Thing": Branding Authenticity in the Luxury Wine Trade', *Journal of Business Research*, 59 (February), 251–8.

——. (2009), 'Tally Ho, Chocs Away! The Morgan Motoring Experience', in Lindgreen, A., VanHamme, J. and Beverland, M. B. (eds.), *Memorable Customer Experiences*. Gower Press: London.

——. and Michael T. Ewing (2005), 'Slowing the Adoption and Diffusion Process to Enhance Brand Repositioning: The Consumer Driven Repositioning of Dunlop Volley', *Business Horizons*, 48 (October), 385–92.

——. and F. J. Farrelly (2007), 'What Does it Mean to be Design-Led?' *Design Management Review*, 18 (4), 10–17.

——. and F. J. Farrelly 'The Quest For Authenticity In Consumption: Consumers' Purposive Choice Of Authentic Cues To Shape Experienced Outcomes', *Journal of Consumer Research*, in press.

——., F. J. Farrelly, and Pascale Quester 'Authentic Subcultural Membership: Antecedents and Consequences of Authenticating Acts and Authoritative Performances', *Psychology & Marketing*, in review.

——., Adam Lindgreen, and Michiel W. Vink (2008), 'Projecting Authenticity through Advertising: Consumer Judgments of Advertisers' Claims', *Journal of Advertising*, 37 (1), 5–16.

——. and S. Luxton (2005), 'The Projection of Authenticity: Managing Integrated Marketing Communications (IMC) through Strategic Decoupling', *Journal of Advertising*, 34 (4), 103–16.

Boisard, Pierre (2003), *Camembert: A National Myth*. University of California Press: Berkeley, CA.

Booker, Christopher (2004), *The Seven Basic Plots: Why We Tell Stories*. Continuum: London.

Boyle, David (2003), *Authenticity: Brands, Fakes, Spin and the Lust for Real Life*. HarperCollins: London.

Bradley, John (2008), *Cadbury's Purple Reign: The Story Behind Chocolate's Best-Loved Brand*. John Wiley: Chichester, UK.

Brady, Chris and Andrew Lorenz (2005), *End of the Road: The True Story of the Downfall of Rover*. Pearson: Harlow, England.

Branson, Richard (2005), *Losing my Virginity: The Autobiography*. Random House: Sydney.

Brown, Stephen (2003), *Time, Space and the Market: Retroscapes Rising*. M. E Sharpe: London.

—— (2007), 'Harry Potter and the Fandom Menace', in Bernard Cova, Robert V. Kozinets and Avi Sankar (eds), *Consumer Tribes*. Sydney: Elsevier, pp. 177–93.

—— (2008), *Fail Better! Stumbling to Success in Sales & Marketing*. Marshall Cavendish: London.

——, Robert V. Kozinets, and John F. Sherry Jr. (2003), 'Teaching Old Brands New Tricks: Retro Branding and the Revival of Brand Meaning', *Journal of Marketing*, 67 (July), 19–33.

Burr, Chandler (2002), *The Emperor of Scent*. Arrow Brown Books: London.

Butterfield, Leslie (2005), *Enduring Passion: The Story of the Mercedes-Benz Brand*. John Wiley: Chichester, England.

Campbell, Colin (2005), *The Romantic Ethic and the Spirit of Modern Consumerism*. Blackwell: England.

Cappannelli, G. A., & Cappannelli, S. (2004), *Authenticity: Simple Strategies for Greater Meaning and Purpose at Work and at Home*. Emmis Books: New York.

Carruthers, Iain (2007), *The Domestic Engineer: How Dyson Changed the Meaning of Cleaning*. Cyan: London.

Caves, Richard E. (2000), *Creative Industries: Contracts between Art and Commerce*. Harvard University Press: Cambridge, MA.

Chalmers, Tandy D. (2007), 'Advertising Authenticity: Resonating Replications of Real Life', *European Advances in Consumer Research*, 8, 442–3.

——. and Linda L. Price (2009), 'Perceptions of Authenticity in Advertisements: Negotiating The Inauthentic', *Advances in Consumer Research Volume 36*, in press.

Charles-Roux, Edmonde (1995), *Chanel*. Harvill Press: London.

Christensen, Clayton M. (1997), *The Innovator's Dilemma: When New Technologies Cause Great Firms to Fail*. Harvard Business School Press: Cambridge, MA.

Collins, Jim and Jerry I. Porras (2004), *Built to Last: Successful Habits of Visionary Companies*. Collins Business: Sydney.

Courtney, Karl (2008), 'Adidas: Walk this Way', *Marketing*, August, 18–24.

Dapin, Mark (2008), 'Nightmare on Ramsay Street', *Good Weekend*, 31 May 26–32.

Davies, Keith (2004), *Defying Gravity: The Fisher & Paykel Story*. David Ling Publishing: Auckland.

Deighton, John. (2003), *Snapple*. Harvard Business School Case 9-599-126.

Dent, Jackie (2003), 'Brand Britain', *The Australian Financial Review Magazine*, 54–8.

Dickinson, Sonia J., Michael Beverland, and Adam Lindgreen 'Building Corporate Reputation with Stakeholders: Exploring the Role of Message Ambiguity for Social Marketers', *European Journal of Marketing*, in press.

Drummond, Scott (2008), 'You Don't Know Jack', *Marketing*, September, 16–22.

Dyson, James (2002), *Against the Odds*. Orion: New York.

Ebenkamp, Becky (2008), 'Cracker Barrel Freshens Old Country Experience', *Brandweek*, 8 December, 13.

Eisenstein, Paul A. (2002), 'The Raging Bull', *Cigar Aficionado*, August, 96–103.

Faith, Nicholas (1988), *Chateau Margaux*. Vendome Press: New York.

Farmer, Lyn (2005/2006), 'Revealing Champagne's Mystique', *Wine News*, Dec/Jan, 34–9.

Fine, Gary A. (2004), *Everyday Genius: Self-Taught Art and the Culture of Authenticity*. Chicago, IL: University of Chicago Press.

Firat, Fuat and Nikhilesh Dholakia (1998), *Consuming People: From Political Economy to Theaters of Consumption*. London: Routledge.

Flavell, Kylie (2008a), 'Only the Lonely', *Marketing*, October, 16–27.

—— (2009), 'Kiss and Make Up', *Marketing*, March, 8.

Fog, Klaus, Christian Budtz, and Baris Yakaboylu (2005), *Storytelling: Branding in Practice*. Springer: Copenhagen.

Forden, Sara (2001), *The House of Gucci: A Sensational Story of Murder, Madness, Glamour, and Greed*. Perrenial Currents, New York.

Foulkes, Nick (2005), *Dunhill by Design: A Very English History*. Flammarion: Paris.

Fournier, Susan (1998), 'Consumers and Their Brands: Developing Relationship Theory in Consumer Research', *Journal of Consumer Research*, 24 (March), 343–73.

—— (2001), *Pokemon™: Gotta Catch 'Em All*. Harvard Business School Case 9-501-017.

Fox, Catherine (006), 'Designer Marketing: Multi-Tasking', *Boss Magazine*, February, 10.

Friedman, Thomas L. (2000), *The Lexus and the Olive Tree*. Farrar, Straus and Giroux: New York.

Fullerton, Ronald A. (1988), 'How Modern is Modern Marketing? Marketing's Evolution and the Myth of the Production Era', *Journal of Marketing*, 52 (1), 108–26.

Gallagher, Leigh (2002), 'Tiffany for All', *BRW*, 18–23 April, 48.

Giddens, A. (1991), *Modernity and Self-Identity: Self and Society in the Late Modern Age*. Stanford University Press: Stanford, CA.

Gilmore, James H. and B. Joseph Pine (2007), *What Consumers Really Want: Authenticity*. Harvard Business School Press: Cambridge, MA.

Gladwell, Malcolm (2002), *The Tipping Point: How Little Things Can Make a Big Difference*. Back Bay Books: New York.

—— (2008), *Outliers: The Story of Success*. Little Brown and Co: New York.

Goffman, Erving (1959), *The Presentation of Self in Everyday Life*. Hammondsworth: Penguin.

Gorman, Leon (2006), *L. L. Bean: The Making of an American Icon*. Harvard Business School Press: Cambridge, MA.

Grandey, Alicia A., Glenda M. Fisk, Anna S. Mattila, Karen J. Jansen, and Lori A. Sideman (2005), 'Is "Service with a Smile" Enough? Authenticity of Positive Displays during Service Encounters', *Organizational Behavior and Human Decision Processes*, 96 (1), 38–55.

Grayson, Kent and Radan Martinec (2004), 'Consumer Perceptions of Iconicity and Indexicality and their Influence on Assessments of Authentic Market Offerings', *Journal of Consumer Research*, 31 (September), 296–312.

—— and David Schulman (2000), 'Indexicality and the Verification Function of Irreplaceable Possessions: a Semiotic Analysis', *Journal of Consumer Research*, 27 (June), 17–30.

Gross, Michael (2003), *Genuine Authentic: The Real Life of Ralph Lauren*. HarperCollinsPublishers: New York.

Grossman, Lev (2005), 'How Apple Does It', *Time*, October 24, 38–42.

Hackett, A. J. and Winston Aldworth (2006), *Jump Start: The Autobiography*. Random House: Auckland, NZ.

Hall, James (2004), 'Reinventing the Real', *Inside Marketing*, May, 42–5.

Hanna, Tim (2003), *John Britten*. Craig Potton Publishing: Nelson, NZ.

Harden, Michael (2006), *Of a Nation: Nestle Peters*. Hardie Grant Books: Melbourne.

Hatch, Brad (2006), 'The Best Advice I Ever Had', *Boss Magazine*, February, 16.

Hatch, Mary Jo and Majken Schultz (2008), *Taking Brand Initiative: How Companies Can Align Strategy, Culture, and Identity Through Corporate Branding*. Jossey-Bass: San Francisco, CA.

Hein, Kenneth (2009), 'Free Giveaways Come at a Cost', *Brandweek*, March 9, 30.

Henley, John and Jeevan Vasagar (2003), 'Think Muslim, Drink Muslim, Says New Rival to Coke', *Guardian*, 8 January.

Hertzfeld, Andy (2005), *Revolution in the Valley: The Insanely Great Story of How the Mac was Made*. O'Reilly Media: Sebastopol, CA.

Hollister, Geoff (2008), *Out of Nowhere: The Inside Story of How Nike Marketed the Culture of Running*. Meyer and Meyer Sport: Maidenhead, UK.

Holt, Douglas B. (2002), 'Why Do Brands Cause Trouble? A Dialectical Theory of Consumer Culture', *Journal of Consumer Research*, 29 (1), 70–91.

——. (2004), *How Brands Become Icons*. Harvard Business School Press: Cambridge, MA.

——. (2005), 'How Societies Desire Brands: Using Cultural Theory to Explain Brand Symbolism', in S. Ratneshwar and David Glenn Mick (eds), Routledge: London, 272–91.

Hume, Marion. (2004), 'Radical Chic', *The Australian Financial Review Magazine*, 36–40.

Irwin, Colin (2005), *In Search of Albion: From Cornwall to Cumbria: A Ride Through England's Hidden Soul*. London: Carlton.

Irwin, Terri (2005), *My Steve*. Simon and Schuster: Sydney.

Jackson, Tim (1998), *Inside Intel: Andy Grove and the Rise of the World's Most Powerful Chip Company*. Plume: New York.

Jarratt, Phil (2006), *The Mountain and the Wave: The Quiksilver Story*. Quiksilver Entertainment: Huntingdon Beach, CA.

Jefford, Andrew (2002), *The New France: A Complete Guide to Contemporary French Wine*. Mitchell Beazley: London.

Jobs, Steve (2005), 'You've Got to Find What You Love', *Stanford Report*, 14 June, retrieved 5 March 2008.

Jones, Deborah and Karen Smith (2005), 'Middle-Earth meets New Zealand: Authenticity and Location in the Making of *The Lord of the Rings*', *Journal of Management Studies*, 42 (5), 923–46.

Joplin, Norman, John T. Waterworth, and Philip Dean (2008), *Britains New Toy Soldiers 1973 to Present: Traditional Gloss Painted Models*. Schiffer Publishing: Atglen, PA.

Kahney, Leander (2004a), *The Cult of Mac*. No Starch Press: San Francisco, CA.

—— (2004b), 'Techno Fetishism', *Macworld*, 68–76.

—— (2008), 'Evil Genius', *Wired*, April, 136–43.

Kates, Steven M. (2002), 'The Protean Quality of Subcultural Consumption: An Ethnographic Account of Gay Consumers', *Journal of Consumer Research*, 29 (3): 383–400.

——. (2004), 'The Dynamics of Brand Legitimacy: An Interpretive Study in the Gay Men's Community', *Journal of Consumer Research*, 31 (September), 455–64.

Kazanjian, Kirk and Amy Joyner (2004), *Making Dough: The 12 Secret Ingredients of Krispy Kreme's Sweet Success*. John Wiley & Sons: Hoboken, NJ.

Keller, Kevin-Lane (1999), 'Managing Brands for the Long Run: Brand Reinforcement and Revitalization Strategies', *California Management Review*, 41 (3), 102–24.

—— (2003), *Strategic Brand Management: Building, Measuring, and Managing Brand Equity*. Prentice Hall: Sydney.

Kelley, Gordon (2008), 'Motorola Phones Sales Crash 38 Per Cent', Trusted Reviews, 24 January, http://www.trustedreviews.com/mobile-phones/news/2008/01/24/Motorola-Phones-Sales-Crash-38-Per-Cent/p1. Accessed 20th April 2009.

Kemp-Robertson, Paul (2008), 'New Marketing Landscapes', *Viewpoint*, 23, 106–17.

Kendall, Kate (2009), 'From Infinity to Divinity', *Marketing*, March, 16–25.

Kiley, David (2004), *Driven: Inside BMW: The Most Admired Car Company in the World*. Wiley: Hoboken, NJ.

Klein, Naomi (2000), *No Logo: Taking Aim at Brand Bullies*. Picador: New York.

Kotchka, Claudia (2006), 'The Design Imperative in Consumer Goods', *Design Management Review*, 17 (1), 10–14.

Kozinets, Robert V. (2001), 'Utopian Enterprise: Articulating the Meanings of *Star Trek*'s Culture of Consumption', *Journal of Consumer Research*, 28 (June), 67–88.

Krass, Peter (2004), *Blood & Whiskey: the Life and Times of Jack Daniel*. Wiley: Hoboken, NJ.

Laban, Brian (2000), *Morgan: First and Last of the Real Sports Cars*. Virgin Publishing: London.

Lane, Anthony (2007), 'Candid Camera', *The New Yorker*, September 24, 165–72.

Levitt, Theodore (1983), 'The Globalization of Markets', *Harvard Business Review*, May–June, 2–11.

Levy, Steven (2000), *Insanely Great: The Life and Times of Macintosh, the Computer that Changed Everything*. New York: Penguin Books.

MacCannell, D. (1976), *The Visitor: A New Theory of the Leisure Class*. Schoken Books: New York.

MacManus, Richard (2006), 'TradeMe: Big Fish in a Small Pond', *ReadWriteWeb*, 21 August. www.readwriteweb.com/archives/trademe_big_fish_small_pond.php. Accessed 22 April 2009.

Mack, Ann M. (2009), 'Betting on the Uncertain', *Brandweek*, 5 January, 10.

Markham, D. (1998), *1855: A History of the Bordeaux Classification*. Wiley: New York.

Mathews, Ryan and Watts Wacker (2008), *What's Your Story? Storytelling to Move Markets, Audiences, People, and Brands*. FT Press: Upper Saddle River, NJ.

McAlexander, James H. John W Schouten, Harold F Koening. (2002), 'Building Brand Community', *Journal of Marketing*, 66 (1): pp. 38–55.

McCallion, Steve (2004), 'Design and Economic Development at Umpqua Bank: An Interview with Ray Davis', *Design Management Review*, 15 (4), 21–8.

McCloy, Nicola (2008), *Made in New Zealand: Stories of Iconic Kiwi Brands*. Random House: Auckland, NZ.

McCracken, Grant (2005), *Culture and Consumption II, Markets, Meaning, and Brand Management*. Indiana University Press: Indiana.

McDade, William (2009), 'Collector's Story', *Toy Soldier & Model Figure*, 129, 24–9.

McDowell, Colin (2000), *Manolo Blahnik*. Cassell & Co: London.

McSpedden, Bani (2005), 'The Complications', *The Australian Financial Review Magazine*, September, 68–72.

—— (2008), 'Among the Chosen: The Japanese Watch gets Emotional', *The AFR Magazine*, 30.

Meabon, Linda L. (2003), *Zippo Manufacturing Company*. Arcadia: Charleston, SC.

Meagher, David (2005), 'Room at the Top', *The Australian Financial Review Magazine*, September, 66–7.

—— (2008), 'So You Think You Can Swear', *The Weekend Australian Magazine*, May 17–18, 24–8.

Miller, Daniel (2008), *The Comfort of Things*. Polity, Cambridge, UK.

Milligan, Andy and Shaun Smith (2002), *Uncommon Practice: People Who Deliver a Great Brand Experience*. Pearson: London.

Moon, Youngme (2003), *In-N-Out Burger*, Harvard Business School Case 9-503-096.

Morris, Evan (2004), *From Altoids to Zima: The Surprising Stories Behind 125 Famous Brand Names*. Fireside: New York.

Muñiz, Albert M Jr and Hope Jensen Schau (2005), 'Religiosity in the Abandoned Apple Newton Community', *Journal of Consumer Research*, 31 (4); 737–48.

Napoli, Julie, Sonia J. Dickinson, Michael B. Beverland and Francis J. Farrelly, 'Keeping it Real: Measuring Consumer-Based Brand Authenticity', *Journal of Consumer Psychology*, in review.

Nathan, John (2001), *Sony*. Mariner Books: New York.

Neumeier, Marty (2003), *The Brand Gap*. New Riders: Boston, MA.

Oldenburg, Ray (1989), *The Great Good Place: Cafes, Coffee Shops, Community Centers, Beauty Parlors, General Stores, Bars, Hangouts, and How They Get You Through the Day*. Paragon House: New York.

Olney, Richard (1991), *Romanee-Conti: The World's Most Fabled Wine*. Flammarion: Paris.

—— (2008), *Yquem*. Flammarion: Paris.

Palepu, Krishna G. and Vishnu Srinivasan (2007), *Tata Motors: The Tata Ace*. Harvard Business School Case 9-108-011.

Pasi, Alessandro (2003), *Leica: Witness to a Century*. W. W. Norton & Co: New York.

Pasols, Paul-GéRard (2005), *Louis Vuitton: The Birth of Modern Luxury*. Harry N. Adams Inc: New York.

Patton, Phil (2002), *Bug: The Strange Mutations of the World's Most Famous Automobile*. Da Capo Press: Cambridge, MA.

Pendergast, Mark (2000), *For God, Country & Coca-Cola: The Definitive History of the World's Most Popular Drink*. Thomson: New York.

Peters, Tom (1994), *The Pursuit of WOW! Every Person's Guide to Topsy-Turvy Times*. New York: Random House.

Peterson, Hal (2007), *Chucks! The Phenomenon of Converse Chuck Taylor All Stars*. Skyhorse Publishing.

Piaggio & C. S.p.A. (2003), *Vespa*. Scriptum Editions: London.

Postrel, Virginia (2003), *The Substance of Style: How the Rise of Aesthetic Value is Remaking Commerce, Culture, & Consciousness*. New York: HarperCollins.

Pridmore, Jay and Jim Hurd (2001), *Schwinn Bicycles*. MBI Publishing: St Paul MN.

Principals-Synovate (2008), *2008 Authentic Brand Index Study*. Melbourne, Australia.

Putnam, Robert D. (2001), *Bowling Alone: The Collapse and Revival of American Community*. New York: Simon and Schuster.

Ragas, Matthew W. and Bueno, Bolivar J. (2002), *The Power of Cult Branding: How 9 Magnetic Brands Turned Customers into Loyal Followers (and Yours Can, Too!)*. Prima Publishing, Roseville, CA.

Rahoi-Gilchrest, Rita (2007), 'The 42 Below Story', *International Journal of Communication*, July–Dec.

Rand, Ayn (1994 [1943]), *The Fountainhead*, Bobbs-Merrill: New York.

Ries, Al and Jack Trout (2000), *Positioning: The Battle for Your Mind, 20th Anniversary Edition*. McGraw-Hill: New York.

Ritson, Mark (2007), 'Aussie Wineries Guilty of French Folly', *Marketing*, 5 December, 23.

Roach, Martin (1999), *Dr Martins*. AirWair: London.

Roberts, Lisa S. (2006), *Antiques of the Future*. Stewart, Tabori and Chang: New York.

Roddick, Anita (2005), *Business as Unusual*. Anita Roddick Books: West Sussex.

Rose, Randal L. and Stacy L. Wood (2005), 'Paradox and the Consumption of Authenticity through Reality Television', *Journal of Consumer Research*, 32 (September), 284–96.

Rosica, Christopher (2007), *The Authentic Brand: How Today's Top Entrepreneurs Connect with Customers*. Noble Press: Paramus, NJ.

Rubython, Tom (2002), 'Passionate Man, Passionate Brand', *Eurobusiness*, July, 46–9.

Savona, David (2002), 'Passing the Torch', *Cigar Aficionado*, August, 163–8.

Schmitt, Bernd H. Rogers, David, L. and Vrotsos, Karen (2004), *There's No Business That's Not Show Business: Marketing in an Experience Culture*. Prentice Hall: Upper Saddle River, NJ.

Schouten, John W. and James H. McAlexander (1995), 'Subcultures of Consumption: An Ethnography of New Bikers', *Journal of Consumer Research*, 22 (1), 43–61.

Scott, Phil (2003), 'Hog Wild', *Cigar Aficionado*, August, 116–25.

Sennett, Richard (2008), *The Craftsman*. Allen Lane: London.

Shaw, Philip (2006), 'Philip Shaw', *Dumbo Feather, Pass it On*, 8, 32–47.

Sibley, Brian (2006), *Peter Jackson: A Film-Maker's Journey*. HarperCollinsPublishers: Auckland.

Simmons, John (2006), *Innocent: Building a Brand from Nothing but Fruit*. Cyan: London.

Sisodia, Rajendra S., David B. Wolfe, Jagdish N. Sheth (2007), *Firms of Endearment: How World-Class Companies Profit from Passion and Purpose*. Wharton School Publishing: Philadelphia, PA.

Smith, Catherine (2008), 'Real Leaders', *Idealog*, 17 (Sept–Oct), 133.

Specter, Michael (2004), 'The Designer', *The New Yorker*, March 15, 104–15.

Spenceley, Nick (2009), 'The Delhi Durbar', *The Standard*, February, 6–9.

Stafford, Patrick (2009), 'Backlash forces Facebook to Back Down on Terms-Of-Use Changes', *Smart Company*, 20 February.

Stebbins, Robert A. (2007), *Serious Leisure: A Perspective for Our Time*. Transaction: New Brunswick, NJ.

Sudjic, Deyan (2008), *The Language of Things*. Penguin Books: London.

Taylor, David J. (2007), *Never Mind the Sizzle, Where's the Sausage? Branding Based on Substance Not Spin*. Wiley: Chichester, UK.

Terrio, Susan J. (2000), *Crafting the Culture and History of French Chocolate*. University of California Press: Berkeley, CA.

Thompson, Craig J. (1997), 'Interpreting Consumers: A Hermeneutical Framework for Deriving Marketing Insights from the Texts of Consumers' Consumption Stories', *Journal of Marketing Research*, 34 (November), 438–55.

Thompson, Craig J., Aric Rindfleisch and Zeynep Arsel (2006), 'Emotional Branding and the Strategic Value of the Doppelgänger Brand Image', *Journal of Marketing*, 70 (1), 50–64.

Tischler, Linda (2006/2007), 'Fast Talk: Karen Walker', *Fast Company*, Dec/Jan, 38–9.

Tonello, Michael (2008), *Bringing Home the Birkin: My Life in Hot Pursuit of the World's Most Coveted Handbag*. William Morrow: New York.

Tupperware (2005), *Tupperware: Transparent*. Stichting Kunstboek bvba: Oostkamp, Belgim.

Turner, Brook (2004), 'A Woman of Influence', *The Australian Financial Review Magazine*, 14–19.

Twitchell, James B. (2004), *Branded Nation: The Marketing of Megachurch, College Inc., and Museumworld*. Simon and Schuster: New York.

Vargo, Stephen L., and Robert F. Lusch (2004), 'Evolving to a New Dominant Logic for Marketing', *Journal of Marketing*, 68 (1), 1–17.

Vinjamuri, David (2008), *Accidental Branding: How Ordinary People Build Extraordinary Brands*. Wiley: Hoboken, NJ.

Wathieu, Luc, Gao Wang and Medha Samant (2007), *Li Ning – Anything is Possible*, Harvard Business School Case Study 9-507-024.

Ward, Arthur (2003), *Airfix: Celebrating 50 Years of the Greatest Plastic Kits in the World*. HarperCollinsPublishers: London.

Wetlaufer, Suzy (2001), 'The Perfect Paradox of Star Brands: An Interview with Bernard Arnault of LVMH', *Harvard Business Review*, October, 116–23.

Wikipedia (2008), 'Amateur', http://en.wikipedia.org/wiki/Amateur, accessed 15 March.

Williams, Richard (2001), *Enzo Ferrari: A Life*. Yellow Jersey Press: London.

Wipperfürth, A. (2005), *Brand Hijack: Marketing Without Marketing*. London: Portfolio.

Wozniak, Steve and Gina Smith (2006), *iWoz: Computer Geek to Cult Icon*. Headline Review: London.

Wright, Karen (2006), *The Road to Dr Pepper, Texas: The Story of Dublin Dr Pepper*. McMurray University: Abilene, TX.

Young, Jeffrey S. and William L. Simon (2005), *iCon: Steve Jobs The Greatest Second Act in the History of Business*. Wiley: Hoboken, NJ.

AUTHOR INDEX

A

Alessi 88, 116,
Aldworth, Winston 78
Anonymous 131, 159, 168
Arnould, Eric J. 16, 22, 23, 33, 59, 82,
    144, 155
Arsel, Zeynep 4, 20, 26, 32

B

Barnes John 54
Berger, Peter 17
Belk, Russell W. 20, 34, 98
Beverland, Michael B. 3, 5, 14, 16,
    17, 19, 20, 21, 25, 26, 27, 37, 48,
    49, 50, 52, 53, 54, 55, 56, 57, 58,
    67, 69, 70, 72, 73,74, 81, 82, 87,
    93, 94, 99, 101, 109, 116, 118,
    120, 121, 123, 124, 130, 144,
    146, 147, 156, 164, 170, 172,
    178, 179
Boisard, Pierre 146
Booker, Christopher 33, 37
Boyle, David 22
Bradley, John 163, 169
Brady, Chris 88
Branson, Richard 47, 96, 132
Brown, Stephen 22, 58, 100, 108,
    121, 122
Budtz, Christian 37, 44
Bueno, Bollivar J. 100
Burr, Chandler 117
Butterfield, Leslie 57

C

Campbell, Colin 69
Cappannelli, G. A. 15
Cappannelli, S. 15
Carruthers, Iain 133, 73, 47
Caves, Richard E. 50, 183
Chalmers, Tandy D. 25
Charles-Roux, Edmonde 48
Christensen, Clayton M. 73, 123
Collins, Jim 179
Courtney, Karl 3
C. S.p.A. 77, 88, 147

D

Dapin, Mark 106, 159, 173
Davies, Keith 130
Dean, Philip 99, 137
Deighton, John 13, 19, 47
Dent, Jackie 31, 72, 88
Dholakia, Nikhilesh 22
Dickinson, Sonia J. 3, 26, 56,
    69, 74, 94
Drummond, Scott 3, 85,
    141, 175
Dyson, James 45, 47, 105,
    133, 146

E

Ebenkamp, Becky 66
Eisenstein, Paul A. 69, 118
Ewing, Michael T. 14, 19, 54, 147

F

Faith, Nicholas 41, 57
Farmer, Lyn 29, 116
Farrelly, Francis J. 3, 5, 16, 17, 20, 21, 25, 26, 50, 57, 69, 74, 82, 94, 101, 108, 120, 121, 124, 144, 156, 164, 172
Fine, Gary A. 16, 73, 124
Firat, Fuat 22
Fisk, Glenda M. 16
Flavell, Kylie 72, 78, 186
Fog, Klaus 37, 44
Forden, Sara 51
Foulkes, Nick 52, 151
Fournier, Susan 55, 59
Fox, Catherine 128
Friedman, Thomas L. 101
Fullerton, Ronald A. 107

G

Gallagher, Leigh 109
Giddens, A. 33
Gilmore, James H. 26, 37
Gladwell, Malcolm 104, 105, 150
Goffman, Erving 34
Gorman, Leon 42, 101
Grandey, Alicia A. 16
Grayson, Kent 16, 22, 82
Gross, Michael 53, 65, 90
Grossman, Lev 112, 167

H

Hackett, A. J. 78
Hall, James 13, 77, 185
Hanna, Tim 80
Harden, Michael 163, 166
Hatch, Brad 122
Hatch, Mary Jo 170
Hein, Kenneth 183
Henley, John 5
Hertzfeld, Andy 57
Hollister, Geoff 126
Holt, Douglas B. 4, 5, 17, 18, 141, 179

Hume, Marion 67, 69, 76, 90, 166, 168, 170
Hurd, Jim 94, 110

I

Irwin, Colin 55
Irwin, Terri 107, 110

J

Jackson, Tim 175
Jansen, Karen J. 16
Jarratt, Phil
Jefford, Andrew 97
Jobs, Steve
Jones, Deborah 59
Joplin, Norman 99, 137
Joyner, Amy 97, 148, 47, 92

K

Kahney, Leander 20, 108, 185
Kates, Steven M. 19, 155, 156
Kazanjian, Kirk 47, 92, 97, 148
Keller, Kevin-Lane 17
Kelley, Gordon 76
Kemp-Robertson, Paul 188
Kendell, Kate 78, 90, 103, 135, 163
Kiley, David 57, 77
Klein, Naomi 5
Koening, Harold F. 155
Kotchka, Claudia 63
Kozinets, Robert V. 58, 100
Krass, Peter 41, 57, 93

L

Laban, Brian 2, 47, 81, 99, 171
Lane, Anthony 52, 53, 137
Levitt, Theodore 4
Levy, Steven 47, 65, 70, 77
Lindgreen, Adam 25, 26, 27, 52, 56, 69, 73, 99, 146, 178
Lorenz, Andrew 88

Lusch, Robert F. 107
Luxton, S. 27, 87, 179

M

MacCannell, D. 17, 110, 111
MacManus, Richard 142
Mack, Ann M. 177
Markham, D. 15
Martinec, Radan 16, 82
Matthews, Ryan 76
Mattila, Anna S. 16
McAlexander, James H. 18, 155
McCallion, Steve 82, 119
McCloy, Nicola 147
McCracken, Grant 22
McDade, William 44
McDowell, Colin 64, 71, 93
McSpedden, Bani 119
Meabon, Linda L. 10
Meagher, David 161, 168, 172
Miller, Daniel 22
Milligan, Andy 166
Moon, Youngme 56, 80, 187
Morris, Evan 63
Muniz Jr., Albert M. 60

N

Napoli, Julie 3, 26, 69, 74, 94
Nathan, John 37, 130
Neumeier, Marty 35, 169, 177

O

Oldenburg, Ray 22
Olney, Richard 98, 148

P

Palepu, Krishna G. 123, 151
Pasi, Allessandro 137, 151
Pasols, Paul-Gerard 93, 163
Patton, Phil 153
Pendergast, Mark 4
Peters, Tom 122

Peterson, Hal 13, 22, 24, 92, 151
Piaggio, 77 88, 147
Pine, B. Joseph 26, 37
Porras, Jerry I. 179
Postrel, Virginia 15, 16, 20, 33, 51, 119
Price, Linda L. 16, 22, 23, 25, 33, 59,
    82, 144
Pridmore, Jay 94, 110
Principals-Synovate 4
Putnam, Robert D. 55

Q

Quester, Pascale 21, 50, 57, 101,
    156,172

R

Ragas, Matthew W. 100
Rahoi-Gilchrest, Rita 79
Rand, Ayn 103
Ries, Al 179
Rindfleisch, Aric 4, 20, 26, 32
Ritson, Mark 68, 88, 169
Roach, Martin 180
Roberts, Lisa S. 129
Roddick, Anita 29, 45, 56, 96, 118,
    127, 131, 134, 161, 162, 169, 170,
    172, 178
Rogers, David L. 157
Rose, Randall L. 16, 17
Rosica, Christopher 40, 107, 147,
    171, 177
Rubython, Tom 112

S

Samant, Medha 128
Savona, David 189
Schau, Hope Jensen 60
Schmitt, Bernd H. 157
Schouten, John W. 18, 155
Schulman, David 22
Schultz, Majken 170
Scott, Phil 18, 23, 25, 92
Sennett, Richard 67, 132

Shaw, Philip 92
Sherry Jr., John F. 58, 100
Sheth, Jagdish N. 33
Sibley, Brian 35, 113
Sideman, Lori A. 16
Simmons, John 78
Simon, William L. 41
Sisodia, Rajendra S. 33
Smith, Catherine 159, 166
Smith, Gina 41
Smith, Karen 59
Smith, Shaun 166
Specter, Michael 123
Spenceley, Nick 115
Srinivasan, Vishnu 123, 151
Stafford, Patrick 35
Stebbins, Robert A. 67, 74, 79
Sudjic, Deyan 22

T

Taylor, David J. 126
Terrio, Susan J. 146
Thompson, Craig J. 4, 5, 20, 26, 32, 155
Tischler, Linda 74
Tonello, Michael 73, 108
Trout, Jack 179
Tumbat, Gulnur 20, 34, 98
Tupperware 22, 90, 126
Turner, Brook 115, 130
Twitchell, James 24

V

Vargo, Stephen L. 107
Vasagar, Jeevan 5
Vinjamuri, David 65
Vink, Michiel W. 25, 26, 27, 52, 69, 74, 99, 146, 178
Vrotsos, Karen 157

W

Wacker, Watts 76
Wang, Gao 128
Ward, Arthur 71
Waterworth, John T. 99, 137
Wathieu, Luc 128
Wetlaufer, Suzy 122, 128
Wikipedia 66
Williams, Richard 57
Wipperfürth, A. 34, 87
Wolfe, David B. 33
Wood, Stacy L. 16, 17
Wozniak, Steve 41
Wright, Karen 68, 90

Y

Yakaboylu, Baris 37, 44
Young, Jeffrey S. 41

BRAND INDEX

#

3M 76, 176
42 Below 78, 79,143,153,154
66 Degrees North 57, 148

A

Absolut 19, 20, 51, 56, 155
Adbusters 20
A Christmas Tale 96
Adidas 3, 14, 80,128
Aero 43
Aero 8, 80, 91, 95
Aero 8 Club, 55, 119, 144, 145
Aeromax 43, 91, 95, 180
Airfix 70
Air New Zealand 95
Ajax 32,44
Alessi 88, 135
Alien 44, 128
Altoids 2, 60, 63,64,65,78,117
American Machine and Foundry
  Company 91
Ansett 95, 96
Antipodes 57,148
A Perfect Mind 44
Apple 2, 16, 20, 24, 33, 34, 36,
  40, 41, 46, 47, 49, 50, 51, 55,
  57, 70, 77, 78, 80, 97, 98, 106,
  107,108,109, 112, 113, 115, 116,
  121, 122, 124, 138, 139, 145, 149,
  150, 160, 168, 180, 185, 188
Apple 1, 40, 41, 50
Apple Newton 60
Armani 23

Art of Shaving 65, 180
Aston Martin DB5, 106
Atari 41
Atlas Bicycles 163
Audi 145
Audio Technica AT-727 Sound
  Burger 124

B

Bacardi 79
Bally 185
Barbie 20
Battlestar Galactica 59
BBC's Troubleshooter 171
Beauty Engineered Forever (B.E.E.), 82
Bee Movie 178
Belgian Trappist Monasteries 25
Beyond Petroleum 5
Big 120
Billabong 74, 171
Birkin 73, 106, 108, 166, 180
Black Phantom 94
Bloomingdales 112
BMW 49, 55, 57, 60, 77, 88, 145,
  146, 170, 180
Borders 24
Boston Consulting Group 82
Boy Scout 19
Brandweek 177
Bringing Home the Birkin 73
British Petroleum (BP) 5
Britten V1000, 80, 106
Bruichladdich 29, 30, 31, 32, 36, 42,
  78, 94, 139, 164, 171, 180, 188
Bugatti 23

Burberry 53, 180
Burton 24, 48, 54, 55
Burt's Bees 65, 40, 147, 177
Buzzy Bee 154

C

Cadbury 52, 145, 149, 162, 163, 164,
    165, 168, 169
Campagnolo 50
Camper 77, 185
Cartier 152
Celtic Nations 31, 36
Chanel 23, 26, 48, 51, 106, 117,
    122, 149
Chanel No. 5 48
Chanel No. 19 117
Champagne Bollinger 27, 69, 97,
    108, 109
Champagne Krug 42, 69, 73, 94, 106,
    108, 109, 172, 180
Chateau d'Yquem 98, 188
Chateau Margaux 26, 41, 42, 57, 67,
    72, 81, 106, 116, 117, 118, 122,
    139, 141, 142, 143, 148, 180
Chateau Mouton Rothschild 149
Chateau Musar 126
Chimay 56, 94,101
Chivas Regal 94
Christian Dior 88, 168
Chronicles of Narnia 26
Chrysler 1, 2, 80
Chuck Taylor 22, 24, 87, 92, 186
Chuck Taylor's All Stars 106
Churchill's 116
Click Clack 129, 134
Click Clack's Airtight Canister 129
Cloudy Bay 136
Coca Cola 4, 34, 97, 179
Cockburn's 116, 170
Coke 51, 52, 179
Columbia Sportswear 65
Commodore 150
Converse 92
Converse White High Top Chuck
    Taylor 22
Cooper's Brewery 43, 101

Coors 19, 156
Corona 18, 179
Countach 54, 118
Cracker Barrel 65
Crayola 60

D

Dare 126
Denimwool 190
Deutz 116 170
Dilmah Tea 57, 74, 75, 148, 164,
    165, 180
Disney 15
Dog Town and Z-Boys 156
Domaine Romanee Conti 148
Dom Perignon 188
Done the Impossible: The Fans' Tale of
    Firefly & Serenity 46
Dove, 187
Dr Grordbort's Rayguns 138
Dr Martens 180
Dr Pepper 58, 68, 89, 183, 184
Dr Who 186
Dublin Dr Pepper 58, 60, 68, 89, 90,
    94, 99, 109
Dummies Manuals 150
Dunhill 52, 53, 139, 150, 151, 180
Dunlop Volley 14, 19, 28, 54, 56, 58,
    74, 75, 80, 147, 154, 155,
    182, 186
Dyson 2, 26, 47(22), 70, 73, 109,
    169, 180
Dyson Airblade 116, 133, 134
Dyson Contrarotator 47, 116, 132, 133
Dyson Dual Cyclone
    22,45,47,105,106, 116 118, 180

E

Eardrops 175, 176
Edmonds 147
Edmond's Cookbook 147
Eames 15
Easy Rider 19, 32
eBay 63, 73, 142, 143

elBulli 49
Emma and Toms 108
Enron 97, 102
Escarpment 114

F

Facebook 20, 23, 34, 35, 143, 169
Fairfax 143
FAO Schwarz 120
Farscape 46, 59
Fellowship of the Ring 113
Ferrari 42, 57, 145
Fiat 1
Fiat 500, 16
Firefly 46, 59
First Gear 99
Fisher and Paykel 60, 169
Fisher and Paykel Dish Drawer 130
Flirtation 31, 36, 188
Ford 1, 2, 69, 80
Ford Edsel 121
Fortnum and Mason 60
Fortune 163
Fosters 44, 85, 86, 95

G

General Motors 1, 2, 102
Giaconda 130
Google 78, 90, 103, 135,
    163, 169
Google Image 187
Google News 135
Grange 85, 86(10), 87 , 92, 95,
    168, 179
Great Bear 165
Great George 165
Great Harry 165
Gucci, 42, 51, 94

H

Hahn 185
Hamley's 120

Handmade 95
Handmade 2, 95
Hard Yakka 57
Harley Davidson 2, 18, 19, 23, 24,
    32, 46, 52, 55, 91, 138, 145,
    179, 187
Harry Potter 58, 121
Harvard Business Review 2
Heritage Foundation 156
Hermes 51, 52, 60, 67, 69, 73, 76, 90,
    122, 152, 160, 161, 165, 166, 168,
    170, 185
Hermes Birkin Bag 73, 106, 108,
    166, 180
Hershey 52, 162
Honda 42, 119, 147
Honest Charlie's 108
Hushpuppies 75

I

Icebreaker 57, 148
IDEO 169
Iliad 33
iMac 47, 50, 77
Imperial Productions 70, 94
ING 80
Innocent 78, 108, 113
In-N-Out Burger 26, 42, 56, 70, 80,
    94, 109, 122, 153, 162, 187
Insanely Great 70
Intel 175, 188, 189
Intel Inside 175, 189
Intel Pentium 175
iPhone 50
iPod 50, 116, 121, 124, 168, 180
iTunes 116
Isetta 77

J

Jack Daniel's 3, 41, 57, 85, 93, 149,
    175, 185
Jaguar 180
J. Furphy & Sons 54
Journal of Management Studies 11

K

King and Country 70
King Kong 26, 110, 135, 138
Krispy Kreme 47, 59, 70, 92, 97, 109, 110, 147
Krug 42, 69, 73, 94 106,108, 109, 172, 180

L

Lamborghini 54, 69, 118
La Trappe 56
Leica 52, 53, 60, 119, 122, 126, 137, 138, 145, 146, 149, 150, 151, 166, 168
Leica C-Lux 2 150
Leica M3 53 106
Leica M-series 119, 180
Leitz 137
Le Mans 112
Levi's 19, 56, 155, 156, 163, 186
LIFEcar 43, 49
Li Ning 128
Links 31
Linux 66, 97
Lisa 188
L.L. Bean 42, 74, 101, 128, 148, 171
Lonely Planet 27, 72, 77
London News 115
Lord of the Rings 26, 35, 44, 45, 59, 110, 138, 180
Loro Piana 190
Louis Roederer 69
Louis Roederer Cristal 106
Louis Vuitton 26, 51, 93, 119, 122, 129, 135, 139, 149, 163, 169, 170, 171, 180
LVMH 98, 122 128, 129, 136, 170

M

Macintosh 50, 70, 106
MacWorld 49, 115, 138
Manchester United 59
Manolo Blahnik 23, 65, 73,106

Marc Jacobs 135
Martinborough Vineyards 114
Mathmos Lava Lamp 106
Mazda 119
McDonald's 4, 153
McDonald's Arch Deluxe 121
Mecca Cola 5
Mercedes-Benz 57, 60, 145, 146, 149, 170, 180
Merino NZ 189, 190
MG 24
Microsoft 2, 65, 76, 78, 97
Mini 16, 180
Misery 101
Miscellany 138
Moby Dick 44
Moleskine 68
Mondo Vino 69
Morgan Motor Company 1, 2, 24, 26, 31, 32, 35, 42, 43, 47, 49, 51, 52, 55, 58, 60, 70, 73, 74, 80, 81, 91, 94, 95, 99, 101, 109, 112, 113, 116, 119, 120(5), 122, 126, 138, 144, 163, 170, 171, 180
Morgan Owners Club 138
Motorola 76
Mountain Dew 18, 179
MTV 186
Myspace 20

N

Neiman Marcus 60, 180
Nestle Peters 166
Never Mind the Bollocks 51
New Coke 97, 121
Newton 188
New Yorker 122
New Zealand's National Museum Te Papa 80
Nike 5, 14, 18, 80, 126, 128, 137, 164, 179
No Logo 5
Nordstrom 60, 107
Norman's Winery 184, 185
Nudie 108

O

Old Number 7 41
Oliva Tobacco Co. 189
Once Were Warriors 154
Opossumwool 190

P

Pacific Brands 14, 19
Palliser Estate 164, 165
PC 31, 36, 96, 97, 98, 165
Peacock, 185
Peat 31
Penfold's 85, 86, 87, 92, 95, 168,
 178, 179
People for the Ethical Treatment of
 Animals (PETA) 44
Pepsi 2
Peters Ice Cream 163, 166
Phil and Ted's 124, 125, 126,
 169, 182
Pinot Noirs 165
Piper Heidsieck 184
Pixar 180
Playmobil 130, 131, 168
Pokemon 55
Pol Roger 69
Porsche 170, 184
Port Charlotte (PC5) 164
Post-it Notes 76
Power PC 77
Prada 42, 123, 145, 180, 184
Premier 137
Pret-a-Manger 166
Proctor and Gamble (P&G) 63,
 65, 117

Q

Qantas Airways 118
Quaker Oats 13, 14, 18, 19, 47,
 65, 80
Quiksilver 24, 50, 51, 55, 57, 74, 78,
 101, 126, 127, 145, 182

R

Racing Champions 98
Ralph Lauren 65, 184
Ramsay's Boiling Point 159, 165
Ramsay's Kitchen 172
Real Groovy Records 78, 112
Recreational Equipment Inc. (REI) 26
Reidel 117
Remington Razors 171
Ringers 35, 110
Ringers: Lord of the Fans 110
Ripcurl 74, 101, 171
Roadster 43
Rocks 31
Rolls Royce 52, 70
Rosemount 92
Rover 88

S

Saatchi & Saatchi 78
Sandeman 116
Schwinn Bicycles 24, 52, 55, 60, 94,
 110, 145, 168
Sci-Fi Channel 59
Sea Shepard 173
Second Hand Lives 103
Seiko 119
Seinfeld 108
Sesame Street 106
Sex and the City 71
Sinclair 150
Singapore Airlines 95
Sixteen 31
Shanghai Tang 60
Smithsonian 22
Snapple 13, 18, 19, 28, 47, 63, 65,
 80, 108
Sony 37, 51, 119, 130, 137, 147, 168
Sony Playstation 168
Sony Walkman 106, 124, 130, 134,
 168
Southcorp 86, 87, 92
Southwest Airlines 161
Starbucks 4, 5, 20, 24, 26, 99, 152

Star of Davidson 23, 25
Star Trek 24, 46, 59, 100, 155
Star Trek Enterprise 100, 155
Star Trek New Generation 100
Star Trek Voyager 100
Star Wars 58, 100, 110
Steiff Bears 120
Story of 42 Below 153
Student 96, 113
Stuff Magazine 53

T

Target 129
Tata Motor 123, 150, 151
Tata Motor's Ace 123
Taylor's 116
Te Koko 136, 137
The Art of Shaving 65, 180
The Body Shop 27, 45, 96, 113, 134,
   161, 163, 164, 165, 170, 172,
   178, 189
The Fountainhead 44, 103, 105
The Great Gatsby 53
The Magical World of Misery 101
The Perfect Storm 44
The Piaggio Historical Archive 77
The Red Star 135
The Signature 164, 165
The Standard 115
Tic Tac 152, 153, 179
Tiffany 109
Tiger Balm 90, 91, 180
Time Magazine 122
Tommy Hilfiger 75
Top Gear 49
Toys R Us 120
TradeMe 142, 143
Trekkies 100
Troubleshooter 81, 171
Tupperware 22, 23, 90, 126,
   156, 164
Twitter 20

U

Umpqua Bank 81, 119
Untouched World 27, 127
Upper Class 180
Ur-Leica 137

V

Vans 24, 51, 100, 101, 126, 145, 156
Vegemite 16, 56
Vespa 51, 60, 77, 88, 91, 126, 146,
   147, 170, 185
Vespa Piaggio Historical Archive 185
Vespa Riders Clubs 147
Victoria and Albert Museum 22
Virgin 47, 50, 51, 79, 96, 101, 102,
   131, 132, 161, 170
Virgin Atlantic 60, 118
Virgin Blue 95, 96, 113
Virgin Brides 78
Virgin Music 126
Virgin Records 96, 113
Vista 76, 96, 97, 109, 188
Vivienne Westwood 23, 130
Vodafone 79
Volkswagen 40, 51
VW Beetle 16, 24, 58, 78, 91,
   100, 153
VW Combi 152

W

Wachovia 119
Wal-Mart 4, 120
Waves 31
W. Britains 42, 44, 60, 70
Wendy's Old Fashioned
   Hamburgers 171
Weta Digital 149
Weta Works 26, 46, 135
Weta Workshop 149

White Grange, 86, 92
Wikipedia 76
Wingnut Films 35, 46
Wired 107, 108
WMD 1, The Weapons Inspectors – 30, 36, 78, 188
WMD II, 30
Works Magazine 169
WorldCom 102
World of Warcraft 115, 137

Y

Yahoo 169
Yalumba 43, 164, 165

Yattarna 86
YouTube 20, 24, 154

Z

Zealander 190
Zippo 7, 10, 11, 27, 52, 60, 188
Zippo Click Club 11
Zippo Visitors Centre 11, 185, 186

SUBJECT INDEX

A

amateurism 7, 13, 65, 66, 70–2, 77, 83
anti-brand discourse 4–5, 20
  see also customer backlash
appearance 67–8, 81–2
artisan 66–7, 76
artisanal amateurism 68, 74, 83
attention to detail 113, 115–18
  see also quality commitment quality leadership
authenticity
  definition, traditional 6, 15–16
  definition, contemporary 6, 16–17
  forms of 27
  see also brand authenticity
authenticity claims, overt 25–6, 178–9
authenticity threshold 25

B

B2B brands 189–190
backstage experience 109–111
balance 26, 27, 179–180
beliefs
  see personal beliefs
bonds
  cultural 145, 152–4
  industry 145, 149–152
  national 145–7
  regional 145, 147–9
  sub-culture 145, 154–7
brand association 18–19, 52–3, 146, 148, 152–3

brand authenticity
  attributes 2, 16–17, 26–7
  authors of 18
    see also brand meaning co-creation
  building 6, 7–9, 14, 25–7, 32–3, 35–7, 65, 83, 88, 106–7, 124, 139 145, 157, 160, 173–4, 176–190
  cues
    see brand cues
  definition, 26outcomes of 3–4, 7–8, 13–14
brand cues 20–1, 24, 25–7
brand culture
  see organizational, culture
brand community 18–19, 21, 24, 55–6, 100, 144–5
  see also fan base
brand equity 3, 7, 13–14, 19, 28, 42, 56, 58, 95, 143
brand extensions 85–6, 100–1, 184
brand historian 184–5
brand identity 17
  see also brand image; *see also* brand positioning
brand image 17, 32, 51, 52–3, 148
  see also brand identity; *see also* brand positioning
brand loyalty 38, 59
brand meaning
  authors 18
  co-creation of 3, 5, 18–20, 32
  evolution of 88
    see also stories

215

brand positioning 14, 35, 36–7, 110, 119, 179
  see also brand identity; *see also* brand image

C

challenging conventions 49, 105, 134, 173
classic 26, 91
  see also timeless design
collective identity 18, 21, 23–5, 33, 53–4
  see also fan base; *see also* brand community
collectors 55, 60, 63–4, 98–9, 114
commercialization
  overt 13, 86, 95, 100, 183–4
  disavowal of 14, 16, 26, 27, 178–9, 183–4
community
  see brand community
  see also sub-culture
conflict 7, 38, 42–6
  see also struggles; *see also* tragedy
continuous improvement
  see quality commitment; *see also* quality leadership
country of origin
  see bonds national
craftsperson 50, 66–7, 86
  see also artisan
craft tradition 68–70, 170
  see also tradition
creation 38, 48–51
culture 152–4
  see also bonds; *see also* heritage; *see also* tradition
culture jamming 20
  see also anti-brand discourse; *see also* customer backlash
customer advocate 44–5
  see also sub-culture
customer, as employee 124–8, 182
customer backlash 20, 97, 156
  see also anti-brand discourse
customer devotion 46, 180
  see also customer love

customer identity goals 16, 18, 20–1, 24–5, 38, 39, 143–4, 186
  see also self-authentication
customer life world 8, 123–131, 139, 181–3
  see also market immersion
customer love 22, 24, 29, 55
  see also customer devotion

D

decoupling 82
design-led 118–120, 129
deterritorialization 23, 33, 58, 144,
differentiation, point of 9, 35, 38, 69, 89–90, 94, 102, 129, 165, 173
  see also uniqueness
distinguishing characteristics
  see uniqueness

E

emotional connection 7, 38, 46, 102, 147
employee
  creativity 160, 167–9
    see also institutionalized dabbling
  immersion 43, 95–6, 160, 169–171, 172,
  knowledge transfer 93, 171
  loyalty 162, 163, 166
  recognition 160, 164–5, 173
  selection 101, 160–2
  welfare 160, 162–4, 173
  quality of 160, 165–7
    see also customer, as employee
enthusiasm 8, 106, 112, 126
  see also passion
espoused values
  see organizationalvalues

F

family 11, 38, 42–4, 101, 172, 185
fan base 3, 18–19, 20, 23, 35, 55, 58–9, 138–9, 144–5

see also brand community
focal activity 89–90, 101
 see also roots
folklore 36, 41
 see also myths
founding
 activity
  see focal activity
 community 9, 99–100, 156
  see also bonds community
 place 57
  see also bonds
 spirit 89, 95–6
 stories 37–42, 51, 70–1
 tradition 94
  see also heritage; *see also* history;
   see also tradition *see also* roots
fun 77–80, 113

G

genuine article 27
genuine intentions 9, 16
 see also honesty; *see also* sincerity
globalization 23, 33, 56, 58,102, 144
gut feeling 130–5, 183
 see also intuition

H

heritage 26, 38, 39, 41, 42, 50, 58,
 146, 179, 184
 see also history; *see also* roots;
  see also tradition
history 26, 38, 39, 43, 51–4, 76, 145,
 149–150, 184–5
 see also heritage; *see also* roots;
  see also tradition
honesty 9, 77, 174, 175–7,187–9
 see also genuine intentions; *see also*
  sincerity
human resource management
 see employees
human qualities 7, 37, 38, 40, 41, 46,
 48, 77, 173–4
 see also personal beliefs; *see also*
  personal values.

hurricane metaphor 35–6, 52, 87
hyperreality 23, 33, 58, 144

I

icons 3, 9, 14, 18, 22–3, 39, 47–8, 53,
 59–60, 75, 145, 149, 152–3
identity
 see customer identity goals
impression management
 see appearance
innovation 8, 38, 39, 48, 58, 70, 80,
 93, 95, 121, 123, 127, 129, 138,
 139, 169, 181, 182
 see also quality commitment;
  see also quality leadership
inspiration
 customers 22, 48
 employees 123, 124, 129, 185, 190
institutionalized dabbling 124, 135–8
 see also employee, creativity
intuition 48, 50, 69, 123, 132, 139
 see also gut feeling

L

leaders, brand 40–1, 48, 49, 159,
 171–3
 dedication 50, 71, 173
 involvement 106, 111–13, 171–2
legends 20, 40, 46–7, 59
 see also myths; *see also* stories
legitimacy 19, 39, 143, 155–6
limited resources 14, 80–1
local status 142–5
 see also bonds
love of craft 8, 50, 113–15, 120
 see also passion
luck 40, 71, 74–6, 83, 188

M

market immersion 8, 123–4, 128–130,
 139, 181–3
 see also customer life world
market orientation 107

market research, rejection of 108,
121–3, 130
market testing, rejection of
see market research, rejection of
marketing expertise, downplay 7, 27,
50, 67, 68, 72–3
see also amateurism;
see also decoupling
marketing cues
see brand cues
moral messages 96–7
mystique 37, 40, 42, 48,
myth 18–19, 31–2, 38, 39, 40, 41–2, 87
see also folklore

N

naivety 82, 126
see also amateurism
national narrative
see bond, national
non-commercial values
see organizational values; see also
commercialization, disavowal of
nostalgia 16, 24, 67, 178

O

off-script behaviour 34, 35
on-script behaviour 34
organizational
culture 118, 169–171, 181
values 38, 42, 155–6, 160, 170–2,
177–8
origin
see roots
original
see genuine article

P

passion 8, 26, 41, 65, 66–7, 73–4, 86,
105–6, 111–15, 160–172
see also love of craft; see also
enthusiasm

perfectionism
see attention to detail;
see also quality commitment;
see also quality leadership
personal beliefs 27
see also personal values;
see also human qualities
personal values 38, 48
see also personal beliefs;
see also human qualities
place 16, 26, 27, 38, 39, 56–8, 102,
110–11, 141–2, 143–4, 148–9
see also bonds, regional
popular culture
see bonds; sub-culture
process transparency
see backstage experience
product 8, 26, 38, 39, 59–60, 180–1
product orientation 107–9, 180–1
production orientation 107–9

Q

quality commitment 26, 39, 50,
112–13, 115–17
see also attention to detail; see also
quality leadership
quality leadership 26, 38
see also attention to detail; see also
quality commitment

R

regional characteristics
see bonds, regional
roots 8, 38, 47, 53–4, 65–6, 77, 85–9,
98–9, 101–2
see also focal activity; see also
founding; see also heritage; see
also history; see also tradition

S

sales orientation 107
self-authentication 33, 58
see also customer identity goals

serendipity 36
  see also luck
service 38, 39, 59–60, 107–9, 177,
  180–1
sincerity 9, 16, 26, 27, 38, 39, 47, 51,
  57, 58, 82, 105, 155–6, 180
  see also genuine intentions; *see also*
    honesty
social construction 16, 17
  see also subjectivity
stereotype 145–6, 157
stewardship 38, 42–3, 93, 171
stories
  authors 3, 7, 32
  outcomes 26, 34, 40, 41, 43, 46,
    50, 53–4, 55–6
  sources 29–31, 83
  themes 7, 38–9
  see also brand meaning
struggles 7, 9, 19, 38, 39, 44–6
  see also conflict; *see also* tragedy
stylistic consistency 26, 88, 90–3
sub-culture 3, 14, 19, 24
  see also bonds, sub-culture
subjectivity 6, 16, 17, 32
  see also social construction

T

time 16, 24, 26, 38, 39, 41,
  52–3, 153
timeless design 26, 92, 180
  see also classic
tradition 8, 16, 26, 38, 43, 49–50,
  68–70, 93–5, 99–100, 116, 157
  see also craft tradition; *see also*
    heritage; *see also* history
tragedy 38, 46–8
  see also conflict; *see also* struggles
triumph 38, 46–8

U

underdog 2, 81
uniqueness 57–8, 63–5, 148–9
  see also differentiation, point of

V

values
  see organizational; values